$6.00

2

D0147983

Implementation

This volume is sponsored by the
OAKLAND PROJECT
University of California, Berkeley

Implementation

HOW GREAT EXPECTATIONS IN WASHINGTON
ARE DASHED IN OAKLAND;

OR,

WHY IT'S AMAZING THAT FEDERAL PROGRAMS WORK AT ALL

THIS BEING A SAGA OF THE

ECONOMIC DEVELOPMENT ADMINISTRATION

AS TOLD BY

TWO SYMPATHETIC OBSERVERS WHO SEEK TO BUILD MORALS

ON A FOUNDATION OF

RUINED HOPES

Jeffrey L. Pressman
AND
Aaron Wildavsky

THIRD EDITION

UNIVERSITY OF CALIFORNIA PRESS
BERKELEY, LOS ANGELES, LONDON

University of California Press
Berkeley and Los Angeles, California

University of California Press, Ltd.
London, England

© 1973, 1979, 1984
The Regents of the University of California

Library of Congress Cataloging in Publication Data

Pressman, Jeffrey L.
     Implementation : how great expectations in Washington
are dashed in Oakland.

     (The Oakland Project series)
     Bibliography: p.
     Includes index.
     1. Manpower policy—California—Oakland. 2. United
States. Economic Development Administration. 3. Oakland
(Calif.)—Public works. I. Wildavsky, Aaron B.
II. Title. III. Series.
HD5726.022P73 1984 353.0084'84'0979466   83–17987
ISBN 0–520–05232–3
ISBN 0–520–05233–1 (pbk.)

Printed in the United States of America

2   3   4   5   6   7   8   9

FOR KATE,
a partner in program negotiation,
AND FOR JUDY,
who accomplishes, fulfills, produces, performs,
executes, achieves, completes,
and otherwise implements

¹im·ple·ment [fr. *implementum* action of filling up, fr. *implēre* to fill up, finish (fr. *in-* + *plēre* to fill) + *-mentum* -ment—more at FULL]

²im·ple·ment la: to carry out: ACCOMPLISH, FULFILL (wondering how he might best ∼ his purpose) (continued to clamor for action to ∼ the promise—*N.Y. Times*) (a committee to ∼ the plans so well formulated); *esp*: to give practical effect to and ensure of actual fulfillment by concrete measures (failure to carry out and ∼ the will of the majority —Clement Attlee) (an agency created to ∼ the recommendation of the committee) (programs to ∼ our foreign policy)

[From *Webster's Third New International Dictionary of the English Language*, unabridged, Philip B. Gove, ed. in chief (Springfield, Massachusetts: G. & C. Merriam Co., 1969), pp. 1134–1135.]

To IMPLEMENT: *Produce*: do; carry out; perform; execute; achieve; accomplish. *Complete*: effectuate; realize; bring about.

[Selected synonyms from *Roget's Thesaurus of English Words and Phrases*, revised edition (New York: St. Martin's Press, 1964.)]

Contents

Acknowledgments

My first debt is owed to Angela Browne, a graduate student in the School of Social Welfare in Berkeley, who co-authored chapters 9, 10, and 11. If this third edition ranges further and probes deeper than before, she deserves the credit.

Interest in implementation is attested to by the many perceptive and detailed critical comments I have received on the new preface and chapters 9, 10, and 11 for this third edition. My thanks for the suggestions adopted and my regrets for those I should have but did not use go to Asoke Basu, Eleanor Chelimsky, Jeanne Nienaber Clarke, Ross Conner, Howard Freeman, Jan-Erik Lane, Martin Levin, Giandomenico Majone, Arnold Meltsner, William Meyers, Robert Nakamura, Dennis Palumbo, Brian Tannenbaum, Joseph White, and Hellmut Wollman.

A special, unfortunately posthumous acknowledgment belongs to a practitioner-cum-researcher, Gordon Chase, whom I never met but who has nonetheless made me aware of how centrally the subject of implementation is connected to learning. More than anyone else, he has made good on the practical promise that Jeff Pressman and I felt inhered in turning attention to implementation.

In a substantial article entitled "Implementing a Human Services Program: How Hard Will It Be?" (*Public Policy* 27 [Fall 1979]: 385–436), Chase wrote that his "interest in predicting implementation obstacles grew out of a relatively painful experience." As administrator of New York City's Health Services Administration, he had good success with methodone maintenance and lead poison control programs. When the mayor asked him to reform the city's prison health system, he began with confidence but was soon frustrated. "Not until some time later," after discarding too easy excuses for himself, "did I realize," he tells his readers with candor, "that 95 percent of the obstacles that made prison reform so hard to implement were predictable before hand." To him, as well as to me, this still seemed "to be an important discovery" (p. 386).

Stated simply, the forty-four precepts he derived from comparing the two easy and the one difficult program—such as "How many transactions will the program manager have with the overhead agencies?" (p. 409) or "Are there dimensions of the program that are predictably going to produce a bad press?" (p. 420)—are quite ordinary. And that is part of the point: ordinary aspects of implementation are often ignored. But when they are put together in a handy chart, each aspect noted simply as being E for easy, H for hard, and M for being of moderate difficulty, the would-be implementer has a useful checklist in anticipating and perhaps heading off trouble.

For such small favors, I hope other implementers will be, as I am, grateful to Gordon Chase.

ASSESSMENT OF THE LEAD, METHADONE, AND PRISON HEALTH
PROGRAMS BASED ON THE 44 "FACTORS FOR CONSIDERATION"

	Lead	Methadone	Prison Health
A. *Difficulties Arising from Operational Demands*			
1. People to be Served			
(a) Number of client transactions	E	M	M
(b) Ease of reaching client	M-H	M	E
2. Nature of Services			
(a) Number of discrete functions	M	E	H
(b) Complexity of discrete functions	E	E	H
(c) Coordination among functions	M	E	H
(d) Replication	M	M	H

SOURCE: Gordon Chase, "Implementing a Human Services Program: How Hard Will It Be?" *Public Policy* 27 (Fall 1979):385–436.

Assessment (*Continued*)

	Lead	Methadone	Prison Health
3. Likelihood and Costliness of Distortions or Irregularities			
(a) Involving clients	M	H	M
(b) Involving services	E	H	M
4. Controllability of Program			
(a) Measurability	E	E	H
(b) Uncontrollable critical elements	E	H	M
B. Difficulties Arising from Nature and Availability of Resources			
1. Money			
(a) Flexibility	E	E	E
(b) Obtaining additional funding	M	E	M-H
2. Personnel			
(a) Nature of personnel in place	M-H	E	H
(b) Numbers, kinds, and quality needed	E	E	H
(c) Availability of personnel in market	E	E	E
(d) Attractiveness of program to personnel	E	M-H	H
3. Space			
(a) Nature of the current facilities	E	E	H
(b) Availability of facilities	E	M	E
(c) Special problems in acquiring or using space	E	H	H
4. Supplies and Technical Equipment			
(a) Availability and usability	M	M	M
(b) Importance of technology	M	H	E
C. Difficulties Arising from Need to Share Authority			
1. Overhead Agencies			
(a) Number of transactions	M-H	E	H
(b) Likelihood of favorable response	M-H	M	M-H
2. Other Line Agencies			
(a) Extent of involvement	M-H	E	H
(b) Critical nature of involvement	M	E	H
(c) Likelihood of harmonious working conditions	M	E	H
(d) Ability to pinpoint responsibility	M	E	H

Assessment (*Continued*)

	Lead	Methadone	Prison Health
3. Elected Politicians			
(a) Capacity to help or hurt	M	M-H	M
(b) Inclination to help or hurt	M	M	M
4. Higher Levels of Government			
(a) Extent of authority	E	M	E
(b) Number of transactions	E	M	E
(c) Nature of politics	E	M	E
(d) Likelihood of favorable response	E	M	E
5. Private-Sector Providers			
(a) Need	E	M-H	H
(b) Availability	E	M	H
(c) Control	E	M	M
(d) Political problems	E	H	M
6. Special-Interest Groups			
(a) Kinds and inclinations	E	M	E
(b) Strength	M	M	M
(c) Likelihood of helping or hurting	M	M	M
7. The Press			
(a) Level of visibility	M	H	M
(b) Power of the press	M	M	M
(c) View of Administration	M	M	M
(d) Controversial dimensions	M	H	M

Participants

Preface to the Third Edition:
IMPLEMENTATION AND EVALUATION AS LEARNING

In recent years there has been a growing emphasis on the implementation and evaluation phases of the policy process. These phases of policy development are attracting special attention for good reason: many policies based on apparently sound ideas have encountered difficulties in practical application. A policy's value therefore must be measured not only in terms of its appeal but also in light of its implementability. But how would we know whether a program embodying a policy had been well or poorly implemented?—by observing the difference between intended and actual consequences, i.e., by evaluation. Indeed, by expanding the task of evaluation beyond the mere measurement of outcomes to their causes, we can obtain knowledge that can be used to alter programs and/or their modes of implementation. Whether used to check progress or to change direction, evaluation includes the analysis of implementation.

Implementation and evaluation are the opposite sides of the same coin, implementation providing the experience that evaluation interrogates and evaluation providing the intelligence to make sense out of what is happening. In writing about the interrelationships between implementation and evaluation in chapter 9, Angela Browne and I point to the part played by implementation in generating the very errors that evaluation must detect and, if possible, correct.

If implementation is based on evaluation of public policy and if evaluation has as its subject matter the implementation of public policy, why are the two subjects separated in scholarly discourse? There are, as we shall see, reasons of convenience for separating the domains to which these twin subjects apply. We can only point in one direction at a time. But there is no reason to avoid discussion of the interrelationships between program action through implementation and program learning through evaluation.

By relating implementation to evaluation, moreover, we become aware of the trend toward conceptual imperialism that characterizes both of these generic aspects of policy analysis. It is all understandable. To be effective, evaluation must be utilized. Gearing evaluation into an organizational context therefore assumes importance. Once evaluators enter the world of action, they become aware of how hard their task is made when objectives that can be monitored are omitted from policy designs. Rather than remain a reactive profession, therefore, evaluators may attempt to control policy design itself. Before they know it, evaluators get into forecasting, attempting to predict how proposed policy designs will fare in an uncertain world. Once they feel a sense of responsibility for policy, evaluators want to see their designs utilized. Thus evaluators become implementers; they generate their own mistakes and become responsible for fixing them. In order to correct malfunctioning programs, evaluators have to know not only what went wrong, and why, but how to improve on program performance. Slowly, imperceptibly, but surely, evaluation becomes policy analysis. All the stages of analysis, from design to implementation to termination, become the evaluator's preserve.

The same sort of aggrandizement occurs in implementation studies, though this is less noticeable because the field has not yet become professionalized. (Legislation may well mandate setting aside funds for evaluation but not as yet for implementation.) Nonetheless, students of implementation (present company included) are eager to make their concerns part of policy design.

As programs are put into practice, it becomes apparent that not everyone is equally affected by them. Program clientele and other interested parties (now known as "stakeholders") take different positions on what exactly shall be implemented in which way. Soon enough the call goes out for multiple implementation studies (as it did for more diverse evaluations) that would encompass a wider range of values. Who should implement and who should benefit become as important as whether the original program should be carried out. New fields of implementation (known as "cut-back management" or, more starkly, "termination") arise to undo what was done under the same program.[1]

It is possible that evaluation, being better entrenched, will subsume implementation as part of a broader view of its subject matter. Then again, evaluation might give way to a still broader designation called policy analysis, which, in turn, might be replaced by the field it once thought to replace, namely, planning. The seamless web of public policy might thus reassert itself with a vengeance, converting all rival conceptual dominions into an imperialized hodge-podge. Now that implementation and evaluation have entered into their mature phase, some might say "mid-life crises," it is time to arrange a working division of labor. No matter where the dividing line ends up, however, implementation will remain the foundation of evaluation.

As programs are altered by their environments and organizations are affected by their programs, mutual adaptation changes both the context and content of what is implemented. The study of implementation is shaken from its safe cognitive anchorage in prior objectives and future consequences that do or do not measure up to original expectations. Evolution overwhelms origins and the search is on for a standpoint above the flux. How the various authors cope with this condition—attempting a still shot of a moving picture—is the subject of our study of the literature on implementation in

1. See Charles H. Levine, "Organizational Decline and Cutback Management," *Public Administration Review* 38 (July/August 1978):316–24; Robert D. Behn, "Closing the Massachusetts Public Training Schools," *Policy Sciences* 7 (June 1976):151–71; Robert Behn, "The False Dawn of the Sunset Laws," *The Public Interest*, no. 49 (Fall 1977):103–18; Robert Behn, "Closing a Government Facility," *Public Administration Review* 38 (July/August 1978):332–38; Robert P. Biller, "On Tolerating Policy and Organization Termination: Some Design Considerations," *Policy Sciences* 7 (June 1976): 133–49; Garry D. Brewer, "And the Clocks Were Striking Thirteen: The Termination of War," with James L. Foster, *Policy Sciences* 7 (June 1976): 225–43; and Peter de Leon, "Policy Evaluation and Program Termination," Rand Paper Series, P–6807 (Santa Monica, Calif.: Rand Corporation, September 1982).

chapter 10. We attempt to bridge evaluation, implementation, and learning in our closing statement in chapter 11.

In a world that changes programs as they are carried out, implementation is the only source of experience that managers can use to test and improve their programs. That is why this Third Edition ends with a discussion of learning. Whether programs adapt well to their environments can be determined only by continuous evaluation. Whether the results of evaluation are used to improve implementation depends both on the ability of evaluators to learn from experience and of implementers to learn from evaluators.

There is no standpoint not subject to human limitations. There is no mode of organizing social life not subject to contradiction or unanticipated consequences. The best humankind can do is to try to learn about the characteristic defects of each way of going about things so that their worst aspects may be ameliorated.

Of course, implementation is a Sisyphean labor. How could it be otherwise? How could mankind ever finally finish its labors? Only if social life (with its conflicting visions of how to live) never changed, a dull man's utopia, could there be an end to implementation.

Learning, which we adopt as our standpoint, is doubly limited; it is never finally achieved because it is always concerned with improving our conception of what we ought to prefer in the light of our failures in achievement. Since learning aims to educate our preferences in the light of our possibilities, what we do and what we seek evolve together.

Learning is the key to both implementation and evaluation. We evaluate to learn, and we learn to implement. Evaluation is a method of inducing learning within an organization geared for implementing. And it is not only evaluators but the program personnel, the implementers, who are to do the learning. Were this not so, were evaluation isolated from implementation, the latter would be blind and the former would be dumb, and neither could change for the better.

Preface

TO THE FIRST EDITION

Late in 1968 our attention was drawn to the Economic Development Administration's employment effort in Oakland by the appearance of a book with the arresting title, *Oakland's Not for Burning*. Written by a major participant in the EDA's Oakland venture,[1] the book appeared to suggest that the city had recently been saved from riot and ruin by the infusion of $23 million in federal funds. Because it created minority employment—thus sending out a beacon light of hope to a troubled nation—the EDA program was touted as a model worthy of imitation. Since Oakland Project members were not aware that the city had been delivered from evil, we inquired into the status of the program and discovered that in 1969, three years after it began, approximately $3 million had actually been spent. At that rate, another twenty years would pass before this emergency operation would have spent the money to create the jobs to employ the people who would prevent (or at least not participate in) riots. Part of the $3 million had gone to the city for the Hegenberger overpass to the coliseum (which we somehow thought would have been built anyway), and the rest had been spent on architects' fees. We indulged briefly in mild fantasies depicting local architects about to overthrow the Oakland City Council in a suave coup d'etat, only to be bought off at the last minute by EDA funds. But further investi-

---

1. Amory Bradford, *Oakland's Not for Burning* (New York: McKay, 1968).

gation suggested that there were no easy targets or evident villains. Implementation of the EDA's program was just more difficult than any of us had thought.

This book begins at the end: We will concentrate on that part of a public program following the initial setting of goals, securing of agreement, and commitment of funds. A new agency called the Economic Development Administration (EDA) is established by Congress. The EDA decides to go into cities for the purpose of providing permanent new jobs to minorities through economic development. Oakland is chosen as an experiment in showing how the provision of public works and building loans can provide incentives for employers to hire minorities. Congress appropriates the necessary funds, the approval of city officials and employers is obtained, and the program is announced to the public amidst the usual fanfare. Years later, construction has only been partially completed, business loans have died entirely, and the results in terms of minority employment are meager and disappointing. Why?

Some programs are aborted because political agreement cannot be obtained. Others languish because funds cannot be secured. Still others die because the initial agreement of local officials or private concerns is not forthcoming. All these conditions were met in the EDA employment program in Oakland, but the program could not be implemented in time to secure the desired results.

In our study of implementation, we have deliberately chosen case material in which dramatic elements that are essentially self-explanatory are ruled out. There was no great conflict. Everyone agreed. There was only minimum publicity. The issue was not one of overriding political importance. Essential funds were on hand at the right time. The evils that afflicted the EDA program in Oakland were of a prosaic and everyday character. Agreements had to be maintained after they were reached. Numerous approvals and clearances had to be obtained from a variety of participants. Failure to recognize that these perfectly ordinary circumstances present serious obstacles to implementation inhibits learning. If one is always looking for unusual circumstances and dramatic events, he cannot appreciate how difficult it is to make the ordinary happen.

People now appear to think that implementation should be easy; they are, therefore, upset when expected events do not occur or turn out badly. We would consider our effort a success if more people began with the understanding that implementation, under the best of circumstances, is exceedingly difficult. They would, therefore, be pleasantly surprised when a few good things really happened.

Implementation in recent years has been much discussed but rarely studied. Presidents and their advisers, department secretaries and their subordinates, local officials and groups in their communities complain that good ideas are dissipated in the process of execution. Yet, except for an excellent book by Martha Derthick,[2] we have not been able to locate any thoroughgoing analysis of implementation.[3] Complaints about implementation do not constitute serious efforts to grapple with the problem.

No doubt a comparative approach to problems of implementation would ideally be preferable to the one we have adopted. But not enough is known about the subject to develop appropriate categories, and there is no previous literature on which to rely for guidance. We do not make any claim to have undertaken a comprehensive analysis of implementation. We are not certain we know what all the problems are, let alone provide solutions to them. But a start must be made somewhere and we hope this is it.

Implementation, to us, means just what Webster and Roget say it does: to carry out, accomplish, fulfill, produce, complete. But what is it that is being implemented? A policy, naturally. There must be something out there prior to implementation; otherwise there would be nothing to move toward in the process of implementation. A verb like "implement" must have an object like "policy." But policies normally contain both goals and the means for achieving them. How, then, do we distinguish between a policy and its implementation?

In everyday discourse we use policy (when referring to decisions)

2. Martha Derthick, *New Towns In-Town* (Washington, D.C.: Urban Institute, 1972).

3. The splendid account of the Elementary and Secondary Education Act by Stephen Bailey and Edith Mosher reveals acute sensitivity to problems of implementation. But it is not their purpose to analyze implementation as a distinct phenomenon. See their *ESEA: The Office of Education Administers a Law* (Syracuse: Syracuse University Press, 1968). Jerome T. Murphy, in the article "Title I of ESEA: The Politics of Implementing Federal Education Reform," *Harvard Educational Review* 41 (1971): 35–63, does address himself directly to the question of implementation. Although this article does not contain as thoroughgoing an analysis of implementation as is found in the Derthick study, the author does provide a number of insights into the problem.

in several strikingly different ways. Sometimes policy means a statement of intention: Our policy is to increase employment among minorities. Policy here is treated as a broad statement of goals and objectives. Nothing is said about what might be done or whether anything has been or will be done to accomplish that purpose. Other times we speak of policy as if it were equivalent to actual behavior: Our policy is to hire minorities, meaning that we actually do hire them. Policy in this sense signifies the goal and its achievement. Both these meanings of policy rule out the possibility of studying implementation. When policy remains a disembodied objective, without specifying actors or the acts in which they must engage to achieve the desired result, there is no implementation to study. When the statement of the objective includes its attainment, implementation is unnecessary.

We can work neither with a definition of policy that excludes any implementation nor one that includes all implementation. There must be a starting point. If no action is begun, implementation cannot take place. There must also be an end point. Implementation cannot succeed or fail without a goal against which to judge it.

Let us agree to talk about policy as a hypothesis containing initial conditions and predicted consequences. If X is done at time t_1, then Y will result at time t_2. If the federal government, through the Economic Development Administration, provides $23 million in loans and grants to enterprises in Oakland, and if these enterprises agree to hire minorities after spending the money, then facilities will be built leading to the creation of new jobs that will go to minorities. Implementation would here constitute the ability to achieve the predicted consequences after the initial conditions have been met.

Implementation does not refer to creating the initial conditions. Legislation has to be passed and funds committed before implementation takes place to secure the predicted outcome. Similarly, agreements with the local enterprises would have to be reached before attempts are made to carry them out. After all, the world is full of policy proposals that are aborted. You can't finish what you haven't started. Lack of implementation should not refer to failure to get going but to inability to follow through.

To emphasize the actual existence of initial conditions we must distinguish a program from a policy. A program consists of governmental action initiated in order to secure objectives whose attainment is problematical. A program exists when the initial conditions

—the "if" stage of the policy hypothesis—have been met. The word "program" signifies the conversion of a hypothesis into governmental action. The initial premises of the hypothesis have been authorized. The degree to which the predicted consequences (the "then" stage) take place we will call implementation. Implementation may be viewed as a process of interaction between the setting of goals and actions geared to achieving them.

Considered as a whole, a program can be conceived of as a system in which each element is dependent on the other. Unless money is supplied, no facilities can be built, no new jobs can flow from them, and no minority personnel can be hired to fill them. A breakdown at one stage must be repaired, therefore, before it is possible to move on to the next. The stages are related, however, from back to front as well as from front to back. Failure to agree on procedures for hiring minorities may lead the government to withhold funds, thus halting the construction. Program implementation thus becomes a seamless web.

Policies imply theories. Whether stated explicitly or not, policies point to a chain of causation between initial conditions and future consequences. If X, then Y. Policies become programs when, by authoritative action, the initial conditions are created. X now exists. Programs make the theories operational by forging the first link in the causal chain connecting actions to objectives. Given X, we act to obtain Y. Implementation, then, is the ability to forge subsequent links in the causal chain so as to obtain the desired results. Once the funds are committed and the local agreements reached, the task is to build facilities to create new jobs so that minorities will be hired.

We oversimplify. Our working definition of implementation will do as a sketch of the earliest stages of the program, but the passage of time wreaks havoc with efforts to maintain tidy distinctions. As circumstances change, goals alter and initial conditions are subject to slippage. In the midst of action the distinction between the initial conditions and the subsequent chain of causality begins to erode. Once a program is underway implementers become responsible both for the initial conditions and for the objectives toward which they are supposed to lead.[4]

4. After numerous discussions, we have come to understand why no one else has apparently tried to distinguish policy from implementation. One person says that he likes to think of implementation as problems that arise when goals are set at high levels of organizational decision but are not realized be-

The longer the chain of causality, the more numerous the reciprocal relationships among the links and the more complex implementation becomes. The first four chapters illustrate the movement from simplicity to complexity. The reader interested in implementation should, therefore, be conscious of the steps required to accomplish each link in the chain. Who had to act to begin implementation? Whose consent was required to continue it? How many participants were involved? How long did they take to act? Each time an act of agreement has to be registered for the program to continue, we call a decision point. Each instance in which a separate participant is required to give his consent, we call a clearance. Adding the number of necessary clearances involved in decision points throughout the history of the program will give the reader an idea of the task involved in securing implementation. We will perform this chore for him in chapter 5.

When objectives are not realized, one explanation is the assertion of faulty implementation. The activities that were supposed to be carried out were not executed or were subject to inordinate delays. Another appropriate explanation may be that aspirations were set too high. Instead of asking why the process of implementation was faulty, we ask why too much was expected of it. Studying the process of implementation, therefore, includes the setting of goals (policy,

---

cause of resistance or distortion at lower levels of organizational performance. We cannot force anyone to accept our choice of words or concepts, but we do think it makes more sense to conceive of "organization" in an extended sense so that it encompasses those whose cooperation is necessary for a program to be carried out. To us, it seems strange to talk of a program as being implemented merely because lower-level participants in the sponsoring organization attempted to carry it out though essential support from others was not forthcoming. Support for a program within an organization is but one stage of implementation as we understand it.

Another person claims that policy and implementation are not distinguishable. Policy includes intended effects—i.e., policy includes implementation. Hence, a policy is not real until the intended changes have taken place. Again, we do not gainsay others the vocabulary with which they are comfortable. But we think that this choice of words confuses rather than clarifies. If policy includes its own implementation, then by definition alone it is not possible to carry out an investigation concerning the implementation of a policy. The important thing, we suppose, is that there are differences between deriving goals or objectives, working out a theory of how to achieve them, embodying that theory in governmental action, and executing it as intended. We think that Webster is on our side but anyone else is welcome to translate his vocabulary into our concerns.

according to its earlier meaning) toward which implementation is directed. By paying attention to the structural position of those who set targets—top federal officials who wish large accomplishments from small resources in a short time—and those who must implement them—career bureaucrats and local participants characterized by high needs and low cohesion—we seek in chapter 6 to uncover the causes of setting targets that are unlikely to be met.

The possibility of a mismatch between means and ends calls into question the adequacy of the original policy design. Perhaps implementation was good but the theory on which it was based was bad. Could a different set of initial conditions have achieved the predicted results? To explore this possibility, we end the book with an analysis of the economic theory underlying the EDA program in Oakland. Perhaps, we suggest in chapter 7, it might have been better to subsidize the wage bill of private firms directly in order to increase employment instead of the more roundabout method of providing grants and loans to construct facilities to create jobs for which minorities would then be hired.

The study of implementation requires understanding that apparently simple sequences of events depend on complex chains of reciprocal interaction. Hence, each part of the chain must be built with the others in view. The separation of policy design from implementation is fatal. It is no better than mindless implementation without a sense of direction. Though we can isolate policy and implementation for separate discussion, the purpose of our analysis is to bring them into closer correspondence with one another.

This book is based on interviews and a variety of documents. The first round of interviewing was done by Louise Resnikoff, a graduate student in the Political Science Department at Berkeley, who submitted a narrative report of events before leaving to pursue her studies in Tanzania. Owen McShane, a graduate student in city planning, conducted further interviews. His report, completed just before he returned to his native New Zealand, concentrated on the legislative history and economic theory behind EDA public works programs. His work is reflected in the fourth and seventh chapters. Jeffrey Pressman conducted yet one more round of interviews, this time reaching into the Washington office of the EDA, and Aaron Wildavsky concluded by reinterviewing major participants.

We are deeply grateful for the invaluable preparatory work done by McShane and Resnikoff. Without the willingness of participants to share their time and information with us, this book would not have been possible. We wish particularly to thank Andrew Bennett, Amory Bradford, Douglas Costle, Eugene Foley, George Karras, and Hugh Taylor for giving us repeated interviews and, in some cases, extensive comments on drafts of this manuscript. Our colleagues at Berkeley—Eugene Bardach, Frank Levy, Bart McGuire, Arnold Meltsner, and Frank Trinkl—made useful suggestions, as did Judith May, who is now at the University of California at Davis. The contribution of Oakland Project members in supplying missing bits of information and bolstering our morale is equally important, though it is so constant and pervasive that no particular person can be singled out. Kate Pressman computed the probabilities and gave useful advice on the charts associated with them. We would like to thank Mary Ellen Anderson and the Oakland Project staff for their skill, helpfulness, and patience in typing numerous drafts of. this manuscript. As always, Pat O'Donnell, the secretary of the dean at the Graduate School of Public Policy, kept the master copy and saw the manuscript through to publication. We hope that everyone who helped us will feel they have contributed to opening up sustained analysis on problems of implementation that for so long have bedeviled participants and puzzled observers.

No book that touches on resource allocation would be complete without an expression of gratitude for indispensable financial support. Part of the early work on this study was done under a grant from the National Aeronautics and Space Administration. From July 1969 to September 1971, the Oakland Project was supported by the Urban Institute, using funds made available by the Department of Housing and Urban Development. The work published herein has been supported in large part under that arrangement. During the last year the project has benefited from the generosity of Melvin Webber and his Institute of Urban and Regional Development.

Permission to reprint the Rube Goldberg cartoons comes from the King Features Syndicate and by courtesy of the Bancroft Library, University of California, Berkeley, where we spent many pleasurable hours.

1

Appearances

On the morning of April 25, 1966, the *Wall Street Journal* ran the following headline: "Urban Aid Kickoff: Administration Selects Oakland as First City in Rebuilding Program."[1] The *Journal* article expressed surprise at the fact that "the Great Society's first package of aid in its drive to save the cities" would "not go to New York, Chicago, Los Angeles or another major metropolis whose poverty and racial tensions have erupted into public demonstration or riot." Rather, the aid would "go to Oakland, California—a city of high unemployment and racial unrest that Federal agents have tabbed a potential powder keg." To help solve the problems of unemployment and racial unrest, the new program would finance public works and business loans that would lead to the creation of jobs for the unemployed, primarily blacks.

A further surprise, according to the *Journal,* was that the "donor will not be the new Department of Housing and Urban Development. . . . It will be an agency with rural antecedents and primarily a rural jurisdiction: The Economic Development Administration of the Department of Commerce. Eugene P. Foley, the enthusiastic, restless and imaginative Assistant Secretary of Commerce who heads EDA, will make the formal announcement this week."

On April 29, Foley formally announced the program at a press conference held at the Oakland airport. Governor Edmund G. Brown

1. *The Wall Street Journal,* April 25, 1966, p. 1.

of California introduced Foley as "the Assistant Secretary of Commerce for Economic Development, who has decided to conduct in Oakland a massive experiment in solving the principal urban problem, unemployment."[2] Foley then read his statement to the press. After discussing Oakland's problems—including an unemployment rate of 8.4 percent, more than twice the national average—Foley announced that the EDA had agreed to offer public works grants and loans amounting to $23,289,000 for various projects in the city. The following public works projects would receive EDA money:

Airport hangar and support facilities (Port of Oakland; to be leased by World Airways)	$10,650,000
Marine Terminal and access roads (Port of Oakland)	10,125,000
30-acre industrial park (Port of Oakland)	2,100,000
Access road to coliseum area (city of Oakland)	414,000
TOTAL	$23,289,000

Foley said that these projects would provide 2,200 jobs when completed, with more jobs following from later "spinoffs." In addition, $1,600,000 for business loans then being considered would create 800 new jobs. Thus, he promised some 3,000 jobs in all.

But how would the EDA make sure that the new jobs would go to the unemployed residents of the inner city who were supposed to be the beneficiaries of the new program? Foley unveiled an innovative procedure: each employer who wished to receive an EDA loan or lease an EDA-financed facility would have to draw up an employment plan. This plan would project the future employment opportunities that would result from EDA financing and would commit the employer to make a concerted effort to recruit hard-core unemployed Oakland residents to fill those positions. An employment review board, including representatives of business, labor, and the poor, would have to review each plan before the EDA could provide a loan or rule favorably on a lease agreement. (In each case, the EDA itself would have to give final approval to the plan.) Every employer would submit a monthly report on hiring to the review board. If the EDA made a finding of noncompliance and subsequent negotiation failed to resolve the dispute, then the matter would be settled by arbitration. Thus, EDA financial aid would be conditioned on performance

2. Quoted in Amory Bradford, *Oakland's Not for Burning* (New York: McKay, 1968), p. 123.

by employers. Hopes in both Washington and Oakland for a successful urban experiment were high.

In 1968, over two years after the initial EDA announcement, a
book appeared which suggested that the experiment had resulted in
some substantial achievements. Entitled *Oakland's Not for Burning,*
the book was written by Amory Bradford, the former vice-president
of the *New York Times* who had served as Foley's special representative in Oakland during the first months of the program. Through
a series of moving passages, Bradford painted a picture of the hope-
lessness and rage he had found in the Oakland ghetto when he arrived there in December 1965. One black leader told Foley and
Bradford at an early meeting that "We hate Whitey because he hates
us, thinks us no better than dogs. Call me 'Nigger,' it gives me respect. I have no respect for Whites, because they have no respect for
me. I just want to be considered human. I'm not responsible for five
hundred years of history, but for getting justice now. If we don't get
it, we'll have a Watts here, and kill and bomb."[3]

In countless meetings with ghetto residents, labor and business
leaders, educators, and government officials, Bradford and his EDA
staff tried to break down the barriers of distrust and suspicion that
divided the groups. To each, Bradford argued that the EDA could
provide vital help in the effort to create jobs for the hard-core unemployed—the key to solving the urban crisis.

Toward the end of the book, Bradford provided an optimistic evaluation of the EDA experiment. He noted that "so many of the other
cities have exploded with serious riots that it is clear we face a national crisis of major proportions. But all through 1966, 1967 and
the first half of 1968 Oakland has not suffered a riot. We must then
ask: What happened in Oakland that saved it from burning, when
most observers thought it would be one of the first to go?"[4] Bradford
admitted that "there are no easy answers to that question," and he
went on to say that the "EDA's purpose in Oakland was not the prevention of a riot." Rather, the EDA's mission was "to attack one of
the main sources of frustration and despair in the ghetto—the inability to get jobs." Still, "the fact that there was no riot in Oakland during those years cannot be ignored, as the country inquires into the

3. *Ibid.,* p. 4.
4. *Ibid.,* p. 204.

causes of riots elsewhere, and seeks to decide on the action needed
to prevent them in the future."[5]

Looking back at the social and political situation in Oakland
during 1966, Bradford identified two developments that "may have
made the difference" in preventing a riot in the city:

The first was the dramatic, massive EDA program, directed at the central
ghetto need, training and jobs. This was an experimental pilot project, something that was not being done on this scale or in this way in any other city.
It was carried out with unusual speed, and was more fully coordinated with
all related Federal, state, and city efforts than is usually the case with a large
Federal program. The second was the local response to this new Federal
approach. Following the change in the city administration, the new Mayor,
John Reading, and the new City Manager, Jerome Keithley, succeeded in
mobilizing first the business community, and then Minority groups and labor,
to respond with effective local action. . . .
This increasingly effective combination of Federal and local action gradually dissolved the deadlock between the ghetto and the establishment.[6]

By the end of 1968, the fame of the Oakland experiment was
spreading throughout the country. An article in the *New Yorker* of
November 30 cited "the allocation of some thirty million dollars to
Oakland by the Economic Development Administration." The article stated that Amory Bradford, in the course of directing the
spending of this sum, had "managed to break a longtime deadlock
between the Oakland ghetto and the local business and government
Establishment."[7] The appearance of success seemed overwhelming.

Appearances, however, can change. On March 16, 1969, a *Los
Angeles Times* feature carried the following headline: "OAKLAND
MINORITY JOB PROGRAM LABELED A 'PRETTY BIG DISASTER.' " According to the article, the once-heralded EDA program in Oakland
had fallen on hard times:

Today, only 20 new jobs have materialized for minorities and the program
is bogged down in a bureaucratic fight over minority hiring.
Critics see it as a classic case of big promises and little action.
"It's a pretty big disaster," says Percy Moore, executive director of Oakland's antipoverty agency. "A lot of commitments were made, but it never
got off the drawing board."[8]

5. *Ibid.*
6. *Ibid.,* pp. 204–205.
7. "The Talk of the Town," *New Yorker,* November 30, 1968, p. 52.
8. *Los Angeles Times,* March 16, 1969, p. 8.

Although an impressive array of public works construction had been planned, only the industrial park and access road had been completed.

The *Times*'s disheartening story uncovered disillusionment on the part of both businessmen and poverty groups. Walter Abernathy, assistant executive director of the Port of Oakland, observed that "our people felt the Federal government was going a little too far in telling us how to run our business." Other critics, with a different perspective, felt that most of the EDA money would "help the Vietnam war effort rather than the poor. World Airways gains much of its revenue for transporting cargo to Vietnam and the Marine Terminal would accommodate increased military traffic."

As for Oakland's black leaders, the article found that the hopes engendered by the 1966 urban experiment were badly dimmed by 1969. Local poverty program director Percy Moore complained that "from the beginning it was business as usual . . . and conditions here are getting worse. The port doesn't particularly care about social issues in the community, and the EDA hasn't used what little muscle it has to get employers to hire from minority groups."

In the same week that the *Los Angeles Times* article appeared, the EDA office in Oakland reported to the City Council that the federal agency had invested $1,085,000 in business loans in Oakland, but that only forty-three jobs had been created. The City Council was not pleased by the news.[9]

Written accounts of the EDA experience in Oakland provide two widely differing views of the program. In the optimistic view, the program had succeeded in forging an alliance between minority groups, business, and labor for the creation of new employment opportunities. In the pessimistic view, the urban experiment had raised expectations but had delivered only meager results. As time passed, the latter view became dominant. Four years after the initiation of the program, few jobs had been created and the major public works projects—the marine terminal and the aircraft hangar—had not been built. If despair and disillusionment in the minority community were in any way related to EDA activities in Oakland, these conditions would only have been worsened by the gap between promise and performance.

9. "U.S. Invests $1,085,000 to Create 43 Oakland Jobs," *Oakland Tribune,* March 16, 1969, p. 1.

In this study, we will go beyond the appearance of quick success or abject failure that have characterized most of the previous discussion of the EDA program in Oakland. After tracing the tortuous course of the program from the time of its inception, we will examine those factors that lay behind the program's frustrations: the difficulties of translating broad agreement into specific decisions, given a wide range of participants and perspectives; the opportunities for blockage and delay that result from a multiplicity of decision points; and the economic theories on which the program was based.

Our goal is not to be Monday-morning quarterbacks, to dissect the EDA's mistakes with the clarity that only hindsight can give. Rather, we will search for the lessons—administrative, economic, and political—that can be learned from the experience of the EDA in Oakland.

The experience of this program, which began with laudable intentions, commitment, and an innovative spirit, shows that *implementation* of a large-scale federal project can be very difficult indeed. Money was duly authorized and appropriated by Congress; the federal agency approved projects and committed funds with admirable speed. But the "technical details" of implementation proved to be more difficult and more time-consuming than the federal donors, local recipients, or enthusiastic observers had ever dreamed they would be.

Promises can create hope, but unfulfilled promises can lead to disillusionment and frustration. By concentrating on the implementation of programs, as well as their initiation, we should be able to increase the probability that policy promises will be realized. Fewer promises may be made in view of a heightened awareness of the obstacles to their fulfillment, but more of them should be kept. That aspiration guides this study.

2

Formulating Policy

Before we trace the tortuous path of this employment program in Oakland, let us examine the background and nature of the EDA itself. How did a primarily rural agency decide to go into Oakland—or into any city at all?

BACKGROUND: THE EDA, THE CITIES, AND OAKLAND

The Economic Development Administration was given life by the Public Works and Economic Development Act, passed into law on August 26, 1965.[1] This legislation was the successor to the Area Redevelopment Act of 1961, which had established a program to aid the depressed areas of the United States. These were areas that had suffered the loss of a major supportive industry, either through the depletion of a natural resource (such as gold) or as the result of a shift in the structure of the economy favoring one resource at the

1. For legislative history, we are indebted to Louise Resnikoff, "EDA in Oakland: An Evaluation" (unpublished paper of the University of California Oakland Project, October 1969); Owen McShane, "Toward a Transitional Economics: A Reappraisal of Urban Development Economics based on the experience of the Economic Development Administration in Oakland, California" (unpublished paper of the University of California Oakland Project, May 1970); and Douglas G. Montgomery, "The Federal Delivery System: Impact on the Community—A Case Study of EDA and the West Oakland Health Center" (paper delivered at the American Political Science Association annual meeting, Los Angeles, 1970).

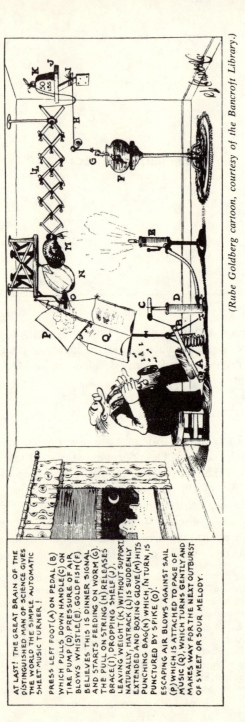

(Rube Goldberg cartoon, courtesy of the Bancroft Library.)

SIMPLE, ISN'T IT?

expense of another (such as oil for coal). The program had been administered by the Area Redevelopment Administration (ARA), the organizational predecessor of the EDA.

Other programs also had a strong influence on the Public Works and Economic Development Act. The Accelerated Public Works Act of 1962 had provided funds for the construction of job-producing public works in "depressed" areas eligible for ARA funds— as well as those other areas that had suffered over 6 percent unemployment during the previous twelve months.

In 1962 Congress had also passed the Appalachian Regional Development Act, which attempted to respond to the extraordinarily severe conditions of poverty that prevailed in the Appalachian region. Most notably, the program provided aid for the development of basic infrastructure, such as roads or flood control systems, which were necessary before any community could hope to attract industry. It also allowed for the formation of a Regional Development Commission which could plan for a region encompassing the many counties of the Appalachian area.[2]

The Public Works and Economic Development Act[3] combined features of all these preceding programs. Noting that "some of our regions, counties, and communities are suffering substantial and persistent unemployment and underemployment," the act proposed to help overcome this problem by providing "financial assistance, including grants for public works and development facilities to communities, industries, enterprises, and individuals in areas needing development."[4] The new act gave the Area Redevelopment Administration a new name—the Economic Development Administration.

Titles I-VI of the act provided for assistance to "redevelopment areas" (counties or cities of 250,000 population or over) and "development districts" (containing two or more redevelopment areas) where both unemployment and underemployment conditions had been persistently greater than those in the nation as a whole. Programs for assistance included direct and supplementary grants for the construction or improvement of development facilities; long-term low-interest loans for development facilities and for commercial and industrial establishments; and technical assistance for planning,

2. McShane, pp. 5–6.
3. Public Law 89–136, 89th Congress, 1st Session.
4. *Ibid.,* Statement of Purpose.

research, and demonstration projects. Title V provided for the establishment and funding of regional commissions.

Although the act did not rule out aid to depressed areas of large cities, it is clear from a reading of the legislative history that its provisions were directed toward the economies of rural areas and small towns. In the debate following introduction of the bill, Senator Muskie argued that certain provisions were the same as in the Appalachia bill because "since it was applicable to the undeveloped counties in Appalachia . . . it could also be applicable to other areas of the country in like circumstances."[5] Senator Yarborough observed in the same debate that "this is one bill which . . . enables the people in smaller cities and towns to share in the economy."[6]

Eligibility criteria made it difficult for cities to qualify for EDA programs. To be designated as a redevelopment area, a county or municipality would have to have registered an unemployment rate of 6 percent for the most recent calendar year. Furthermore, unemployment would have had to be at least (a) 50 percent above the national average for three of the preceding four years, or (b) 75 percent above the national average for two of the preceding four years, or (c) 100 percent above the national average for one of the last two years. In all qualifying time periods, the jobless rate must have exceeded 6 percent.[7]

Although parts of cities might have qualified on the basis of distressing unemployment statistics, eligibility had to be gained on the basis of city-wide figures. (In recent years, the criteria have been changed to make it easier for cities—or parts of cities—to qualify.[8]) Thus, in 1966 only eight cities of over 250,000 population—Oakland, San Diego, Philadelphia, Newark, Miami, Cleveland, Toledo, and Buffalo—were eligible for EDA programs.

Legislative eligibility requirements did not constitute the only constraint limiting the EDA's urban role. From the beginning, the

5. *Congressional Record,* U.S. Senate, May 26, 1965, p. 11795. Quoted in McShane, p. 81.

6. *Ibid.,* p. 11793.

7. *Public Works and Economic Development Act,* Sec. 401.

8. The "Javits-Farbstein Amendment" of 1967 designated as "redevelopment areas" those parts of cities that were eligible for OEO special impact programs. In 1969, a further amendment was passed that would allow the secretary of commerce to designate areas that exhibited characteristics of dependency, chronic unemployment, or rising community tensions. (See Montgomery, pp. 8–11.)

Federal Bureau of the Budget (now Office of Management and Budget) has taken a skeptical view of the EDA's involvement in large cities. A Budget Bureau official put the case clearly during a 1970 interview:

The EDA said to us, "There's so much to be done in the cities—we've got to get involved." But we've got a lot of programs already for cities—in HUD, HEW, and so on. The EDA just does not have the resources to become involved in cities. Their budget is a small one. [In 1966 the EDA appropriation was $332,421,000; in 1967 it was $295,816,000; in 1968, $274,834,000.] If they do get involved in urban programs, to do the job right they'd have to spend a huge hunk of money in one city. A program like the Oakland one could take up 10 percent of the agency's budget. Spending that much would be politically disastrous.

This official identified a distinctive role for the EDA:

Nobody's doing much in terms of middle-sized cities. You have Agriculture helping rural areas, you have HUD helping urban areas, but what about middle-sized cities? Say 2 to 5,000 to 150,000. This was an area that appeared to us to warrant EDA's attention. A total package of $1 million can have a fair impact on a 10 to 15,000 size city. Now, for these reasons we have tried in terms of recommendations to keep the EDA out of the cities.

The Budget Bureau's recommendations cannot be taken lightly by an agency mindful of next year's funding needs.

Seemingly undaunted by legislative and administrative obstacles, Eugene P. Foley (who became assistant secretary of commerce in charge of the EDA in October 1965) was determined to plunge the new agency into a concerted urban program. An EDA internal evaluation of the Oakland program, written in 1968, reveals that,

while many people in the Department, including Secretary Connor, viewed the EDA program as essentially rural, Foley apparently wanted to go where the action was—into the cities. Foley strongly believed that EDA should orient its program to the inner city core areas *where the majority of the nation's unemployed and underemployed lived.* (In fact, at one point, Foley believed that EDA should really be housed in HUD rather than Commerce.) His trips to Oakland reinforced his beliefs and resulted in his becoming caught up in the whole syndrome in which black people lived. He wanted to do something about it and wanted to do it in a hurry.[9]

Having decided to make a significant effort to attack urban un-

9. *EDA in Oakland, California: An Analysis* (prepared by Urban Affairs Division, Office of Policy Coordination, Economic Development Administration, October 1968). Hereafter referred to as EDA internal report.

employment, why did Foley and his aides choose to concentrate that effort on *one* city? One constraint on this decision was surely the lack of available time in which to spend the EDA's first appropriation; it appeared that the money could be allocated more quickly if it were concentrated in one city, rather than divided among a few. The authorization of $500 million had been passed by Congress in August 1965, and an appropriation of $300 million was passed in October for the fiscal year ending June 30, 1966.

During November and December, the new agency was being organized and staffed. "Very few projects had been approved" by January 1966, according to Amory Bradford, "though many applications were beginning to flow in as the new program became known."[10] Only four months remained in which to process nearly $300 million worth of projects, since any not completed and approved by the end of May could not go through the required legal and fiscal machinery in time to be funded out of the 1966 appropriation, which would expire on June 30. Bradford points out that the agency had a certain incentive to spend its allotted funds, for "if EDA failed to use all of its current appropriation, the next year's appropriation would almost certainly be cut by the Budget Bureau and Congress to a figure far below the $500 million authorized in the statute."[11]

Speaking of the first EDA appropriation, Foley remarked, "I had to spend it awfully fast."[12] An immediate major project provided a way to spend the EDA's appropriation quickly. As a Budget Bureau official observed, "Gene's decision to go to Oakland was a godsend, a smart move. This would be a big bang and it would also commit a lot of money."

Foley lists other reasons for his decision to focus the EDA's efforts on one city: "I could never have found the staff to spread around to numerous cities. Besides, I wanted one significant experiment." By concentrating a major program on one urban area, Foley hoped to achieve an early, dramatic success that would establish the EDA as a pathbreaker in the alleviation of urban misery. If the experiment worked, he would have a tangible accomplishment, visible and humanitarian, to his credit. (Normally, we would expect an

10. Bradford, p. 26.
11. *Ibid.*
12. Interview with Eugene P. Foley, July 23, 1970. Subsequent quotations from Foley are also taken from this interview.

"experiment" to include some specification of what is to be tested and how the results are to be evaluated. But the EDA's sense of urgency did not permit this kind of preparation.)

Why was Oakland chosen to be the one city? There appear to have been a number of reasons for the selection:

(1) Previous ARA contacts and experience in Oakland.—Because of its persistently high unemployment rate, Oakland had been designated as a redevelopment area under the ARA in 1964. In that year Oakland filed an Overall Economic Development Program, a planning document that was needed to qualify for ARA assistance. Raeburn Hay, of the ARA Business Loans Office, had gone to Oakland to discuss the kind of assistance his agency could offer the city.

In meetings with Mayor Houlihan and Norvel Smith, director of the Oakland Economic Development Council (the city's community action agency), Hay encouraged the city representatives to apply for ARA funds for a skills inventory of Oakland's unemployed.[13] The application was rejected by the ARA's Washington office, on the grounds that conducting skills inventories was a function of the Labor Department.

After turning down the city's first technical assistance application, the ARA sent Andrew Bennett of the Technical Assistance Office to Oakland to pursue other potential projects. Through his efforts, the Adult Minority Employment Project was given funding by the ARA. At that time, the project consisted of two staff members who were supposed to work with unions and businesses on job development. Although this was not a large effort, the EDA felt that it had to do something to mollify Houlihan and Smith, who were angered by the rejection of the skills inventory application.

The ARA also funded a consultant's study of the potential for economic development at the Port of Oakland, with an emphasis on marine terminal facilities. The port, which had been established under the city charter as an independent agency with authority over port facilities and the airport, was preparing applications for federal funding. At the same time, a few local businessmen had submitted applications for the ARA business loans program. Thus, when Foley arrived at the EDA, there was a "shelf" of potential projects for Oakland ready for funding. The ARA had had both experience and contacts in the city.

13. EDA internal report, p. 1.

(2) Oakland's potential for riot.—Foley recalls that "there was a general opinion in the government that Oakland was a tinderbox—the next Watts—the next to blow." Indeed, it was the view of a 1965 White House interdepartmental task force that Oakland was the most likely of fifteen explosive cities to "blow."[14] High unemployment, particularly in black areas, and racial tension were felt to be critical conditions that might lead to a riot.

Shortly after Foley came to the EDA, he received a number of staff papers describing a "potentially explosive" situation in Oakland and recommending an EDA program for the city. Among these was a paper by Anne Gould, the EDA training coordinator, based on a trip she had made to Oakland in late August and early September 1965. While most of the recommendations in her September memorandum concerned training program possibilities in Oakland, she also described the general social and economic conditions she found in the city.

Miss Gould's tone was ominous: "racial tension does exist. . . . there is sufficient mistrust, disaffection, and frustration building up in the Negro community to make the situation potentially explosive." But it was her view that there was still time to avert disaster "if we begin *at once* with some tangible programs that will reach the residents of the affected communities."[15] Even if the EDA's main purpose in Oakland was not the prevention of a riot, there is no question that Oakland's apparent potential for a violent explosion was an important reason for its selection as the recipient of the EDA's major urban effort.

(3) Oakland's unemployment statistics.—With an unemployment rate of 8.4 percent (compared to a 4.1 percent national average), Oakland's designation as an EDA eligible area seemed secure. Furthermore, Oakland appeared to be of manageable size; Washington officials felt that "Oakland's unemployed population was small enough in absolute numbers to be impacted upon by an EDA investment."[16]

(4) Oakland's political situation.—In reviewing his reasons for choosing Oakland, Eugene Foley pointed out that "Oakland had a Republican administration. If anything went wrong with an EDA

14. *Ibid.,* pp. 8–9.
15. *Ibid.,* p. 3. Italics in the original.
16. *Ibid.,* p. 9.

program, if we were arguing with a mayor, I did *not* want some Democratic mayor—like Daley—to be able to pick up the phone and call President Johnson. With a Republican mayor, I thought the federal government would at least not be against us." Oakland's weakness vis à vis the federal government thus became an advantage in drawing Foley's attention.

For a number of reasons—economic, administrative, and political—Oakland qualified admirably for the EDA's urban experiment. It had a high unemployment rate, and this condition—coupled with racial distrust—was felt by federal officials to mark the city as a prime target for a riot. Also, the ARA had had previous experience in the city and projects had already been developed. Finally, Oakland officials could not go over the EDA's head to the president.

Before beginning work on developing an Oakland program, Foley and his chief aides had made a number of crucial decisions—to launch a major EDA urban effort, to concentrate the program on one city, and to designate Oakland as the particular target. Let us now examine the City of Oakland and the ways in which the EDA effort there initially took shape.

HOPEFUL BEGINNINGS (1965–66)

OAKLAND—THE MEDIUM FOR THE EXPERIMENT

In 1966, when the University of California's Survey Research Center carried out a survey of poverty in Oakland, the total household population of the city was 365,490. The racial composition of the city, summarized in Table 1, shows a large minority population. Among people defined as below the poverty level—earning below $2,500 per year for a single individual and below $4,000 for a family

TABLE 1: Racial Composition of Oakland, California, 1966

Ethnicity	Number	Percent
White (excluding Spanish surname)	201,180	55
White (with Spanish surname)	35,200	10
Negro	110,050	30
Other nonwhite	19,060	5
Total persons	365,490	100

SOURCE: Survey Research Center, University of California, *Poverty and Poverty Programs in Oakland: Selected Results from the 701 Household Survey of Oakland,* William L. Nicholls, II, Study Director (Berkeley, 1967), p. 26.

of four—minority groups (black people and Mexican-Americans) were overrepresented. Whereas blacks made up 30 percent of the city's total population, they constituted 45 percent of the poverty population. Mexican-Americans, who made up 10 percent of the city's population, were 14 percent of the poverty population.

The most relevant statistics from the EDA's point of view were those concerning unemployment. Table 2 shows that Oakland's unemployment rate was over twice the national average. And other data from the survey showed clearly where the burden of joblessness rested. Among blacks and Mexican-Americans, the unemployment rate was found to be 12 percent, as opposed to 6 percent among whites and 8 percent among "orientals and other non-whites."[17] In the affluent Oakland hills, unemployment was 3.9 percent; in the West and East Oakland ghettoes, the figures were 14.3 percent and 14.4 percent, respectively.[18]

TABLE 2: Oakland's Unemployment Rate Is Significantly Higher than the National Average[a]

| Rates | Percent of Civilian Labor Force Unemployed | |
	Oakland	United States
Crude Rates[b]		
Total (all civilian workers)	8.4	4.1
Males, 20 years and over	4.8	2.3
Females, 20 years and over	8.3	3.9
Both sexes, 14 to 19 years	30.5	13.0
Seasonally Adjusted Rates[c]		
Total (all civilian workers)	7.7	4.0
Males, 20 years and over	4.6	2.5
Females, 20 years and over	7.5	3.9
Both sexes, 14 to 19 years	26.7	12.4

[a]Figures based on 1966 "701" study of Oakland. Section 701 of the Federal Housing Act of 1954, as amended, provides funds for urban planning assistance.
[b]For Oakland, the sample unemployment rate based on all cases included in the 701 survey. For the United States, the mean adjusted unemployment rate for May, June, July, and August.
[c]Mean seasonally adjusted rates for May, June, July, and August. For Oakland, an approximate seasonal adjustment was made for interviews completed in each month, based on U.S. seasonal adjustment figures.
Source: Stanford Research Institute, *Human Resources Development for Oakland: Problems and Policies* (Menlo Park, 1968), p. 10.

17. Stanford Research Institute, *Human Resources Development for Oakland: Problems and Policies* (Menlo Park, 1968), p. 12.
18. *Ibid.*, p. 16.

In dealing with the problems posed by poverty, unemployment, and racial tension, Oakland's elected officials have faced a number of obstacles. One is the fragmentation of governmental authority: the Redevelopment Agency, Housing Authority, School Board, and Port Commission are all outside the control of City Hall. (In 1967 the poverty program's community action agency, the Oakland Economic Development Council, declared its independence from local government, though the city took over again in 1971.)

City government itself is based on the council-manager form, under which the City Council is supposed to formulate policy and the city manager is supposed to administer that policy. The mayor, who is elected separately, is one of nine councilmen. Although the council-manager model assumes that "policy" will direct "administration," the relationship between policy and administration in Oakland has been strongly affected by the resources available to the politicians on one hand and the administrators on the other. The advantages of the administrators are considerable.

First of all, the mayor and councilmen are not intended to serve full time at their jobs; the city manager, in contrast, is enjoined by the charter "to devote his entire time to the duties and interests of the City."[19] Salary levels underscore this difference: the mayor earns only $7,500 and each councilman earns $3,600 per year, but the city manager's annual salary is $38,940. It would be a rare councilman or mayor who could afford to spend full time on his job.

This imbalance between the political and administrative sides of Oakland city government is further increased by a disparity in the staff and informational resources available to the council and manager. For the entire city council is served by just one secretary, who answers the phone, arranges appointments, types letters, and administers the Christmas program of the Municipal Employees' Choir. The mayor is not much better off, with one administrative assistant and three secretaries.

The city manager, in sharp contrast, may utilize the manpower and information resources of all city departments under his control —police, fire, public works, and so forth. Furthermore, the manager has three full-time staff assistants in his own office who help him keep abreast of departmental communications. The finance and budget directors, who serve under the city manager, provide him with in-

19. *Charter of the City of Oakland,* Sec. 27 (4) m.

formation regarding department allocations and utilization of city funds. As a result, the city manager tends to know more than anyone else about city government structure, processes, and substantive policy. For an elected public official in Oakland who wishes to exercise leadership, the built-in obstacles are enormous.

Perhaps even more discouraging to the exercise of political leadership has been the nature of Oakland's political system itself. The lack of politically oriented interest groups and party activity has meant that leaders—or potential leaders—have been deprived of a source of both information about and support for public policies they might wish to propose.

EDA officials who were interviewed in 1970 felt that Oakland's governmental and political system constituted one of their most difficult problems in the implementation of their program in that city. We shall examine the connections between this federal program and the Oakland political system in a later chapter. But let us return now to the hopeful beginnings of the EDA Oakland program in the seemingly distant past of 1965–66.

FIRST IMPRESSIONS

On December 9, 1965, Eugene Foley, the assistant secretary of commerce, and Amory Bradford, who had expressed an interest in helping EDA urban projects, made their first visit to Oakland. Instead of going to City Hall or the Port of Oakland, Foley and Bradford went to a meeting of the East Oakland Parish. John Frykman, Pastor of St. John's Lutheran Church in East Oakland, had assembled a dozen people—including black community organizers and members of the parish staff—to tell Foley about Oakland. Curtis Lee Baker, an outspoken black man, took a dim view of the outsiders' visit: "What did it cost to bring you rich White men out here? We'd rather have the money. We've had enough studies. What we need now is justice, action, jobs!"[20]

Later in the day, Bradford and Foley went to a Teamsters hiring hall and talked to blacks who were looking for jobs. Then came a tour of the West Oakland ghetto, guided by Curtis Baker and Elijah Turner, a CORE officer. The overall impression they gained was a

20. Bradford, p. 5.

bleak one; blacks in the Oakland ghetto faced uncertain employment prospects and suffered from poverty and woefully inadequate housing.

A month later, on January 7, 1966, Foley and Bradford returned to Oakland. On the next morning they were to attend a "mass meeting" called by Curtis Baker to tell the federal representatives more about the needs of the unemployed. Although the recreation hall that was to have been the meeting place had been "closed for painting" (Baker and his friends suspected a City Hall move against them), Foley was able to talk informally to those assembled on the grass outside the hall.

Bradford felt that thoughts were expressed frankly and easily between the EDA officials and poor black people, and he wrote in his book:

I noted then something that surprised me, but which has since been confirmed again and again. The poor and the unemployed see their problems more clearly, and better understand the mechanisms of society that create their problems, than the great majority of outside, trained experts whose job it is to provide solutions. Also, even when illiterate, they express their knowledge with a simple clarity and force, unencumbered by complicated theory, which cuts through many useless preconceptions.[21]

Assistant Secretary Foley was also impressed by his visits to the Oakland ghetto. After the January 8 meeting Bradford wrote in a letter that "Foley is going to make Oakland a pilot project in concentrating all Federal resources to create new jobs by bringing in new business, public works, training, and ending discrimination in hiring." Foley had asked Bradford to "head this up, negotiating with business and labor and all groups involved, and coordinating the efforts of all government agencies"[22]— a large order indeed.

Why, in their initial trips to Oakland, did Foley and Bradford neglect visiting City Hall? Foley offers this explanation: "I didn't want to alienate the black community by seeming to come in as part of the Establishment. I wanted to meet black people first." This strategy, however, did alienate Oakland's Mayor John C. Houlihan, who complained bitterly about Foley's choice of initial contacts when the mayor visited the assistant secretary in Washington on January

21. *Ibid.,* p. 17.
22. *Ibid.,* p. 22.

13.[23] Although angered by the rebuff, Mayor Houlihan—who was actively trying to promote economic development in Oakland—agreed to set up a meeting of local leaders on January 28 and 29 to hear about Foley's proposed pilot program.

THE OAKLAND TASK FORCE AND ADMINISTRATIVE INNOVATION

At a breakfast meeting with Foley on January 13, the day of Mayor Houlihan's visit, Amory Bradford agreed to take over personal direction of the EDA project in Oakland. Foley assigned to the project a group of staff members—mostly young—who he felt were both capable and committed to urban programs. They included Andy Bennett of Technical Assistance and Anne Gould, the training coordinator, who had been instrumental in directing Foley's attention to Oakland in the first place. Other members of the group assigned to Oakland were:

Jay Schwamm, an investment banker who had been retained by Foley as a project consultant charged with increasing the role of private investment in economic development.

Blair Butterworth, the son of a career diplomat and a graduate of Princeton, who came from the Peace Corps in Ghana to be western area supervisor in charge of EDA offices in the western states.

Douglas Costle, an attorney in the EDA general counsel's office, who was Bradford's Washington liaison and then his assistant in Oakland. Costle had spent two years working with the Civil Rights Division of the Justice Department.

Richard Daschbach, of the Business Loans Division, who was charged with stimulating interest in the loans program. Daschbach was also a lawyer; he had begun his Washington career as an assistant to Representative Hale Boggs of Louisiana.

George Karras, of the Office of Public Works (and in 1972 director of that office), who was to analyze public works projects for their job-creating possibilities and technical soundness. Karras, who came out of the labor movement, was now committed to EDA service as a long-term career.

Bill Leland, assistant for Equal Opportunity, who was to concentrate on civil rights questions.

23. *Ibid.,* p. 29.

Foley believed that "about 90 percent of the people in government are for retrenchment. The challenge is to pick out the 10 percent who can do something. You have to move directly and circumvent the bureaucracy if you really want something." For these reasons Foley changed the normal bureaucratic procedure in order to expedite the Oakland project: "I advised my administrators that Oakland had the highest priority. Any request from Bradford had the highest priority; Bradford was able to call me directly and calls would always be put through."

The members of the Oakland task force were similarly inclined toward nonbureaucratic innovation. Bradford says,

All were the antithesis of the stereotyped bureaucrat cautiously protecting his career. Their approach right down the line was: "What needs to be done? How can we do it best, and faster?" When the answers were clear, they were all willing to risk their careers and their health and sacrifice their personal lives, to get the job done well and quickly. Something happened to us all in Oakland, once we became identified with its problems, that created a rare combination of shared dedication, excitement and satisfaction.[24]

Members of the task force interviewed in 1970 remembered the "exhilaration," "excitement," and "feeling that we could really turn things around" that pervaded the EDA project in 1966.

There were those who did not share the enthusiasm for the Oakland project shown by Foley, Bradford, and the members of the task force. Bradford admits that the high spirit of the project team "puzzled, and annoyed, some of their uninitiated associates and bosses in Washington, until they came to Oakland and caught the fever themselves."[25] (Unfortunately for the project, there were many EDA officials in Washington who never "caught the fever." The 1968 EDA internal evaluation said that "Foley's arrangement had created intra-agency antipathies between his task force agents and their program superiors."[26])

The magnitude of the departure from normal bureaucratic channels should not be exaggerated. As one task force member pointed out,

24. *Ibid.*, p. 30.
25. *Ibid.*, p. 31.
26. EDA internal report, p. 52.

Foley did by-pass people—like [Secretary of Commerce] Connor—in his decision to go into Oakland and commit the funds. But, after we went in, the paperwork, review, and analysis was done by regular EDA Washington staff. Although it is true that, in business loans, Daschbach did do a lot of running himself, and although Foley did put gold stars on certain projects he wanted expedited. My job was expeditive: cajoling, persuading, etc. I did not evaluate projects; technical project evaluation would be done by EDA staff.

It is important also to note that EDA task force members split their time between Washington and Oakland and were not relieved of their regular Washington duties. During this time they were also working on legal opinions, loan applications, and public works construction in their respective EDA divisions.

Thus, the administrative break with normal channels was far from complete, but there is no question that it engendered substantial resentment among EDA staff members in Washington. Holdover staff members from the ARA, who had prepared plans for projects all over the country, now found that Oakland had highest priority. An urban program was being initiated—and quickly—in an agency whose staff was primarily oriented toward rural areas.

DUNSMUIR

A few days before the Dunsmuir House meeting at which the EDA representatives were to confer with Oakland's civic and business leaders, one Oakland institution had the opportunity to present an early case to the EDA. Monroe Sullivan, a staff member of the Port of Oakland, had initiated engineering and architectural studies that would lead to the port's submission of applications for EDA aid. Then Sullivan worked up a brochure to present the projects to EDA staff. He called Blair Butterworth to arrange for an appointment, and Sullivan met with the EDA task force in Foley's office shortly before they left for Oakland. With Oakland's congressmen George Miller and Jeffery Cohelan in supportive attendance, Sullivan made a detailed presentation of the port's needs and its plans for meeting them with EDA assistance.[27]

When the task force met with Foley on January 26 to review the program for the upcoming meetings, a number of the staff proposed that the EDA efforts be coordinated carefully with those of all other

27. Bradford, p. 34.

federal agencies, both in Oakland and in Washington. But Foley objected, on the grounds that it would delay the project "longer than Oakland can afford to wait." Instead, he said that the EDA should proceed as fast as it could and let coordination follow later.[28] Foley was fond of repeating a story about Mayor Jimmy Walker of New York. A Democratic candidate for city council, who was worried about his chances for election, expressed that anxiety to Walker. So the mayor took the candidate for a ride on a tugboat and pointed to the garbage following in the boat's wake. "You see the way this boat is pulling in that garbage?" asked Walker. "Well, that's how I'm going to pull you in on Election Day." In a similar manner, explained Foley, the EDA would be out front and the other agencies would be pulled along. Prior coordination would be unnecessary.

Even if the EDA had decided to coordinate its policies with other departments, what would "coordination" have meant for designing policy? Who would coordinate whom? Toward what ends would the coordination be directed? And which part of the EDA—Washington offices, task force, regional office—would be involved in coordination?

Dunsmuir House is a stately white-columned mansion in a park at the edge of Oakland, which has served from time to time as a city conference center. The EDA had left the question of whom to invite to the January 28 conference in the hands of Mayor Houlihan. He assembled about forty business and governmental leaders, including representatives of the port, the chamber of commerce, the Oakland Economic Development Council (OEDC), and the Planning Commission. The newly named city manager, Jerome Keithley, was there —as well as the heads of some city departments. But aside from the mayor, no city councilmen were present.

Because of EDA concern about the lack of representation from labor and minority groups, last-minute invitations were issued to Robert Ash, executive secretary of the Alameda County Central Labor Council, and to Judge Lionel Wilson, chairman of the OEDC. Judge Wilson and Norvel Smith were the only blacks present.[29]

In introducing the federal officials, Mayor Houlihan showed that he had not buried his hard feelings toward them. He said that the city "had suffered from the oral contributions of the people in the

28. *Ibid.*
29. *Ibid.*, p. 38.

streets" and the visits of "the gratuitous activists, and the Federal
Hawkshaws [who] come in and embrace the poor. All this has kept
the fans of discontent going" and was "stirring in a mudhole."[30] But
then Houlihan changed his tone and declared that he was "full
of hope and desire" for the EDA program and ready to help it along.

Foley, somewhat angered by the introduction, nevertheless managed to keep his temper and to pledge a "creative federalism." He
said that past experience with central direction from Washington had
shown that it did not "allow for adapting programs to the personality
of the community. Creative Federalism requires more and more decisions to be made at the local level, with only policy direction from
Washington." Foley then emphasized the EDA's central mission in
the city: "Our constraint, very simply, is that we must create new and
permanent jobs for the unemployed and the underemployed. Here,
that means the Negro."[31]

The EDA program was then presented in detail. Andy Bennett
discussed technical assistance. George Karras outlined the public
works program, and Dick Daschbach described business loans. Bill
Leland reviewed the statutory requirements for equal opportunity
hiring.

After the presentations were over, City Manager Keithley raised
a perceptive and troubling question, one that would haunt the EDA
in the days and years ahead: "Aren't we skirting the problem? We
are getting a lot of good information, but how do you connect with
the long-term unemployed? We still have not heard a formula on
guaranteeing that the right people get the right job."[32] The search
for that formula would prove difficult.

On the second day of the conference, Foley announced that he was
"prepared to set up a pilot project in Oakland, to see if a massive in-
jection of money can create permanent jobs for the hard-core unemployed. We are talking about $15,000,000, and possibly upward
if you can spend it wisely in a short length of time."[33]

Where had the figure of $15,000,000 come from? An early EDA
participant recalled that "Karras had told Foley, 'Well, you can commit fifteen million dollars safely.' Foley was wondering what figure

30. *Ibid.*, p. 39.
31. *Ibid.*, p. 40.
32. Ibid., p. 43.
33. *Ibid.*

he should announce and they decided to pick a figure they knew they could safely commit and also one that was big enough to really make people listen to them."

Oakland's civic and business leaders did listen to the EDA team, although they showed considerably more interest in business expansion than in creating jobs for the unemployed.[34] Still, given the $15,-000,000 "carrot," the federal representatives hoped that progress could be made in the latter area.

THE EMPLOYMENT PLAN

During February the EDA staff in Oakland wrestled with the question of how to tie business development to jobs for the long-term unemployed. There was no unanimity within the EDA organization on the necessity of tying financial aid to job guarantees. One field representative, who had not been at Dunsmuir, told a concerned Oakland minister that "there were no EDA regulations that required the recipient of a grant or loan to employ the long-term unemployed, and that instead it was just expected that the jobs created would eventually result in such employment." [35] Like the businessmen, he apparently expected an abstraction called "the entire community" to benefit from economic growth. Prosperity meant more jobs, and minorities somehow would share in them.

Bradford felt that a general standard of "maximum possible employment" of ghetto residents was too vague and that the EDA ought to try to gain more specific commitments. He therefore searched for a way to link the jobs more closely to the local unemployed. The task force had first thought of assembling a high-level committee that would establish and enforce employment standards. But they soon decided that such willing and able leaders were not to be found in Oakland at that time. The answer Bradford settled on was that of an employment plan in which each applicant for EDA assistance would be required to enumerate and describe jobs that he thought would result from that assistance. Furthermore, each employer would have to tell the EDA what he would do to recruit the hard-core unemployed and what training would be required. All this would be submitted to a local committee—and then the EDA—for

34. A situation that was noticed by Bradford, Foley, and the rest of the EDA task force at Dunsmuir.
35. Quoted in Bradford, pp. 72–73.

review and approval before the EDA would agree to provide assistance.

If approved, the employment plan would become part of the contractual agreement between the EDA and an employer; noncompliance with the plan would be a condition of default in the loan or the lease of EDA-improved facilities. (Several employers objected strenuously to the penalty clause which made noncompliance a default enabling the EDA to terminate a lease or call a loan. In August Bradford and his Oakland colleagues decided to substitute arbitration for the stringent penalties of default.)

The Employment Plan Review Board was an integral part of the process Bradford envisioned, for that body would both rule on applications for assistance and provide a continuing system of surveillance over approved projects.

Participation of the poor, although never mentioned in the EDA act, was important to Bradford and to some of his colleagues in the EDA. One task force member explained that "You had to have a committee representing the poor themselves. A countervailing structure to City Hall was important to recognize the legitimacy of the claims of the poor. Bradford and I had gone to a lot of poverty program target area meetings. We were impressed by what we'd seen —impressed by the eloquence of target area representatives."

Within the Oakland poverty program in 1966, representatives of the poverty target areas were fighting for and gaining a greater voice in the program. Bradford and the task force came to feel that poor people should also have the dominant voice on the Employment Plan Review Board. Accordingly, they decided that a majority of the members of that board should be designated by the target area poverty groups.[36]

Although Bradford found enthusiasm in Oakland for his employment plan proposal, some EDA officials in Washington were less happy about it. The agency's lawyers wondered about its looseness; business loan experts worried about the wisdom of saddling already hard-pressed loan recipients with additional obligations; public works administrators viewed the plan as an unnecessary complication in the difficult task of project management. Many were convinced that the whole process was too cumbersome and harsh to be

36. Bradford, p. 83.

put into effect. The final decision, however, rested with Eugene Foley. During the last week of March, Foley sided with Bradford and approved the plan.

A CHANGE OF MAYORS

Other events were occurring in Oakland during February 1966. Mayor Houlihan was charged with embezzling over $90,000 from an estate that he, as a lawyer, had been administering; the mayor resigned on February 15. Two weeks later, the City Council elected one of its members—John H. Reading—to be mayor. Reading, a "nonpartisan" Republican, was a successful businessman who was dedicated to civic service. Though he had an intense dislike for politics, he soon gave promise of being an activist mayor.

Foley, Bradford, and their EDA assistants were impressed with Reading's first actions in office—nominating (unsuccessfully) a black man to fill his old seat on the City Council, seeking out contacts in the ghetto, and vociferously supporting the EDA and other employment-related projects. An EDA participant recalled that "Reading at this time began to look like a very strong mayor. . . . We had a tremendous asset in a potentially strong mayor."

PROJECT DECISIONS: PUBLIC WORKS

When the processing of applications begun in February, time was a pressing concern of the EDA staff. If the appropriation was not spent by June 30, the EDA would lose the money and its future appropriations might be reduced. Because of the time needed for legal and fiscal processing, project proposals would have to be completed by the end of May. Given this constraint, there was not sufficient time to carry out an extensive search of possible sponsors of public works projects.

Besides, there was one applicant that had already made contact with the EDA. "Following the results of the technical assistance project," an EDA staff member pointed out, "it appeared that the port was ready. So we immediately put together port-related projects." The port also had other advantages: autonomy, ownership of a large area, tremendous growth potential, and previous favorable evaluations by the ARA.[37] And EDA officials felt that the port was the

37. McShane, pp. 40–42, discusses these at some length.

institution in Oakland most adept in filling out federal applications. (To him that hath the ability to fill out the forms shall be given.) In any event, given the time constraint, the port appeared to be the only show in town. As an EDA man put it, "The EDA had to spend its funds by June of 1966. The port had the projects and the others didn't."

The city government did submit applications for a range of public works—sewers, streets, and so forth—but it was turned down on the grounds that such projects would not generate sufficient employment. The only city project to be approved was an access road to the newly built coliseum. This project's approval was seen by the EDA task force as an effort on the part of their agency to get city administrators to respond to the program; they never expected that the access road would create many jobs.

In Washington the staff of the Office of Public Works assessed the projects as vehicles for job creation. They made employment estimates based on known and anticipated growth of major project users. The potential recipient's job plans also played a role in these projections. Job estimates were discounted if they would take a long time to materialize or if they were unrelated to the projects under consideration.[38]

At the beginning of April, according to a task force member, "there was a ranking of all programs . . . in relation to employment. Now, for example, building the Hegenberger extension by the city, we put that way down the list because there was really not much employment in it." There was some disagreement on relative ranking; employment prospects were very difficult to predict.

Finally, projects worth $23,289,000 were selected to announce on April 29. By what process was that figure chosen? "There was a phone conversation between Washington and Oakland," Bradford says, "and we drew the line at a certain point in the ranking. There was a stop right under the ones I really wanted and above the ones that I didn't want. The cluster above the line were ones that I was really anxious to get through."[39]

38. Letter from George Karras, director of the EDA Office of Public Works, to Jeffrey Pressman, November 17, 1970.
39. Pressman interview with Amory Bradford, October 27, 1970.

RESEARCH ASSISTANCE

In developing their Oakland program, the EDA task force had the assistance of the sociologist Floyd Hunter, whose consulting firm of Social Science Research and Development Corporation received an EDA planning advance of $72,000 in March. Hunter had been brought into the project by Foley, who says he "was impressed by his [Hunter's] book on Atlanta and by Hunter personally. I thought he could be a critical independent scholar—watching our performance and criticizing us where appropriate." Hunter appeared to have appropriate credentials, since he was an academic and recognized as a critic of Oakland's city government, having written a report on the city's housing situation that had angered City Hall. (This, it was felt, would help to keep the EDA free of the "establishment" label.)

At the beginning, Bradford thought that "Hunter was helpful . . . telling me about Oakland, being a guy I could talk to."[40] Later, Hunter would significantly expand his role in the EDA project.

THE ANNOUNCEMENT

After the successful projects had been selected, but before they had been announced, port officials expressed their concern about part of the employment plan procedure. Specifically, they had serious reservations about the requirements that the employment plan provisions be included in lease and sales of port property developed with EDA funds.

Some of the EDA's Washington staff, who had never liked the employment plan idea in the first place, argued that the federal agency should seek to reach agreement with the port on this point before the April 29 announcement. But Bradford held firm; he urged Foley to "simply announce our employment conditions and leave it to them to accept or reject the entire offer. I was certain that once the offers had been publicly announced it would not be feasible for them to reject $23,000,000 of needed development funds because of the EDA requirements that jobs go to the local unemployed."[41]

40. *Ibid.*
41. Bradford, p. 122.

Foley agreed, and Bradford's strategy proved to be at least partially correct: the Port accepted EDA's conditions. But whether it accepted the conditions as wholeheartedly as it accepted the funds remained to be seen.

By the time of the April 29 announcement, a three-way agreement between the EDA, the port, and World Airways had been forged as a precondition for the start of a $10 million hangar project. The EDA would make a grant and loan to the port for building the hangar; World Airways would lease the facility for forty years for a rent that would cover the port's financing and other costs and increase with its earnings there. Finally, as part of the lease's conditions, President Ed Daly of World would agree with the EDA on an employment plan to provide jobs for unemployed Oakland residents, who would be trained at government expense to qualify for them.[42]

From the beginning, the success of the EDA program depended on agreement among a diverse group of participants with differing organizational objectives. The port and World Airways saw federal funds as an aid in increasing their capital facilities, while the EDA Oakland task force was primarily interested in the rapid development of jobs for unemployed minorities. Even within the EDA there were disagreements between advocates of the employment plan and those who felt that enforcement of the plan would make rapid completion of the projects more difficult.

To recapitulate, Foley declared in the April 29 announcement that the EDA had agreed to offer public works grants and loans totaling $23,289,000; 60 percent of the total would be grants and 40 percent would be loans. The projects were: airport hangar, $10,650,-000 (to Port of Oakland; to be leased by World Airways); marine terminal, $10,125,000 (to Port of Oakland); port industrial park, $2,100,000 (to Port of Oakland); and access road to coliseum, $414,-000 (to city of Oakland). Other public works projects were awarded to the Port of Oakland at later dates. They included: air cargo terminal, $184,000 (approved February 1, 1966); twenty small aircraft hangers, $76,000 (approved June 15, 1966); and auxiliary airport tower, $223,000 (approved February 1, 1967).[43]

42. *Ibid.,* p. 160.
43. Source of figures: Resnikoff, p. 37.

SPRING AND SUMMER: FLESHING OUT THE EDA PROGRAM

The EDA program began to take shape in the spring and summer of 1966. Amory Bradford initiated employment plan discussions with World Airways in May, and in June Mayor Reading organized a series of seminars to acquaint local businessmen with all federal loan programs.

EDA officials were still worried about the city's ability to develop an overall economic development plan; the first plan, done by Stanford Research Institute, was criticized by EDA officials as "providing inadequate directions as to what to do in Oakland's economy." Also, the EDA was skeptical about the city's ability to form a "broad-based committee" to monitor and amend such a plan. In an effort to find out more about Oakland's economy and politics, and to try to identify a group of people who might offer support to its program, the EDA in July awarded Floyd Hunter a $400,000 contract to make an "economic power structure" study of the city and to evaluate certain ongoing programs. From the beginning, EDA officials were unclear about what an overall development plan was, why such a plan was needed, and how a power structure study was related to the plan.

On October 5 the Oakland program suffered a severe jolt when Eugene Foley announced his resignation as head of the EDA. In a later interview, Foley said he quit "because I could see the way the wind was blowing. Commerce was cracking down on EDA—the White House had decided that EDA should not be spending money in cities. Vietnam was eating everything up." Although the Oakland team was surprised and depressed by Foley's departure, there were hopeful developments in Oakland that kept alive a spirit of optimism. By the end of the summer, an eight-member Employment Plan Review Board had been formed, with one representative from each of the five poverty target areas and one each from labor, management, and the EDA.[44]

44. The labor representative, Norman Amundsen, had been selected directly by the Alameda County Central Labor Council; representing management was Ken Thompson, who had talked to EDA officials on a number of occasions since the Dunsmuir meetings. Cesar Flores Mendez, a businessman, was appointed by the "Spanish-speaking" target area committee. The members from each of the other target areas were black housewives: Mrs. Ruby

The first meeting, to organize the committee, was held on September 8. At the next meeting, on October 8, the committee reviewed the Employment Plans of three Oakland applicants for business loans. (We will discuss the experience of this program in chapter 4). Bennie's Candies, Rainbow Car Wash, and Colombo Bakeries were all successful before the committee. (Bennie would receive a loan of $64,000 which he said would help him create 25 jobs. Rainbow would obtain $135,000 for a projected 35 jobs; Colombo would receive $423,000 for a projected job increase of 158.)[45]

At its third meeting on November 12, the board approved two additional employment plans. The first was based on a business loan of $241,000 to Sierra Cotton Mills, which planned to add sixty-six new employees over a two-year period and to provide on-the-job training. The second employment plan presented at the meeting was that of World Airways. After projecting a list of "Additional Personnel to be Hired, 1967–1971," the World employment plan stated that "World and the appropriate governmental agencies undertake to make training opportunities available to the fullest extent possible to unemployed and under-employed residents of Oakland."[46] (By October it had been agreed that World Airways would set up and operate a training program, with the government paying the cost. The program would be funded under Section 241 of the Manpower Development and Training Act, which provided support for programs in EDA-designated areas. EDA officials had decided against locating the training program at the East Bay Skills Center, "partly because it would be better to locate it at the airport, but more because the Skills Center was still suffering from administrative confusion."[47] The training program had always been regarded by EDA officials as a critical ingredient in the capacity of the hangar project to create jobs.)

World Airways further promised to use realistic tests in recruiting for the training programs, in an effort to "avoid the cultural bias found in many existing tests or qualifications." Finally, the plan

---

Baker, West Oakland; Mrs. Jewel Manley, North Oakland; Mrs. Willie Thompson, Fruitvale; and Mrs. Marjorie Woods, East Oakland.

45. For a more detailed account of this meeting, see Resnikoff, pp. 25–27.

46. Employment Plan of World Air Center, Inc. and World Airways, Inc., approved by the EDA on December 14, 1966.

47. Bradford, p. 162.

stated that "preference will be given to qualified residents of the city of Oakland in the filling of positions resulting from the expansion of operations" by World.

The plan recognized fully that predicting future events is an uncertain enterprise: "This Plan is based upon the method and scope of operation now contemplated by World in the hangar which is to be constructed at the Port of Oakland. If World's method and scope of operation is changed, World shall have the right to amend this Plan consistent with its stated objectives, . . . subject to EDA approval." And again:

World and EDA recognize the extreme complexity of predicting business expansion, designing new training programs which will meet FAA standards, developing instructional and institutional forms which will allow previously unskilled and unemployed Oakland residents to move rapidly into highly skilled positions in a growing industry, and assuming that these persons will be sufficiently trained and qualified to take responsibility for the lives of air travelers utilizing World's services.

Even with these conditioning paragraphs, the plan seemed hopeful enough to the review board, which approved it at the November 12 meeting.

That meeting was the last appearance of Amory Bradford as an EDA consultant. He wrote in his book that "Approval of the World Airways Plan, by a Board that had learned to function well, rounded out all that I had set out to do when I began in Oakland in January, nine months earlier. It was time to go."[48] In Washington, Bradford gave a detailed briefing on Oakland to Ross Davis, who had succeeded Foley as head of the EDA.

As 1966 came to an end, there were unmistakable stirrings of activity in Oakland. Mayor Reading had sponsored a job fair in September to bring job developers and job seekers together. (An EDA technical assistance grant had helped the city to cover the small deficit incurred.) Then the mayor moved to establish a manpower commission that would support job training and placement efforts in the city. On December 14 the EDA and World Airways formally signed the employment plan agreement, which promised to create a significant supply of new jobs.

Some difficulties did develop in the EDA program in the last half of 1966, but for the most part they appeared to be "technical" ones

48. *Ibid.*, p. 169.

that did not raise fundamental questions of discrimination or willingness to hire the unemployed. During the summer, an EDA consultant had objected to the method by which the port was filling the area to be used for the marine terminal. In the consultant's opinion, the material being used for filling the bay—material that came from Bay Area Rapid Transit construction sites—contained a great amount of objectionable debris.[49] Because of this, and because the EDA determined that the proposed tenant of that area, Matson Navigation Company, would not provide sizable new employment, the port decided to move the EDA-financed project to a different area. (The Matson Company, frankly admitting that it did not plan extensive new hiring, had requested to be separated from the port's arrangement with the EDA.)

There were also disputes in 1966 between the EDA and the port over reimbursement of in-house engineering expenses and the method of disbursement of federal funds. But these, once again, appeared to be technical issues that could be worked out.

What seemed important was that the EDA had made a substantial financial commitment to Oakland and that that commitment was tied to the creation of jobs for the hard-core unemployed. Foley, Bradford, and the task force had supplied the initial push that had attracted nationwide publicity; now all that remained was the carrying out of the plans.

49. EDA project progress report, April 10, 1968.

3

Trials of Implementation

Although EDA officials had thought that designing the innovative policy, committing funds, and obtaining initial local agreements were the most crucial parts of the program, the implementation of the program proved surprisingly difficult. This chapter will show how the "technical details" of implementation, which had not initially been a source of concern, combined to delay the program and frustrate its sponsors' hopes.

IMPLEMENTATION: MARINE TERMINAL

Before construction of the 7th Street Marine Terminal could begin, a number of thorny issues had to be resolved. One of these issues was the quality of filling material that the port was planning to put in San Francisco Bay. After a summer of dispute on the matter in 1966, Walter Butler (the EDA's consultant) conducted an investigation and found that "practices not always conducive to sound engineering have persisted on the filling portion of this project. Debris, garbage, timber, etc. have found their way into the Terminal area fill. The project generally seems to have suffered from lack of co-ordinated planning."[1] Butler also found that the structural stability of

1. Letter from Walter Butler to Henry Brooks, chief EDA Public Works engineer, September 2, 1966.

the dikes was "marginal." Throughout the last half of 1966, the port and the EDA continued to disagree about the quality of bay fill.

Another subject of dispute concerned advance funding. On June 17, 1966, Ben Nutter, executive director of the port, had written to Foley requesting that the port be reimbursed for " 'in house' engineering expenses where, for small items and under urgency conditions, the Port staff is available to do the work."[2] (In order to expedite the application, the port had used its own staff for preliminary engineering work.)

On July 15, 1966, J. Monroe Sullivan of the port wrote to the EDA about a troubling provision of the Oakland city charter that would make the port dependent on advance funding from the federal government. A section of the charter had been interpreted to mean that the port might raise money by issuing revenue bonds and by issuing certificates of indebtedness. In effect, said Sullivan, this prohibited the port from borrowing money unless there was a pledge of revenues from the facility involved. And in this case, the port had pledged revenues from the industrial park (and surplus revenues from the hangar and marine facilities) to the EDA. Because the charter made it difficult for the port to borrow money for work on these projects, Sullivan wrote, "our goal . . . is to make sure that the interim financing is available out of EDA funds when it is needed."[3]

Difficulties concerning interim financing were causing delays in the project. The EDA's general policy is never to advance grant funds for interim development and construction financing. On a few occasions loans have been advanced to some applicants, usually Indian reservations, who were unable to obtain interim financing on their own. But in normal cases, the applicants must secure their own interim financing. The EDA includes the interest on the grantee's borrowed interim financing as part of the legitimate project cost. (The strict policy on interim financing is designed both to encourage the recipients' initiative in raising money and to protect the EDA from spending money for a project that might never be completed.) On July 18 an EDA representative held a discouraging meeting with port officials where he was told "that no work was in progress on any of the projects, as no plans, specifications, contract docu-

2. Letter from Nutter to Foley, June 17, 1966.
3. Letter from Sullivan to Jack Beddow, EDA Office of General Counsel, July 15, 1966.

ments were available. The Port does not have sufficient funds to contract with A/E [architect/engineer] for preparation of same."[4] Federal policy and local requests could not easily be reconciled. Ross Davis, the EDA administrator who was later to take over direction of the agency, wrote a sharp reply to the port commissioners on July 19. Based on federal regulations, Davis said, "It is EDA policy not to disburse any Federal funds until contracts have been awarded for an entire project. . . . We have previously stated to you, and your staff, the fact that reimbursement for in-house engineering or other functions performed by your regular staff is not an authorized project cost item."[5]

Still, the port continued to press its claims. At an August 31 conference in Oakland, the port proposed that EDA deposit grant/loan funds in a special joint account to pay authorized construction and administrative costs based on a quarterly estimate of construction placement and other project expenses. The EDA replied to the port proposal by telegram on September 9:

WE DO NOT BELIEVE THAT SUCH AN ARRANGEMENT CAN BE JUSTIFIED OR IS CONSISTENT WITH ESTAB. GOVT. CONTRACTING POLICY. HOWEVER, DUE TO THE REQUIREMENTS OF THE OAKLAND PROJECTS AND TO THE REQUIREMENTS OF THE CITY CHARTER, WE WILL CONSIDER A MONTHLY DISBURSEMENT OF FUNDS, ONCE ALL CONTRACTS FOR EACH PROJECT HAVE BEEN LET. . . .[6]

No advances of federal funds would be forthcoming, but approved construction costs incurred by the port for a particular month could be covered by the EDA after the month was over. Furthermore, loan (not grant) funds would be advanced to the port for architect and engineering services.

Now, it seemed, the terminal project could go on. But other difficulties remained: the soils dispute continued through October, and Matson Navigation Company (the prospective tenant of the terminal) stated that it would be unable to provide sufficient new employment. (Matson had also been far from enthusiastic about the EDA's employment plan idea.) For these reasons, the port decided to bypass

4. Memo from Walter F. Rasp, EDA engineer, to Orrin Fayle, chief of construction management, Office of Public Works, July 18, 1966.
5. Letter from Ross D. Davis to port commissioners, July 19, 1966.
6. Telegram from Orrin Fayle, EDA, to Ben Nutter, Port of Oakland, September 9, 1966.

both the soils and Matson problems by moving the EDA-financed project to the western end of the diked construction area.

No further action was taken until late January 1967, when the port submitted an application to relocate the EDA project. This time, the project included a glass tourist-type restaurant. On April 12, 1967 the EDA approved the change in project location; two days later, the port submitted its architecture/engineering (A/E) agreement to the EDA. The federal agency approved the agreement on June 25. But once again progress was slow. A subsequent EDA report noted that, after approval of the A/E contract, "the Engineer did not start on the work for several months because his forces were busy on other work for the Port of Oakland."[7] Not until the fall of 1967 did the architect/engineer start work.

In November 1967 other kinds of problems were developing. Cliff Holden, an engineer who had become the EDA project manager in Oakland, wrote in a memo:

I had a call from Mr. Champ Corsen of the Naval Facilities Engineering Command, San Bruno, today. . . . He read me some correspondence that had been going on between the Port of Oakland and the Navy in regard to serious navigational hazards caused by construction of this project. This is a matter that the Port has never told the EDA about. . . . When the existing dike was built the pattern of the currents in the entrance channel to the Naval Supply Center was changed. . . . It is difficult for ships to navigate.[8]

The military would be heard from again.

On January 17, 1968, the port requested that the terminal project be broken into two phases, which included dredging and filling as phase 1 and construction of the remainder of the terminal as phase 2. The port also requested a $2,000,000 loan advance to finance phase 1.[9] On January 30 EDA Oakland recommended to Washington that the January 17 letter from the port be approved. But on February 6 John Davidson of the EDA Western Area Office in Seattle sent a letter to George Karras in Washington objecting to the Oakland office's memo. By the next day, the Public Works Office in Seattle had agreed to support the port's letter of January 17, provided they

7. EDA project progress report, April 10, 1968.
8. Memo from Cliff Holden to Western Area Office, November 22, 1967.

9. The 1967 and 1968 sections of the marine terminal chronology are based in part on a memo written in December 1968 by Frederick A. Ricci, who was an EDA staff member in Oakland at that time.

were given a resolution by the port commissioners in which the board agreed to build the restaurant at a later date if enough funds were not available at the time for opening the bids. In response the port passed such a resolution on February 20, and on February 21 the Western Area Office threw its suport behind the loan advance. Washington responded favorably.

At this point, the Navy reentered the story to add an additional protest to the terminal project. On April 1, 1968, Rear Admiral F. E. Janney, director of the Shore Installations Division, wrote a strong letter to the EDA's Office of Public Works. During the previous year, the navy had objected to the terminal project because of its effects on ship navigation. Now the issue was airplane safety. Admiral Janney declared that "the Navy is seriously concerned over the possible adverse effects that construction of the proposed Port of Oakland pier extension and associated equipment would have on the flight safety and operational capability of Naval Air Station, Alameda. Of particular concern are the mobile crane at the western end of the new pier and the masts of ships which may be berthed at the pier."[10] The matter was pending before the Federal Aviation Administration, and all sides waited eagerly for that body to rule. Meanwhile, the Port of Oakland had requested another change of plans. On April 7, 1968, the port submitted a plan to construct a larger, revolving resturant at a cost of over $1,000,000 and to eliminate the south wharf and transit sheds. The public works officer at the EDA's Western Area Office replied on May 20 that his office felt that the elimination of the south wharf was a "major change in scope." Therefore, on May 31 the Western Area Office sent a letter to the Port of Oakland stating that the letter of April 7 constituted a "major revision" and that a new project application would have to be submitted for approval by EDA head Ross Davis. The port answered the Western Area Office on May 31 by saying that it only wanted to use $630,-000 of project funds for a restaurant. This was the amount of money available after a crane was eliminated because of the navy objections.

While controversy swirled around the design of the terminal, progress was being made on preparations for dredging and filling. The port submitted plans for dredging and filling to the EDA on

10. Letter from Admiral Janney to Frank A. Cirillo, Office of Public Works, April 1, 1968.

April 29, 1968. Bids for this part of the project were advertised on July 15, but on August 19 all bids were returned unopened because the port could not get a dredging permit from the Army Corps of Engineers. (A disagreement between the Bay Area Rapid Transit District (BARTD) and the port was the reason for the delay in corps approval; BARTD had charged that the dredging for the 7th Street terminal was too close to its dikes in the bay.)

As the summer of 1968 wore on and the disagreement between the port and the Western Area Office concerning the proposed change in plans remained unresolved, other complications arose. On August 1 the United States General Accounting Office (GAO) questioned the EDA's awards to the Port of Oakland on the basis that the 60–40 grant/loan ratio might be too generous. The GAO felt that the port was strong enough to get funds elsewhere, but the EDA replied that other factors—like the special needs of the area—justified the port contracts.[11] Later that month the San Francisco Department of Public Works complained that the port's dumping could affect water contact sports in the bay.[12]

As 1968 ended and a new administration prepared to come to power in Washington, the future plans for the terminal lay in doubt. In the areas of dredging, filling, financing, design, and relationships with other governmental institutions, the technical problems surrounding construction of the marine terminal had proved to be formidable. What had appeared initially to be a relatively straightforward program now involved new and unforeseen participants—the navy, the GAO, local government bodies—whose agreement was necessary if the program was to continue.

IMPLEMENTATION: WORLD AIRWAYS HANGAR

Progress on the marine terminal, although beset by numerous problems, was actually smooth compared to the evils that affected the other major public works project—the aircraft maintenance hangar. Although the hangar project had been approved on April 29, 1966, no action was taken for several months while the port negotiated a lease with the proposed tenant (World Airways) and the

11. EDA report of meeting with GAO, August 1, 1968.
12. Letter from San Francisco Department of Public Works to U.S. Army Corps of Engineers, August 19, 1968.

employment plan was prepared and accepted. The architect/engineering agreement was submitted to the EDA on February 6, 1967, and approved March 6. On May 6 the port entered into a contract with Charles Luckman and Associates (an architecture/engineering firm). But not until August 14, 1967, did the port notify the Luckman firm to start work.

Opinions differed over the reason the A/E did not begin work sooner. "There is no apparent reason for this delay," an EDA progress report stated in April 1968, "other than the fact that the Port spent some time going through the process of requesting and receiving an advance on the project loan to finance drawings which were revised to meet the requirements of World Airways."[13] Ben Nutter, executive director of the port, offered another interpretation of the delay. After the port had signed the contract with Luckman in May, World Airways had retained Luckman to develop industrial engineering information for a general building program. According to Nutter, this study would outline specific project criteria for designing the hangar, and the building program was not received until August 1967, causing the delay.[14]

When Charles Luckman and Associates had completed an initial plan on April 2, 1968, they had some bad news for both the port and the EDA. John R. Campbell of the A/E firm notified Ben Nutter that there were some increased construction costs.[15] The construction cost for the hangar in 1966 had been estimated at $9,262,600. Now the figure had leaped to $13,425,840; thus, the total construction cost increase was $4,163,240. The Luckman representative enumerated the reasons for the cost increase:

(1) Building Cost Escalation of 13.5 percent.—There had been a time lapse caused by discussions with the EDA about the manner of funding. The preparation of the World Airways building program had taken time. Cost increase, $1,250,451.

(2) Fire Protection Requirements.—Insurance companies had complained that the port's original plans for the hangar did not include sufficient protection against fires. The necessary requirements were defined by the insurance carriers. Cost increase, $866,000.

13. EDA project progress report, April 10, 1968.
14. Letter from Nutter to Lambert O'Malley, EDA Public Works, April 2, 1968.
15. Letter from John R. Campbell to Nutter, April 2, 1968.

(3) Improvements.—As the result of the building program and subsequent decisions by World Airways, the configuration of office areas was changed and there was an increase in utilities. Cost Increase, $889,762.

(4) Aircraft Requirements.—Fences were added to the later plan, along with improved paving for heavier planes. Cost increase, $1,-157,027.

Immediately after receiving the new estimates from the Luckman firm, Ben Nutter wrote to Lambert O'Malley (then the EDA's public works director) to tell him about the changes.[16] It could not have been pleasant reading for the EDA:

	1966	1968
Cost of construction (estimated)	9,262,600	13,425,840
Total project cost (estimated)	10,650,000	15,196,520

After disclosing the new figures, Nutter had a request to make: "We respectfully request that EDA consider making available the additional funds required to complete this project, as outlined in the . . . estimate of project cost as revised April 2, 1968." On May 27 the port submitted an application to the EDA for an additional assistance grant of $2,214,000, which would provide financing for approximately half of the overrun estimated at that time. The port later explained that it would finance the other half of the hangar overrun by issuing revenue bonds on the open market.[17]

For the next few months, the port and the EDA argued about engineering considerations lying behind the increased costs. At a July 26 meeting in Oakland, EDA officials asked why the roof of the hangar had to be eighty-five feet high. They were told that this height was required to remove and work on the tail section of the new 747 airplanes.[18]

By August 30 EDA regional officials had come out in favor of the port's request for additional assistance, provided "that the employment plan of World Airways and the training programs that it necessitates will assure that members of the hard-core poverty group in Oakland will be trained and hired."[19] On September 13 an optimistic

16. Letter from Nutter to O'Malley, April 2, 1968.
17. See letter from Nutter to Valmer Cameron, EDA Western Area Office director, June 17, 1968.
18. EDA memo on meeting of July 26, 1968.
19. Memo from Davidson to Bill Rae, Western Area Office, August 30, 1968.

Davidson wrote that Charles Patterson, the Oakland representative, "has assured me that the employment plans were satisfactorily solved and that we can now send the overrun recommendation to Washington."[20] Patterson added on September 17 that World's "efforts to meet its requirements under the Employment Plan" were "consistent with EDA's expectations."[21]

EDA officials in Washington, D.C., were much less enthusiastic at this time about World Airways' employment performance than were their counterparts in the field. A World Airways compliance report of June 1968 had indicated that, while total employment at World Airways had increased by 98 employees (from 1004 in March 1967 to 1102 in February 1968), the total number of minority employees dropped from 129 to 111.[22]

The internal report on Oakland completed by the Urban Affairs Division of the EDA in October 1968 recommended that any increased financial assistance for the hangar should be conditioned on approval of a revised, stronger employment plan for World Airways. (Provision for renegotiation of the plan in the case of a "change of circumstances" was contained in the original employment plan agreement. The alterations on hangar design and costs were felt by the report to constitute such a change.) A revised plan would include (a) the delineation of employment categories with explicit job qualification requirements; and commitments from World Airways (b) to employ graduates of the East Bay Skills Center, an existing training program, and (c) to support the development of training programs and to make available on-the-job training for positions requiring less than EDA or federal contract compliance certification.[23]

The report stated that the "EDA should attempt to extract these commitments from World Airways without agreeing to any additional financial assistance,"[24] but the writers of the report recognized that this might be difficult. Additional money might be useful as a bargaining counter. (In this case, the bargaining was somewhat complicated. The port, which was in charge of building the hangar,

20. Davidson memo, September 13, 1968.
21. Letter from Charles J. Patterson to Russell Stevens, area attorney, September 17, 1968.
22. Compliance Report ED-613, cited in letter from Ross Davis to Robert Mortensen, president, Board of Port Commissioners, February 26, 1969.
23. EDA internal report, p. 79.
24. *Ibid.*, p. 80.

had asked for additional funding. The EDA would be trying to use its control over this funding to force concessions from World Airways, the lessee and future beneficiary of the hangar. Attempting to control funding for one institution to force changes in the behavior of another would prove to be an exasperatingly indirect process.)

Even if the EDA did decide to grant the overrun request and to use it as a bargaining counter, there were a number of shapes such a decision might take. The report outlined some of the alternatives for EDA: (1) approve the overrun request in a 60–40 grant/loan ratio; (2) in line with GAO complaints, reduce the grant ratio to 56.3 percent for supplemental grants to *all* of the Oakland projects, including the hangar; (3) reduce the grant/loan ratio to 50 percent on the hangar project. Of course the EDA had other alternatives: (4) deny the overrun request; or even (5) withdraw support completely from the hangar project.

Noting the small rate of progress in both construction and job creation, the internal report pointed out that the EDA could withdraw on any of the following conditions of the original loan and grant agreement: finding that representations in the application were incorrect or incomplete in any material respect; determining that the borrower has failed to proceed with reasonable diligence in the financing or construction of the project; or determining that the scope or character of the project has changed substantially so as to adversely affect accomplishment of the project as intended.[25] The report suggested that, in the case of the hangar, the EDA might be able to justify the complete termination of the project.

On December 18, 1968, George Karras and Louis Phillips (of the EDA's Office of Policy Coordination) met with members of the port's staff in Oakland to discuss the hangar project. At the meeting Karras and Phillips outlined the EDA's concern about the project's progress and the realization of the goal of creating jobs for the hardcore unemployed and underemployed residents of Oakland.[26] In response to the EDA's questions, the port and World Airways sent letters to Karras that discussed employment and training activities. Both letters were dated December 31. Ben Nutter emphasized the port's commitment to the Oakland minority community. Edward J.

25. *Ibid.*, p. 71.
26. Noted in the EDA Oakland file, compiled August 15, 1969.

Daly, president of World Airways, sent an enclosure entitled "Developing Jobs for the Unemployed and Underemployed: Affirmative Action by World Airways, Inc." This pamphlet described World's role in helping to establish FIPCO and Sons, Inc., a black-owned and black-managed corporation that would service and clean aircraft. Furthermore, the enclosure stated that World's president was serving as Oakland metropolitan chairman of the National Alliance of Businessmen and that World was active in the JOBS program. Also, World had cooperated with the Urban Coalition in contracting with a black-managed firm to produce slipper socks for use on World's commercial charter flights. Finally, World had supported the Opportunities Industrialization Center (the black-directed training program started by Leon Sullivan) in its operations in Oakland.

Still, Washington EDA officials were skeptical. At the end of 1968 they were considering the bleak alternatives open to them on the hangar project. If they approved funding for the overrun, the EDA would be still further committed to the project and there would be no guarantee that costs would not rise again. If they denied the overrun, the whole project would be in stalemate. If they canceled the hangar project completely, the money that had been allocated would revert to the federal treasury. The project appeared to be bogged down in a quagmire from which there was no promising exit.

IMPLEMENTATION: TRAINING PROGRAM

In the eyes of EDA officials, the hangar project could only produce jobs for the unemployed if it were linked to an effective training program for those who would work at the hangar. In October 1966 it had been agreed that World Airways would set up and operate a government-funded training program for airline maintenance personnel. The program would be set up under Section 241 of the Manpower Development and Training Act (MDTA), which provides funds for EDA-designated areas.

Although the idea of job training sounds straightforward, the process under Section 241 of the MDTA is incredibly convoluted. Opportunities for delay or termination of a proposal are present at many points along the way. This is how the process works: First, the group proposing a training program must demonstrate that there is a need for employees in a certain type of industry. The relevant state's department of employment must conduct a survey of the industry in order to evaluate the need. If such a need is proved, the proposal goes to the local MDTA advisory committee, which is composed of representatives of management, labor, and minority groups. That committee must approve the proposal, and the department of vocational education of the state must certify that the proposed training institution is acceptable. Then the proposal must go to the chief elected official of the political subdivision for his approval (in this case, the mayor of Oakland).

Following local approval, the MDTA proposal travels to the state capital, where the state's department of employment and department of vocational education must approve it. (The department of employment is a delegate agency for the U.S. Department of Labor; the department of vocational education is delegate agency for the U.S. Department of Health, Education, and Welfare. Because Section 241 of the MDTA requires joint approval by the EDA *and* the federal Departments of Labor and HEW, the process is further complicated.)

From the state capital, the proposal goes to the federal regional offices of Labor and HEW. (In this case, the regional offices are located in San Francisco.) Then the proposal is sent to Washington, where it must be approved by the EDA and the departments of Labor and HEW.[27] Federal officials who were interested in 1970 were quick to point out that the EDA does not have direct control over Section 241 funds; it must secure the approval of Labor and HEW for any training program under this section.

In the case of the World Airways training proposal, the MDTA Advisory Council in Oakland approved a plan on November 30, 1966, that would train 510 aircraft maintenance personnel. On March 13, 1967, Norman Amundson, chairman of the council, wrote to Alexander Trowbridge, acting secretary of commerce, to ask what had happened to the proposal.[28] Trowbridge turned the letter over to Ross Davis of the EDA, who wrote Amundson, "We are aware that such a proposal is being developed. . . . This project is still in Cali-

27. We are indebted to Hugh Taylor of the EDA for helping us to understand this difficult procedure.
28. Letter from Norman Amundson to Alexander Trowbridge, March 13, 1967.

fornia; when it arrives in Washington it will . . . be given prompt consideration by the Interagency Review Committee."[29]

A copy of Davis' letter was forwarded to Albert Tieburg of the California Department of Employment; Tieburg then explained to Davis that the proposal had been sent by his office to the state Department of Education four months earlier. The state employment official said he hoped "that the necessary work on these proposals will be completed in the very near future so that they may be forwarded for funding."[30] In May 1967 an *Oakland Tribune* article featured Amundson's charges that "Red tape and inter-agency jealousies are delaying critically-needed job training for Alameda County's unemployed."[31]

When the training proposal finally reached Washington, it proved impossible for the EDA, Labor, and HEW to agree jointly to support it. The EDA was worried about the costs per trainee; HEW felt it would be too much of a financial opportunity for World. Later, the Manpower Development and Training Act was amended to give statutory preference to established skills centers in the competition for federal MDTA funds. Because the East Bay Skills Center was on the HEW list of established skills centers, HEW would have a powerful argument against a separate training center for World. Success in HEW's terms meant training and finding jobs for poor people, and conducting that process through skills centers. A rival training institution would necessarily diminish the number of possible placements.

Although federal officials vary somewhat in their interpretations of how the training proposal was killed, by 1968 it was clear that the three federal agencies could not get together to approve the project. Finally, World Airways withdrew its proposal. A key part of the EDA Oakland project had been dismantled. Like the construction of public works projects, the creation of a training program eventually required a long string of clearances by actors with different perspectives. Although the EDA wanted to set up a separate training school for airline mechanics, HEW defined success in terms of en-

29. Letter from Ross Davis to Norman Amundson, March 28, 1967.
30. Letter from Albert Tieburg to Ross Davis, April 21, 1967.
31. "Expert Raps Delay in Job Program," *Oakland Tribune,* May 14, 1967, p. 5.

hancing established skills centers. Given these divergent organizational objectives, the building of agreement—which was necessary for the furtherance of the program—became a difficult task.

EDA ADMINISTRATION, 1967–68: FROM EMERGENCY DELAYS TO ROUTINE HOLDUPS

While EDA projects in Oakland were running into local difficulties of engineering and financing, it became clear that the federal agency itself was becoming less interested in Oakland. "The departure of Foley in the Fall of 1966," the agency's internal report declares, "followed shortly thereafter by a number of key staff people who had helped run the program in its first year, marked a dramatic shift in the emphasis of the Oakland program. . . . When the Oakland program was placed in normal agency channels in Washington, its priority and singular importance diminished."[32]

After 1966 Oakland ceased to be the favored project of the EDA. A number of reasons are given for this: resentment of the task force by senior staff members whose channels had been bypassed; disapproval of the project by the secretary of commerce and the White House; overidentification of the project with Eugene Foley personally. Ross Davis, who succeeded Foley, feels that it is a mistake to expect the federal agency to be a constant initiator of action: "Of course, from Washington it seemed that nothing in Oakland was moving for much of 1967 and 1968. And I was worried. But tradition has it that it was the locals who were supposed to move things, not the feds."[33]

When Amory Bradford left Oakland in November 1966, Doug Costle took over the operation of the local EDA office on an interim basis. Costle devoted much of his time to the development of an interagency Federal Executive Board (FEB) task force, which would examine the federal delivery system in Oakland. The FEB task force idea had originated in the EDA. During 1966 that agency had encouraged other federal departments to participate in and contribute financially to the study and they had done so.

Costle left the EDA in January 1967, and the permanent operation of the Oakland office was taken over by Charles Patterson, a

32. EDA internal report, pp. 51–52.
33. Interview with Ross Davis, July 17, 1970.

black ex-Peace Corps official. The EDA internal report contrasts Amory Bradford's conception of his role in Oakland—"negotiation, discussion, and dialogue with all segments of the community"—with Patterson's decision "not to spend his time negotiating with black militants and other target area residents because of his conviction that there was nothing left which EDA could promise or deliver."[34] The report notes that Patterson devoted much of his time to the chairmanship of the FEB task force (which produced a published report in August 1968), and it records his view that "the publicity given the EDA program raised the expectations of the people in the Oakland ghetto far beyond EDA's capacity to deliver."[35] With promises already made and the difficulties of implementation increasing, Patterson felt his position growing increasingly difficult.

In Washington Ross Davis responded to Patterson's difficulties by making some administrative changes: "Patterson had the advantage of being black. I thought that would help him, but Patterson wasn't enough. So I appointed an ad hoc group in Washington in the first half of 1967 to keep in touch with Patterson. I really had great confidence in Patterson, but after a year, it became apparent that things were not moving."[36] A succession of EDA staff men—Michael Coleman, Blair Butterworth, and Fred Ricci—were sent to Oakland to back up Patterson in the office. And Davis asked Jonathan Lindley, deputy assistant secretary for policy coordination, to do an evaluation of the entire Oakland project (which resulted in the internal report).

What finally created a sense of urgency in Washington regarding the Oakland project was the port's request in mid-1968 for an overrun on the airplane hangar. "That," says Ross Davis, "perforce brought our attention back to Oakland."

Washington, D.C., and Oakland were not the only places where administrative difficulties occurred during 1967 and 1968; the role of the Western Area Office in Seattle constituted perhaps the biggest question mark of all. Technical assistance programs were handled directly between Washington and Oakland, but Seattle was charged with "limited program authority" in the public works and fully dis-

---

34. EDA internal report, p. 56.
35. *Ibid.*
36. Ross Davis interview.

bursed business loans projects.[37] Although the area office did not have the authority to approve or deny funding requests, it was supposed to facilitate "project management."

In a series of memos to Washington, D.C., the Seattle office searched for a definition of its role. On December 15, 1966, for example, John Davidson of the area office wrote: "This memo is for the purpose of (1) providing data to the project files in the WAO and in Washington D.C., (2) to indicate Area Office understanding of who is handling the project, (3) to request closer coordination between headquarters and the Western Area Office in work assignments to consultants."[38] Davidson's complaint was that "WAO had not been informed about the assignment of a consultant to the project." Walter Butler Company had been retained by the Washington office to do a further study of the terminal project, and Davidson felt that Seattle should have been in on the decision.

The response in Washington was not sympathetic to the regional official. Chief Public Works Engineer Henry Brooks wrote a memo to George Karras:

We find no data or comment from the Western Area Office which might be helpful in evaluating the proposed revised project. . . . It is difficult to understand why Mr. Davidson did not know Walter Butler was serving as consultant on this project. . . . Mr. Davidson has raised this question several times and each time it has been explained to him that when a consultant has previously been employed to assist in a project, we have felt it wise to continue the relationship to avoid confusion and maintain some consistency in relation to the projects.[39]

In a later memo to Karras, Brooks was even more blunt: "I hate to waste your time and my time on this trivial complaint by John Davidson, but I feel somehow he must understand our operations here."[40]

A continual concern of the area office was the nature of the "special relationship" between Washington and Oakland. In February 1968 Davidson wrote to Karras that he had talked with Patterson and the two had agreed that:

(1) The Oakland office would send all construction management matters to the WAO through Mr. Holden, Project Manager

37. EDA internal report, p. 52.
38. Memo from Davidson to Washington EDA, December 15, 1966.
39. Memo from Brooks to Karras, December 22, 1966.
40. Memo from Brooks to Karras, December 27, 1966.

(2) At any time that Mr. Patterson has a special concern about a project matter, particularly with regard to policy or the need for a rapid decision, he will make his recommendations directly to the Area Office.[41]

To the present time, the role of the Western Area Office remains unresolved.

Charles Patterson resigned from the EDA in December 1968 to take a position as vice-president of World Airways. He was replaced by Hugh Taylor, an employment expert who had served at the East Bay Skills Center and as director of Mayor Reading's Manpower Commission. The position into which Taylor now stepped was not an enviable one: Washington's attitude toward the Oakland program was unclear; implementation of the projects themselves was moving slowly, if at all; and the Western Area Office in Seattle was asking for greater authority over Oakland. Thus, within the EDA itself, organizational units had differing perspectives with respect to the Oakland projects.

EDA RECEIVES—BUT DOES NOT ACCEPT— THE POWER STRUCTURE STUDY

One area of continuing disappointment to the EDA was its attempt to discover a decision-making apparatus in Oakland that could throw its weight behind federal projects. In the summer of 1968, Floyd Hunter presented the federal agency with his power structure study of Oakland. But Hunter's study—which included a defense of his power-structure methodology and a ranking of Oakland's most powerful decision makers—did not provide the EDA with the means of assembling a local force of allies. And federal officials were disturbed by the study's strong criticism of local officials. When the EDA asked Hunter to revise the study, the author refused. The agency then countered by threatening court action for nonfulfillment of contract unless the revisions were made.

POLITICAL DEVELOPMENTS IN OAKLAND

When he left Oakland in the fall of 1966, Amory Bradford wrote a memo to Ross Davis that, among other things, described Bradford's impressions of Mayor John Reading's leadership:

The new Mayor, John Reading, . . . immediately accepted the major

41. Memo from Davidson to Karras, February 6, 1968.

premise of our program, the need to solve the problems of unemployment, by providing jobs, as his main goal. The announcement of our funded projects at the end of April gave him a good solid platform from which to launch his own efforts to mobilize the business community. He has taken full advantage of this, and we have worked closely and effectively with him. His activities have convinced the ghetto residents that he is trying, and that he cares about solving their problems. This has made all the difference.[42]

In January 1967, when Mayor Reading appointed his Manpower Commission, the EDA provided him with a technical assistance grant of $35,000 a year for two years to staff the commission. The EDA regarded the mayor as a prime asset.

But during 1967 and 1968 life became exceedingly difficult for Mayor Reading. The OEDC (community action agency) decided to declare its independence from the city in 1967; its militant new director, Percy Moore, advocated an aggressive kind of community organization that was hostile to City Hall. The model cities program which came to Oakland in 1968 appeared to be offering still more potential resources to groups in the black community who opposed the mayor. Also in 1968, a black boycott of downtown merchants over a police issue was denounced by the mayor.

Politics in Oakland were becoming more strident, more polarized, more hostile. The mayor, who had hoped to work with ghetto leaders in an atmosphere of rational persuasion, was deeply shaken. He could not understand the confrontation politics in which black leaders, searching for an opponent against whom to organize, repeatedly attacked the mayor as the leader of a reactionary city government. In fact, Reading had few resources with which to meet demands or punish enemies. And his troubles were not only with the black community. The federal government, to which the mayor turned for expanded assistance in the manpower field, repeatedly refused his requests. In the fall of 1968 Mayor Reading was withdrawing from active leadership and was strongly considering not running for reelection in 1969. The EDA was losing its supposed major asset of mayoral leadership.

DISAPPOINTING PROGRESS

In October 1968 the EDA took stock of its early group of public works projects (see Table 3). The results were a far cry from what

42. Memo from Bradford to Davis, October 21, 1966.

had been expected two years earlier. Not only had the two prime projects—marine terminal and aircraft hangar—failed to produce jobs; they were not even under construction. And the industrial park had managed to generate only about ten new jobs for Oakland residents.

Some progress was being made. The small hangars would be completed on December 3, 1968, and the air cargo terminal would be under construction a few months later. But overall, the EDA program looked disappointing, except for one public works project (the West Oakland Health Center) which we will discuss in chapter 4.

As 1968 drew to a close, the EDA program in Oakland was at a low ebb. Business loans had not resulted in many jobs, and public works projects were not even built. Delays were being caused by the difficulty of obtaining clearances on matters that had not been foreseen at the outset. And the general agreement on policy was dissolving into specific disagreements on the steps needed for implementation.

The major decision that now had to be made concerned the cost overrun on the airplane hangar. The project was the most expensive part of the Oakland program, and it had been expected to be the centerpiece of the whole experiment. The EDA's decision would not be long in coming.

EDA SAYS "NO" (JANUARY-FEBRUARY 1969)

During Ross Davis' last months as head of the agency, in early 1969, the EDA's stance began to harden. On January 27 Davis wrote to the port commissioners, reiterating that the EDA's principal mission was to create job opportunities for the unemployed and underemployed.[43] Thus far, Davis said, the port and World Airways had not been sufficiently committed to this mission. "Before EDA can commit additional development resources in partnership with the Port of Oakland," he declared, "we should have adequate and detailed assurances that you intend and are able to carry out the objectives of our Oakland investment."[44]

Such assurances, Davis suggested, could be provided by an effective employment plan for the port itself and a revised plan for World

43. Letter from Ross Davis to port commissioners, January 27, 1969.
44. *Ibid.*

TABLE 3: Progress on Implementation Goes Slowly: The Status as of October 1968 of EDA Public Works Projects

Project Title	Date Approved	Amount ($)	Under-/Over-run ($)	Status	Jobs Projected	Jobs to Date
Port of Oakland: 7th Street marine terminal	4/29/66	10,125,000		Awaiting new design and impact projections	175 plus indirect jobs	0
Port of Oakland: Block B industrial park	4/29/66	2,100,000	Underrun 490,000	Completed October 1968	420	Approximately 10 net new Oakland jobs*
Port of Oakland: aircraft maintenance hangar	4/29/66	10,650,000	Overrun 4,428,000	Plans, financing under negotiation	1,200	0
Port of Oakland: 20 small aircraft hangars	6/15/66	76,000		Under construction	12	0
Port of Oakland: air cargo terminal	2/1/66	184,000		Plans and specifications under review	12	0
City of Oakland: four-lane access road	4/29/66	414,000		Completed November 1966	Indirect	—
Port of Oakland: auxiliary airport tower	2/1/67	223,000		Design completed; will be constructed when main hangar is started	—	—

*One firm located in area as of October 1968 was previously located in smaller quarters in Oakland.
Source: Resnikoff, "EDA in Oakland: An Evaluation." Figures from 1968 EDA report.

Airways. EDA staff would help the port and World devise accept-able plans. On January 31 Assistant Secretary Davis sent the port commissioners a set of guidelines that the EDA wanted to be incor-porated into the new plans. The port was to pledge an on-the-job training program for minorities, and it was to promise to hire a "professional full-time Equal Employment Opportunity officer" to work with port tenants and encourage the hiring of minority unem-ployed. World Airways was to submit new employment projections and was also to promise to hire an equal employment opportunity officer.[45]

Robert E. Mortensen, president of the board of port commission-ers, reacted angrily to Davis' decision that further employment plans would have to be approved prior to approval of the overrun. On February 7 he wrote Davis that "The project has been inordinately delayed and today we have progressed no further than the prelimi-nary design stage. We have attempted to keep this project moving toward realization. However, it appears to us that EDA may not share our sense of urgency in causing the project to be implemented. I believe our impression is supported by EDA's delay in processing our additional assistance application."[46] Davis responded to Morten-sen on February 11, saying that the port commissioner's letter was in no way responsive to the EDA position. The assistant secretary stated that he looked forward to meeting with port officials in the hope that some understanding could be reached.[47]

A meeting did take place, on February 14, between EDA officials, the Port of Oakland, World Airways, Mayor Reading, and Oak-land's Congressmen Cohelan and Miller. According to Davis, "the Port said that they'd wait and deal with the Republicans. I said you don't know what the Republicans will do and maybe you'd better deal with me."[48] With a new EDA head soon to be named, the port reasoned that a less rigid attitude might come to the agency. Neither side was willing to change its posture. The next day Ross Davis sent the port commissioners a list of minimum requirements for an em-ployment plan. It would have to provide for an employment officer,

45. EDA guidelines, January 31, 1969. Included in letter from Davis to Peter M. Tripp, president, Board of Port Commissioners, January 31, 1969.
46. Letter from Mortensen to Davis, February 7, 1969.
47. Letter from Davis to Mortensen, February 11, 1969.
48. Davis interview.

intensive recruiting of minorities, and the making of changes in civil service requirements to facilitate minority hiring.[49]

Meanwhile, the estimated cost of the hangar continued to rise. On February 18 Mortensen notified Davis that new projections set the eventual cost at $16,234,000, a rise of over $1 million since early 1968. Further EDA assistance would be necessary, said Mortensen.[50] The next day Mortensen sent Davis the port's "Tentative Statement of Employment Policy," which pledged that the port would "assist the City in establishing an Equal Employment Opportunity Program and a position of Equal Employment Opportunity Officer for the City including the Port of Oakland."[51] (The EDA had asked the port to create such a position for the port itself.) The plan also pledged that the port would work with community groups to recruit and hire more minorities.

World Airways was somewhat less cordial in its response to the EDA's demand. World's attorney, Jerome C. Byrne, wrote to Davis that the employment plan agreement would have to be replaced. Byrne explained:

This Agreement provides for an arbitration provision. My research indicates that agencies of the United States Government are not permitted to agree to arbitration of disputes without specific statutory authorization. I would be happy to provide you with my research in this area if you so desire. At any rate I assume that you will agree that EDA and World should not enter into any agreement that is not in accord with federal law.[52]

Because of these legal doubts (which EDA lawyers have challenged) and because World's MDTA training program had never materialized, Byrne proposed that an "amended" employment plan and agreement be adopted. The attorney enclosed in his letter the draft of a new employment plan which was rather vague in its promises and projections for hiring minority unemployed:

To the extent that the graduates of the East Bay Skills Center and other such training programs meet World's qualifications for employment and to the extent that World has openings for employees for entry level jobs, World will give precedence to the hiring of such graduates. . . . World and EDA

49. Letter from Davis to Board of Port Commissioners, February 15, 1969.
50. Letter from Mortensen to Davis, February 18, 1969.
51. "Tentative Statement of Employment Policy: Port of Oakland," February 1969. Enclosed in letter from Mortensen to Davis, February 19, 1969.
52. Letter from Byrne to Davis, February 20, 1969.

recognize the extreme complexity of predicting business expansion and recognize the speculative nature of training programs of organizations such as the East Bay Skills Center as to their ability to train the unemployed and the under-employed for entry level jobs in the airline industry. Recognizing these problems, World will, however, exert its best efforts to obtain qualified personnel from the sources heretofore mentioned, but cannot hold out any promises that any particular number of personnel will be hired from such sources.[53]

It was clear that the EDA and World were moving even farther apart.

On February 26, 1969, Ross Davis announced his long-awaited decision: the request for the overrun would not be approved. In a letter to Robert Mortensen of the Port Commission, Davis declared:

> *As EDA has repeatedly stressed, the agency is not in the business of building aircraft hangars or other facilities for port authorities or business firms, particularly firms that have financial resources to build such facilities without government assistance. EDA is in the business of creating jobs for the unemployed, the underemployed and the poor. In Oakland, California, this means jobs primarily for Negroes and Mexican-Americans.*[54]

Davis criticized the performance of World Airways and the port in the area of jobs. There were, for instance, no Negroes or Mexican-Americans holding professional jobs within the Port of Oakland in 1968, according to an Oakland civil service report. The assistant secretary believed that attempts by the port and World to frame employment plans were unsatisfactory. The port had failed to provide for an equal opportunity officer in its own staff, and it had not committed itself to seeking changes in (and exemptions from) civil service requirements. Furthermore, the plan itself was "tentative"; it had never been approved by the port commissioners. World's new plan, in Davis' view, was "less satisfactory than the original Employment Plan Agreement of December 1966." The proposed revisions, he said, had failed "to enumerate the specific actions which World plans to undertake to hire the hard core unemployed Negroes, Mexican-Americans, or other minority groups in the Oakland community."[55]

On the same day, Davis wrote to World Airways President Ed-

---

53. Revised employment plan of World Airways, February 20, 1969.
54. Letter from Davis to Mortensen, February 26, 1969. Emphasis in original.
55. *Ibid.*, p. 6.

ward J. Daly to inform him of the decision. The assistant secretary asserted that "Despite EDA's extraordinary efforts to assist both the Port of Oakland and World Airways to come forward with Employment Plans responsive to the needs of Oakland's unemployed and underemployed residents, both the Port and World have failed to meet the minimum assurances that EDA sought."[56]

During the next month—Davis' last as head of EDA—some progress was made in creating an employment program at the port. On March 24 the port commissioners took the word "tentative" out of their employment policy. They agreed, furthermore, to give the Oakland city government $5,000 toward the $19,000 annual salary of a newly hired manpower consultant who was to "manage minority and disadvantaged employment programs for the city and the port."[57] Still, the EDA program was basically in a stalemate as the Nixon administration prepared to appoint a new head for the agency. Robert A. Podesta, an investment banker from Chicago, was named to replace Ross Davis as assistant secretary for EDA. Oakland's EDA recipients waited anxiously to see what the attitude of the new administration would be.

A CHANGE OF ADMINISTRATION, 1969–70

Soon after taking office as assistant secretary, Podesta put his chief aide, Richard L. Sinnott, in charge of the Oakland program. Sinnott remembers that, "At that time, we had $30 million of commitments and $7 million of expenditures. We just put a freeze on Oakland projects, and treated each project—the hangar, the 7th Street terminal, the hotel—as a new application. The change in scope in all three gave us legal grounds to do so."[58] Podesta, Sinnott, and their staff decided to examine carefully the whole Oakland commitment. They "visited Oakland on a number of occasions—with the mayor, community leaders, black people, and the port."[59] To all these groups, the EDA officials gave the message that the agency would continue to insist on job creation for the unemployed as a necessary condition for the receipt of funds.

56. Letter from Davis to Daly, February 26, 1969.
57. "Port Takes Plunge on Hiring Policy," *Oakland Tribune,* March 25, 1969, p. 15.
58. Interview with Richard L. Sinnott, August 5, 1970.
59. *Ibid.*

During most of 1969 the terminal and hangar projects were held in abeyance while the EDA studied the problems surrounding those projects and possible ways of solving them. (The option of discontinuing the projects entirely continued to have supporters in the agency also.) Decisions had to be made on the following: Should the EDA approve the Port's plan for a revolving restaurant at the terminal? Should the EDA agree to increased funding for the hangar, in return for a binding employment agreement with World Airways? Or should the EDA refuse the overrun in any case?) What time limits should be placed on compliance with EDA conditions?

IMPLEMENTATION: MARINE TERMINAL

The Port of Oakland approved a new affirmative action policy in September 1969 that committed the port to hire an equal employment officer. That official would seek unemployed and underemployed candidates for port employment, propose training programs, assist the port in "seeking realistic employment standards," and direct counseling programs.[60] In early 1970 Joseph Barnett, a black employment specialist, was named to fill the new post. While the EDA considered the port's revolving restaurant plan, some progress was being made in 1969 on other parts of the terminal project. In April the navy withdrew its objections to the proposed construction when the port agreed to eliminate an offending crane.[61]

In June the Umpqua Company of Oregon was awarded a contract for filling and dredging at the terminal project. (The contract-awarding process was not without its problems. Twice before, bids had been thrown out by port attorneys. In the first instance, there was a problem with a minor amendment to the bid document. In the second instance, the low bid by Umpqua had been disallowed when it was discovered that the affidavit of noncollusion had not been dated properly. After some extended legal jockeying, Umpqua's bid was finally approved.) The filling and dredging began in mid-July, over three years after the announcement of the project.

As the year progressed, the new leaders of the EDA began to have serious doubts about the wisdom of approving the port's long-stand-

60. Port of Oakland statement of employment policy, September 8, 1969.
61. See letter from Admiral Janney to Frank Cirillo of the EDA, April 7, 1969.

ing request for a revolving restaurant. It would be a fancy project, they observed, which might make EDA look extravagant. The jobs produced would be low paying. Finally, the proposed lessee had had a disappointing record of minority hiring. But the EDA, under Ross Davis, had already decided to approve the revolving restaurant. If the new EDA leadership wanted to change the agency's policy, how could they justify such a decision? Fortunately for those in the EDA who opposed the revolving restaurant, an answer to the dilemma was at hand. As one federal official described it: "This is how we got out of Phase 3. We had actually approved final plans and specs including it. But we knew that there would be an overrun, a big one, for Phase 2 [construction of the terminal itself]. If the overrun was big enough, the Port would have to request money from Phase 3. And that's what happened. The restaurant was dropped as a *quid pro quo*."

On December 11 Assistant Secretary Podesta wrote to the port, announcing the EDA's decision not to participate in funding the revolving restaurant. The next day, the port's executive director, Ben Nutter, wrote to Podesta to acknowledge the decision. Nutter also had a request to make:

The construction bids for Phase II of the Seventh Street Main Terminal project have exceeded the EDA approved budgeted amount for this phase of the construction project. In response to your decision, we request that the $600,000.00 plus the 5% construction contingency of $30,000 budgeted for Phase III restaurant and public facilities construction be made available for Phase II construction and thereby serve to reduce our overage for this phase of the project.[62]

The EDA acceded to the request. By shifting funds from the revolving restaurant to cover an overrun on basic terminal construction, the federal agency was able to free itself from participation in a potentially embarrassing venture. The revolving restaurant might still be built, but the EDA would not be responsible for it.

In late December two construction contracts for the terminal project were awarded by the port. Ben C. Gerwick Company won a contract for $2,152,543 for construction of wharves, and Rothschild and Raffin, Inc. signed a $4,776,000 contract for constructing roads, a cargo transit shed, and utilities.[63]

62. Letter from Nutter to Podesta, December 12, 1969.
63. "$6.9 Million in Port Jobs OK'd," *Oakland Tribune,* December 25, 1969, p. 6.

During the next year the long-awaited construction of the 7th Street terminal actually began to take place. By December 1, 1970, the EDA's Office of Public Works reported that the terminal was "78 percent complete." Two transit sheds, the paving of 7th Street and the container area, and the installation of some sewers were yet to be completed.[64] But after four and a half years of waiting, a marine terminal *was* being built.

IMPLEMENTATION: WORLD AIRWAYS HANGAR

If the marine terminal project was beginning to show some signs of progress, such was not the case with the EDA's most difficult project, the airline hangar. On August 29, 1969, the port requested that the EDA deviate from its established policy of two-stage (design-construction) competitive bidding and allow the port to negotiate a contract with one firm for both design and construction. The EDA's Office of Public Works took a dim view of such a procedure, feeling that there would be no "checks and balances" between designer and builder if one firm did all the work. Besides, the EDA wanted to review the final plans before construction bids were let.[65] The Office of Public Works was frank to note that some of its misgivings "result from disappointment with regard to the Port and the manner in which it has dragged its feet in the past three years."[66] Once again, memos were written that explored the justification for terminating the project altogether.

By early 1970 the EDA leadership had decided not to cut off the project at that point, but to attach additional stringent conditions to continuation of support for the hangar. On February 2, 1970, Deputy Assistant Secretary Sinnott wrote to Ben Nutter to inform him that the port's request for design-and-construction contracting had been denied: "The EDA program is one which should respond with some dispatch and with some meaning to the target population. This project has not met that test. At this stage, therefore, we are not prepared to agree to a construction procedure which on the surface suggests short cuts and time saving, but which adds to the uncertainty of the kind of facility that will eventually be constructed."[67]

64. Information received from the EDA Office of Public Works. See Table 6.
65. Memo from George Karras to Richard Sinnott, January 13, 1970.
66. *Ibid.*
67. Letter from Sinnott to Nutter, February 12, 1970.

Although Sinnott declared that the EDA intended to "fulfill its commitment," he specified that fulfillment would only take place under certain conditions: the cost of construction had to be under $9,550,000; original job expectations had to be met; final plans and specifications—including the lower cost—had to be completed by December 31, 1970. Sinnott pointed out that "close to four years have transpired since this grant and loan offer was accepted and we cannot permit this offer to remain open indefinitely." This was the EDA's hardest line to date.

Responding to the EDA's demand that the cost of the hangar be drastically cut, the port switched the A/E assignment from Charles Luckman to the firm of Strobel and Rongved of New York. The new firm promised to design "a Ford, not a Cadillac,"[68] and proposed a reduction in the hangar's building size of 16 percent. Preliminary plans and specifications submitted to the EDA in June 1970 estimated the cost at $9.2 million, well within EDA guidelines. The EDA approved preliminary plans and specifications on June 30. The Port Commission approved the revised project in early July, although Commissioner Robert Mortensen voted against the proposal on the grounds that there was no guarantee that the EDA would ever agree to finance the hangar. "I can't act affirmatively on hearsay," Mortensen declared. "After three years there is still no EDA approval and no employment agreement from World."[69] EDA officials, after a brief period of enthusiasm about the new low cost estimates, began to doubt in the late summer whether they were realistic.

World Airways' employment intentions continued to provide still another focus of controversy. John E. Corrigan, director of the EDA Office of Equal Opportunity, went to Oakland to try to work out an acceptable affirmative action employment plan with World. The airline company submitted a long document on May 15, but Corrigan's staff found a number of weaknesses in it: the geographical area for hiring was considered to be the East Bay area, not Oakland; there were no concrete programs spelled out for training minorities to fill professional jobs; there was inadequate specification of the sources of minority recruitment.[70]

68. "Jumbo Jet Hangar Proposal Approved," *Oakland Tribune,* July 3, 1970, p. 18.
69. *Ibid.*
70. Staff criticisms enclosed in letter from John E. Corrigan to General Howell M. Estes, Jr., vice-president of World Airways, July 2, 1970.

Not only was World's affirmative action program considered to be inadequate in its plans for minority hiring; federal officials were also critical of its treatment of women. Quentin S. Taylor, director of civil rights for the Federal Aviation Agency, wrote Corrigan on June 19: "I am greatly concerned about the statement on page 111, under 'Child Care Assistance,' which says that 'female employees are not among those training positions.' This appears to be a violation of the new OFCC [Office of Federal Contract Compliance] sex guidelines. . . . It does not appear that sex would be a bona fide occupational qualification for trainee positions in the aircraft trades."[71] The gulf between World Airways and the EDA was not getting much narrower—four years after the hangar project (the "keystone" of the EDA program) had been announced.

While relations between the EDA and World Airways remained cool during 1970, those between World and the port became frigid. On November 18 the *Oakland Tribune* announced in a headline: "PORT TO CANCEL WORLD AIR AGREEMENT IN DISPUTE." The article said that "Oakland port commissioners will cancel the license agreements of World Airways for hangar and office space in an attempt to get the airline into negotiations on increased rental fees. . . . That action by the board yesterday followed a report by port staff members who said they did not receive any response from World regarding a month-old notification of proposed increases." One of the World projects affected, said the *Tribune*, would be the EDA-financed hangar, which had been "three years in discussion and design."[72] Finally, in June of 1971, although disagreements between the port and World had not been fully resolved, the port awarded construction contracts for the hangar.

SOME LOCAL INITIATIVES

When Hugh Taylor became head of the EDA Oakland office in December 1968, he felt that "the most important thing was to get promised performance before we get any new promises."[73] When contracts for construction of the marine terminal were about to be let in late 1969, Taylor tried to ensure that construction jobs would go to minority workers. Office of Federal Contract Compliance (OFCC)

71. Letter from Quentin S. Taylor to John E. Corrigan, June 19, 1970.
72. *Oakland Tribune*, November 18, 1970.
73. Interview with Hugh Taylor, November 30, 1970.

guidelines required pre-bid affirmative action plans to be approved, and Taylor and his assistant, James Clark, decided to use that provision to secure minority hiring. "That guideline is only a piece of paper; it depends on what you do to enforce it," Taylor remarked.[74]

In late 1969 Oakland EDA officials began to work with the port in organizing the bidding process. At a pre-bidding conference on November 14, Taylor and Corrigan of the EDA—together with an enforcement officer from OFCC—took a hard line with potential contractors. The federal officials explained that all bids had to be accompanied by affirmative action plans. On November 25 the bids were opened, and on December 2 the bidders were invited in again for a preaward conference. At that meeting EDA representatives told the bidders that the federal agency was interested in minority contracting—joint ventures with minority subcontractors and subcontracting with minority enterprises. All general contractors and subcontractors would have to have affirmative action programs or payments would be suspended by the EDA.

When the bids and affirmative action plans were examined, the EDA decided that the low bidder for the roads and sheds part of the project—Rothschild and Raffin, Inc.—did not have a strong or specific enough affirmative action proposal. EDA Oakland officials would not approve the awarding of a contract to Rothschild and Raffin until changes were made in the plan.

Under EDA proddings, Rothschild and Raffin produced an affirmative action plan that was more specific than those signed by previous EDA beneficiaries. The contracting firm named the minority-owned subcontractors with whom it would work, and it named specific percentages of minority workers who would be employed. In a letter to the port, Rothschild and Raffin stated,

In the minor excavation for the underpass we propose to use one half minority men. In order to accomplish this, we will need the complete cooperation of the Federal Agencies. For trucking we propose to use Soul Trucking, the bulkheading will be done by predominately minority carpenters and laborers from Oakland. The concrete underpass will also be framed and poured by minority carpenters and laborers from Oakland. There is a small building on which we have asked minority subcontractors—Oliver Shavies and Archie Tademy—to submit a proposal. We have also asked them to submit a proposal for the foundation of the warehouse. We are attaching copies of

74. *Ibid.*

those letters. . . . We will have an Oakland minority worker in the job office, to take care of the time keeping and job paper work. We are enclosing copy of our usual reporting form of breakdown of ethnic groups on the project. We also enclose manpower projection of the various items of work.[75]

With reference to construction of transit sheds, architectural building, and wall panels, Rothschild and Raffin announced its intention to have the work done "using a black crew from the Oakland area."

Potential subcontractors for the project were also required to list the number and race of people they would employ. For example, E. H. Morrill Company pledged that

The employee composition for E. H. Morrill Co. on the Port of Oakland job will be as follows:
Four plumbers:
  1 foreman
  1 negro journeyman
  1 negro apprentice
  1 non-minority journeyman
Three laborers:
  3 minority laborers
The cooperation of Plumbers' Local 444 has been assured by Mr. Hess.[76]

EDA Oakland officials were now requiring more of contractors than a simple pledge to "try their best" on hiring minorities; potential recipients of EDA funding now had to promise that they would employ certain numbers of minority workers.

Yet, as EDA participants constantly pointed out, enforcement of plans is difficult. One agency official estimated that about 300 construction jobs had been created at the terminal project by November 1970, about 60 percent of which were held by minority workers. But he added a cautionary note: "That's about 60% on peak days, with a lower percentage on non-peak days. And out of those 300 jobs, only about 70 are craftsmen's jobs. That is the focus of the struggle— for jobs on the permanent staff. They can hire blacks for short time periods and move them around from project to project, but permanent jobs are what we want to get. Future agreements should try to secure permanent jobs on a construction company's staff."

Although the EDA had declared that payments would be sus-

75. Letter from R. B. Rothschild to the Port of Oakland, December 16, 1969.
76. Letter from David D. Nolan, attorney for E. H. Morrill Co., to Rothschild and Raffin, December 15, 1969.

pended for noncompliance with the affirmative action plans, Washington EDA officials have not been as ready as their Oakland counterparts to use these sanctions. Thus, although Oakland EDA officials were successful in negotiating far more specific affirmative action agreements for minority hiring, implementation and enforcement of those plans still posed problems in 1972.

In his time as EDA Oakland representative, Taylor has been active in supporting technical assistance projects that go directly to minority groups. In 1969 the EDA awarded a technical assistance grant of $94,000 to a Mexican-American group for the planning of a Spanish-speaking community center. Taylor and Clark of the EDA office were also instrumental in stimulating a joint HUD-EDA-Department of Labor project (the "Prep" program), which funds a minority contractor's association (General and Specialty Contractors Association) to refurbish homes in the West Oakland ghetto and to train minority youth. In a separate project, the EDA provided General and Specialty Contractors with a fifteen-month $75,000 grant to organize and provide technical assistance to minority contractors.[77]

Although some concrete gains were made after five years of EDA activity in Oakland, progress was slow. An agency official echoed a continual EDA concern when he discussed the need for supportive action in the local community: "We need enforcement activities; we need people to make demands for employment opportunities. And these demands ought to come from the local community." In the early days of the EDA Oakland program, federal officials had assumed that community groups would put pressure on aid recipients to force them to hire minorities. But the "non-group, non-political" nature of Oakland's social environment has meant that the sources for such pressure have been largely nonexistent. In an effort to alter this situation, local EDA officials have been supportive of the efforts of an ad hoc committee for minority employment in the downtown civic center project. The EDA hopes eventually to complete a loan agreement with a hotel company that will move into the project.

PROGRESS REPORT: DECEMBER 1970

On December 1, 1970, the EDA Office of Public Works released a report on the progress of its projects in Oakland. Table 4 shows the

77. Taylor interview.

TABLE 4. *Status of EDA ... Projects ... Summary, Sept. ... 19 ...*

EDA Project Number	Description	EDA Funds				Jobs		Current Status
		Approved		Disbursed		Anticipated	Actual	
		Grant	Loan	Grant	Loan			
07-1-00046	7th St. marine terminal	$6,075,000	$4,050,000	$4,284,200	$4,050,000	175	1,000	78% complete; two transit sheds, paving of 7th Street and container area, and some sewers yet to be completed
07-1-00049	industrial park	1,260,000	840,000	962,521	700,000	420	30	100% complete
07-1-00050	aircraft maint. hangar	6,390,000	4,260,000	0	675,000	1,276	N/A	Preliminary plans complete and under review by EDA consultant
07-1-00051	small aircraft hangar	76,000	76,000	74,497	76,000	12	0	100% complete
07-1-00052	air cargo terminal	244,000	184,000	219,000	184,000	20	250 (Relocated)	Work completed; Port of Oakland and contractor have pending lawsuit for alleged delays by contractor
07-1-00160	access road	414,000	0	414,000	0	N/A	N/A	100% complete
07-1-00294	aircraft control tower	133,800	89,000	0	10,000	indirect creation of jobs	N/A	Design complete; further progress dependent on construction of 07-1-00050
07-1-00541	West Oakland Health Center	765,000	765,000	742,451	737,208	130	160	100% complete except for transfer of 2 parcels of land; EDA funds for acquisition of these parcels are being held by EDA until transfer is effected

Source: Economic Development Administration, Office of Public Works.

status in terms of money expended, construction completed, and jobs produced of projects at that time. A number of cautionary words about this table are in order. The 1,000 actual jobs listed for the marine terminal are jobs involved in the "operation of the entire terminal,"[78] not just the one-third of the terminal that is EDA financed. (These jobs are actually in the *other* two-thirds of the terminal, in the non-EDA part that has been completed.) Out of the 1,000 jobs, an agency representative estimated that 350 have gone to minorities. The EDA feels justified in counting these jobs as EDA-induced, because if the EDA had not come in, the port would not have built the 7th Street terminal.

The 30 jobs at the industrial park are all for American Toy Company, and the 250 jobs for the air cargo terminal are for Universal Airlines. This airline company relocated at the air cargo terminal and an EDA official noted that "most of these jobs are not new." There were no available records on the number of these jobs held by unemployed minorities. The access road was felt by an EDA man to be the kind of project "that would not generate jobs in and of itself. But it may generate indirect jobs." These jobs would be very difficult to measure.

The chart does show some gains in the 1968–1970 period: construction on the marine terminal was under way and was 78 percent complete; the West Oakland Health Center had been completed and 160 jobs had been created, with about 150 going to minorities. An EDA representative estimates that 65 of these workers came from the ranks of the hard-core unemployed. (Implementation of the West Oakland Health Center is discussed in chapter 4.)

Thus, EDA officials estimated that the following numbers of jobs were created for minorities: 350 at the marine terminal and 150 at the West Oakland Health Center, for a total of 500. (We have been unable to obtain figures on the number of jobs for minorities created at American Toy Company and Universal Airlines.) In addition, construction of the marine terminal provided approximately 180 construction jobs for minorities.

Five years after the hope-filled genesis of the EDA Oakland program in late 1965, there were still major obstacles to fulfillment of the agency's goal of providing jobs for the hard-core unemployed of the inner city. World Airways and the EDA had still not agreed on a

78. Information received from Office of Public Works, December 6, 1970.

final plan for construction of the hangar, which was supposed to create 1,200 jobs and to be the most important segment of the program. Furthermore, the training programs that were to prepare the hard-core unemployed for employment had become snarled in the bureaucratic jungle of intergovernmental and interagency relations. Finally, in the projects that had been completed (like the industrial park) or were under construction (like the marine terminal), the EDA was not finding it at all easy to enforce employment demands. (By May 1971, construction of the terminal had been completed, and in June contracts were finally let for constructing the hangar. But the question of jobs lay ahead.)

It might be argued that, even though the EDA experienced difficulties in the implementation of its public works program, the agency did provide some unanticipated long-term benefits to poor people in Oakland. For example, EDA officials in the city aided in the development of the Opportunities Industrialization Center and the mayor's Manpower Commission. Also, agency representatives used technical assistance money to aid minority contractors. But we have found it difficult to identify specific unanticipated increases in minority employment that can be ascribed to the EDA. Besides, the public works effort was always felt to be the heart of the agency's Oakland program.

In *Oakland's Not for Burning* Amory Bradford describes the reaction of the members of the Oakland EDA task force to the project announcements of April 29, 1966: "As we listened, all of us who had been working on this felt a sense of tremendous relief. We had done all that we had set out to do, and more, and we had done it on time."[79] The congressional appropriations, agency commitment of funds, approval of projects and acceptance of the employment plan idea had all gone quickly and according to plan. But the "technical details" of financing, construction, and relations with other governmental agencies—combined with continued disagreements between the EDA and its potential beneficiaries about employment policy—had provided continual problems for five long years. Chains of unanticipated decision points, requiring numerous clearances by different actors, had provided the occasions for frustrating delays. The hopeful "experimental program" of 1966 had become a painful example of the problems of implementation.

79. Bradford, p. 124.

4

Two Smaller Programs:
Business Loans and the Health Center

The public works effort was not the only EDA program attempted in Oakland. At his April 1966 news conference, Assistant Secretary Foley had announced that a program of loans to businesses would create 800 new jobs in the city. EDA leaders saw the business loans program as a way of involving private sector firms of various sizes in the effort to provide jobs for the unemployed. But contradictory and restrictive legislative criteria, administrative conflicts, and disappointing performances by local firms combined to erect insuperable hazards to implementation of this program in Oakland.

By the end of 1968 EDA officials were becoming increasingly frustrated and depressed by delays in their Oakland program. They began to wonder if a project would ever be completed. So they seized on an existing neighborhood initiative in order to help bring a health center to West Oakland. Although this center was not part of the 1966 EDA initiative, we include a brief account of it at the end of this chapter to provide a little illumination in an otherwise bleak scene. Later, when we want to contrast a program that has succeeded with others that did not, we will have something with which to work.

BUSINESS LOANS: GOING FROM THE MERELY DIFFICULT
TO THE REALLY IMPOSSIBLE

Policy implementation is made difficult when experience reveals that legislators want incompatible things. They want to help people in areas of low employment by attracting new industries or expanding old ones. But they do not want to subsidize competitors against their own people. When their constituents complain that government funds are being spent to support business competitors, the congressmen naturally write in provisions stating that aid to industry must not compete with existing firms. Since most conceivable enterprises compete in some way with others, the dilemma is passed on to the administrators who discover that they cannot apply the criteria with any consistency. This is one moral of the EDA business loans program.

Both the legislation and the information leaflets of the EDA claim that private enterprise is the key to remedying unemployment in depressed regions. A message from the assistant secretary of commerce on an information folder says, "The federal government, through EDA, can help with this task, but only private enterprise can get the unemployed off the relief roll and onto a payroll." In the United States Senate, following introduction of the public works and economic development bill, Senator Proxmire explained that he liked the bill because it stressed "private enterprise and private development," did not provide for a "gigantic federally controlled and directed public works program," and "basic investment decisions [would] be left up to the private sector of our economy."[1]

And yet the appropriations heavily favor public works expenditure over the business loans program.[2] Why? The idea behind funding public infrastructure is to make a depressed area more attractive to private industry. Public spending is seen as pump priming for the private economy in the area. During the introduction of the public works and economic development bill to the Senate, most of the supporting evidence emphasized that the new bill was to replace the Accelerated Public Works Act program which was expiring at the time. At this stage, public works financing was seen primarily as a means of creating jobs to ease unemployment until the anticipated effect of the tax cut became apparent. The emphasis on public works

1. U.S. Senate, Congressional Record, May 26, 1965, p. 11799.
2. The annual appropriations, from 1966 to 1970, provided $500 million in grants, $170 million in loans. While private business may only receive loans, public works projects may receive grants and loans.

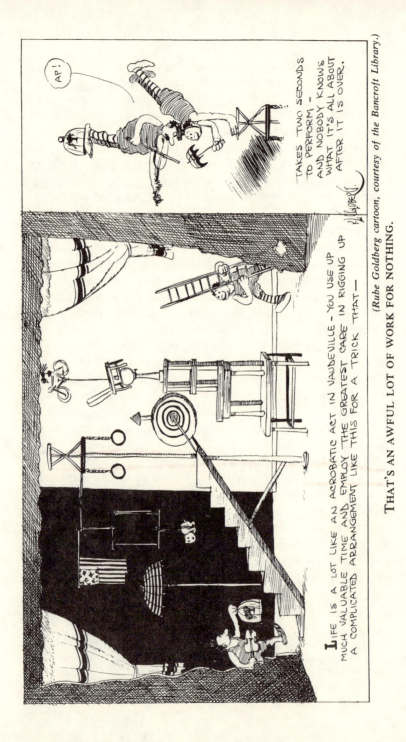

(Rube Goldberg cartoon, courtesy of the Bancroft Library.)

THAT'S AN AWFUL LOT OF WORK FOR NOTHING.

spending as a means of encouraging the development of private enterprise arose as the bill went through the legislative process.[3]

We shall see that those federal and local actors who had dealings with Oakland's business loan program had numerous reasons for becoming disillusioned with it. How did this program, which initially engendered so much support both in Congress and at the local level, eventually engender both bitterness and disillusionment? One answer would seem to lie in a dilemma central to such intervention programs.

The use of public money to stimulate private enterprise rather than to mount public works programs has considerable appeal for many congressmen and their constituents. But in practice such programs soon cause resentment among that same constituency because they inevitably subsidize, or in other ways assist, some firms while ignoring others. William C. Heyn, giving evidence before the Senate Public Works Committee, described the dilemma when he argued that "It is unfair to existing industry to use their tax money to subsidize new industry which will compete for their markets" and that, "since industrial development is a highly competitive activity, it is unfair and discriminatory for the Federal Government to take sides in behalf of some areas, thereby working against other areas to create competition for their products and jobs."[4]

From the time the Area Redevelopment Administration (ARA) began its business loans program, this problem was aggravated by the fact that the average unemployment level was quite high. It is difficult to redistribute jobs from the rich to the poor regions when even the richest regions are short of jobs themselves. Levitan points out that "it is difficult to defend government financing of new capacity when established firms operate below their optimum level because of inadequate demand,"[5] and Miernyk observes that, "When the level

3. U.S. Senate, Congressional Record, May 26, 1965, pp. 11787–11799.

4. U.S. House of Representatives, Public Works Committee Hearings, Public Works and Economic Development Act of 1965, 89th Congress, 1st Session, April 26-May 3, 1965, statement of William C. Heyn, assistant to the president, New Holland Machine Co., Division of Sperry-Rand, New Holland, Pennsylvania, on behalf of the National Association of Manufacturers, p. 156.

5. Sar Levitan, *Federal Aid to Depressed Areas* (Johns Hopkins University Press, 1964), p. 247.

of unemployment is rising, and when unemployment is widespread, little can be done to alleviate the chronic unemployment of the depressed areas."[6]

The severe criticism leveled at the ARA because of the charge of robbing Peter to pay Paul resulted in the introduction of constraining legislation into the Public Works and Economic Development Act of 1965. The chairman was fully aware of the touchiness of this issue when he emphasized, in his introductory statement before the Senate Public Works Committee, that the bill was not designed to "take from one area for the benefit of another," or to "shift job opportunities from our more prosperous communities to the less prosperous," or to "enhance the growth potential of one region to the detriment of another."[7] The legislation reflects this concern by placing restraints on the business loans program. "No financial assistance under this Act shall be extended to any project when the result would be to increase the production of goods, materials, or commodities, or the availability of services or facilities, when there is not sufficient demand for such goods, material, commodities, services, or facilities, to employ the efficient capacity of existing competitive commercial or industrial enterprises."[8]

This is not an easy requirement to administer. At a hearing before the Special Subcommittee on Economic Development Programs, Mr. Edmonson (chairman) asked Ross Davis (assistant secretary of commerce for economic development) how his staff was handling it.[9] Davis replied that the vagueness of, and difficulty of quantifying, such terms as "sufficient demand," "efficient capacity," and "existing competitive enterprises" was making "translation from concept to a specific practical situation quite difficult." He asked, for example, under what economic circumstances and over what period of time "sufficient demand" was to be interpreted.

6. William H. Miernyk, quoted from testimony before U.S. Senate Committee on Labor and Public Welfare, Subcommittee on Labor, Hearings on Area Redevelopment, 84th Congress, 2nd Session, p. 154.

7. U.S. Senate, Public Works Committee Hearings, Public Works and Economic Development Act of 1965, p. 2.

8. Public Works and Economic Development Act, 1965, Sec. 702.

9. U.S. House of Representatives, Hearings Before the Special Subcommittee on Economic Development Programs, 90th Congress, 1st Session, April 11, 1967, pp. 15–17.

To legislators the issue was simple. As Congressman Cleveland explained, "I wonder if it would not be helpful to you if we worked that from the other end? Put yourself in the place of a Congressman. The telephone rings. It is a constituent. The constituent wants to know from his Congressman why the Government is building a motel right next to his motel when he only has half of his available motel facilities used. This constituent is paying taxes."[10]

The EDA administrator is being asked to evaluate businesses to ensure that they are not competing with other firms, are not taking jobs from other areas, and are only producing new jobs in the economy and that the capacity of all other producers in that field is fully taxed, all within a frame of reference undetermined in both space and time. The administrator would also be aware that during the ARA operation the funding of businesses that offended in any of these regards had resulted in much criticism being directed at the agency and its staff.[11] Under these conditions, it is not so much surprising that loans took so long to process (a common complaint of local businessmen) as it is remarkable that any were processed at all.

PROJECT DECISIONS

The affection of Congress for employment, as we have seen, was real but not total. New jobs for the poor were good so long as they did not displace other people. The men who administered these provisions, however, did not share all the qualms and pressures felt by the legislators. Congress may have written the language, but the administrators were doing the translating.

Not surprisingly, EDA administrators took a dim view of the statutory criteria for loans. Figure 1 shows the incredibly complex and contradictory decision path which, according to the legislation, the EDA would have to follow. Faced with this administrator's nightmare, the business loans division of the EDA devised some shortcuts. A former loan official of the agency declared, "We didn't really fol-

---

10. *Ibid.*, p. 17. Sundquist notes that "ARA-financed motels in depressed areas were made to appear as threats to every existing motel for miles around," p. 106, in *Politics and Policy: The Eisenhower, Kennedy, and Johnson Years* (Washington, D.C.: Brookings Institution, 1968).

11. Levitan, pp. 124–130.

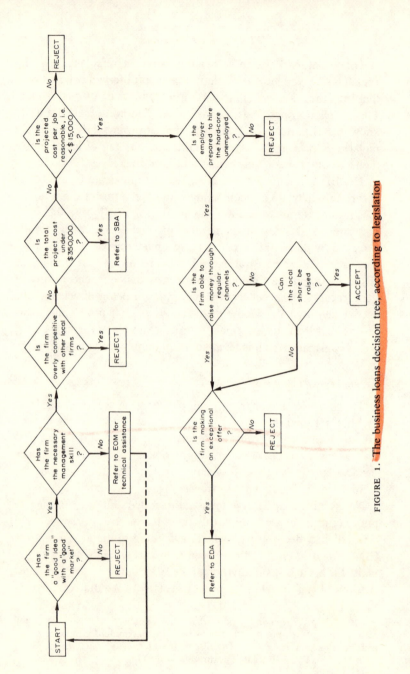

FIGURE 1. The business loans decision tree, according to legislation

low the statutory criteria—all that stuff about not being competitive and not being able to get money from any other source. That was put in by Congressmen who wanted to ruin the program. What we did pay attention to was whether the firm was a dying industry or had excess capacity. In these cases, we wouldn't give loans."

For the Oakland experiment, EDA loan procedures were altered significantly. Normally, EDA field coordinators would develop a project. If an application was filed, it was then sent to the EDA in Washington. A project review committee there met with its counterpart from the Small Business Administration's Washington office. That committee reviewed the application. If the committee's decision was favorable, the SBA was given a set of instructions and asked to conduct a credit investigation. (For the most part, SBA staff members served as the EDA loan division's field personnel. This "delegate agency" device was an economy measure that had been advocated by the Budget Bureau.) After the credit investigation, the SBA wrote a report and sent it to the EDA field office. The EDA reviewed the credit information and made a judgment on job-producing capacity. Finally, the application would come back to the loan director's office for approval or disapproval. A former loan official observed that "the whole thing took about six months. It's true that the target was ninety days. But very few took less than ninety days—the average was about six months."

For Oakland, the process was different:

We put an EDA loan specialist—Daschbach—directly into Oakland. We coordinated efforts with SBA in San Francisco. Our specialist developed a project and reported back to EDA on the project being developed. We'd then discuss the application with Daschbach, a deputy here in the office, and the head of business loans for the western U.S. For Oakland, we ignored the EDA area office and the SBA-EDA Project Review Committee. SBA completed the field investigation and the report was sent directly to EDA.

There were two steps for Oakland: (1) Daschbach and SBA would submit a field report; (2) Washington EDA would examine it. The process of decision was shortened (fewer people were involved) and concentrated (less geographic distance per encounter). Daschbach viewed his own role as that of a promoter, defending projects against the attacks of lawyers, financial engineers, and other agency officials.

Thus we see that the bureaucracy assigned an expediter to circumvent its own restrictions.

For Daschbach, the major criterion for approving applications was the relation of jobs to dollars. The ratio had to be less than $15,-000 per job. The EDA loan office sets up cost/job guidelines to evaluate job-producing potential and to ensure that EDA participation in a project will be kept within bounds; applicants are encouraged to seek money from other sources as well.

The problem was that there were not very many good applicants, that is, businesses that the EDA felt would provide new jobs for inner-city unemployed. Staff members interviewed remembered that only "about a dozen" good applications ever came in. Faced with a paucity of good applications, the EDA in its decisions "went for diversity," according to a former agency official. "We decided to make a loan to one Negro entrepreneur, one project that would provide jobs for the low end of the labor scale, and one business that would provide reasonably skilled jobs." This official noted that "criteria were not something we started with and judged things by. We formulated the criteria *after* we saw what Daschbach brought in. We figured out some things that might be done and decided to get one example of each." (There was no funding constraint; the EDA was far below its permissible loan total of $10 million for Oakland.)

The EDA decided to approve loans for Bennie's Candies (the black entrepreneur); Rainbow Car Wash (for the lower end of the economic scale); and Colombo Bakery ("reasonably skilled jobs"). Also approved was a loan to Sierra Cotton Mills; a loan to Berkeley Instruments (electronic telemetry manufacturing) had been approved in January. The awarding of all these loans could not, of course, be made officially until the approval of employment plans by the review board was secured; this was not done until the fall.

The 5 percent local share provided some difficulty in the administration of the loan program; the EDA legislation required that the local community make a cash contribution as a means of promoting community involvement and participation in the program. The ARA had had a similar requirement, and in 1965 Mayor Houlihan had asked that the business community become involved in the federal economic development program. He established the Oakland Economic Development Foundation (OEDF), which was a group of businessmen who were to provide the local share required for federal loans.

Numerous members of the 1966 EDA staff in Oakland criticized the OEDF as being an obstacle to the loan program ("Those people didn't even believe in federal programs"). When the foundation was asked to give its approval to the first two business loan applicants (Colombo Bakery and Sierra Cotton Mills), the foundation turned down both applications, arguing that Colombo did not need low cost federal loans for its expansion and that Sierra was a bad risk. Bradford did not accept this explanation and claimed that the foundation "had little feel for the problems of expanding small businesses and new ventures" and that "they seemed to feel that anyone who applied for a government loan because he could not get financing through commercial channels was a bad risk."[12]

In order to avoid further such delay, neither the Bennie's Candies nor the Rainbow Car Wash proposals were presented to the foundation for approval. The OEDF was one example of "citizen participation" that didn't work.[13]

THE OUTCOME OF BUSINESS LOANS

Table 5 presents the disappointing results of the EDA business loans projects, as of October 1968.

Colombo Baking Company appears to have used the loan "to finance expansion and automation rather than employment positions."[14] The EDA internal report states that "it is apparent that Colombo did not need a loan from EDA. Clearly Colombo was in a financial position to seek and get commercial money or possibly finance the proposed expansion itself."[15] The report outlines Colombo's minimal progress in the field of job creation:

Colombo had 109 employees when they applied for an EDA loan to finance bulk flour storage facilities. Colombo now employs 117. During that period one employee left (a Negro who became a minority entrepreneur—without government assistance). Of the new hires, three have been Negroes. One

12. Amory Bradford, *Oakland's Not for Burning* (New York: McKay, 1968), p. 62.
13. Pp. 73–76 of this chapter were adapted from Owen McShane, "Toward a Transitional Economics" (unpublished paper, April 1970).
14. *Ibid.*, p. 53.
15. EDA internal report, p. 44.

TABLE 5: EDA Business Loans in Oakland Produce Few Jobs at High Cost: EDA Expenditures and Resulting Jobs

Name and Type of Firm	Total Project Cost ($)	EDA Loan ($)	Projected Jobs	Projected Total Cost/Job ($)	Projected EDA Cost/Job ($)	Actual Jobs	Actual Total Cost/Job ($)	Actual EDA Cost/Job ($)
Colombo Baking Co. (rejected by OEDF)	650,000	423,000	158	4,114	2,677	8	81,250	52,875
Bennie's Candies	99,000	73,000	25	3,960	2,920	10	9,900	7,300
Rainbow Car Wash	207,000	135,000	35	5,914	3,857	25	8,280	5,400
Sierra Cotton Mills (rejected by OEDF)	—	376,000	66	—	5,697	BANKRUPT		
Berkeley Instruments (electronic telemetry manufacturing)	120,000	78,000	25	4,500	3,120	BANKRUPT		
National Plug (scrap paper reprocessing)	—	45,000 (undisbursed)	25	—	1,800	WITHDREW		
Value Engineering (pipe fabrication)	450,000	280,000 (undisbursed)	26	17,308	10,769	WITHDREW		
Hyatt Hotel Corporation	13,000,000	4,000,000 (not yet disbursed)	763	17,038	5,242	BEING PROCESSED		

Source: Owen McShane, "Toward A Transitional Economics," pp. 55, 58. Figures based on 1968 EDA internal report.

of the four other Negro employes was upgraded through use of on-the-job training assistance (Federal money). This young lady was moved from a job in the bakery to the outer office as receptionist.[16]

Bennie's Candies is owned by Bennie Smith, a black entrepreneur who wanted to expand from an over-the-counter family business into a larger commercial enterprise. His EDA loan was for plant and equipment, but the equipment expenditure—for a candy machine—was a disaster. The 1968 EDA report is critical of the SBA's joint role in the process:

The SBA's engineering review failed to adequately evaluate the capacity of a jam-making machine to dispense molten peanut praline batter. SBA's failure to include a clause in the purchase contract with Food Machinery Corporation which would have required performance of the equipment, and SBA's disbursement of money for final payment on the equipment before evaluating its ability to meet its requirements have brought Bennie near the point of failure.[17]

In simpler terms, the brand new candy machine failed to work.

The EDA business loans office tried to get their agency to provide Bennie with technical assistance (in the form of management men) to help him with financial affairs. But the agency's technical assistance officials argued that this would be a subterfuge for giving him working capital, which the agency was not supposed to do. If a man needed all that assistance, they reasoned, then he was obviously not a good businessman. Bennie had to get working capital from the SBA, which let the money out "in drips and drabs," as Bennie said. Instead of giving him the entire working capital loan of $25,000 to put in the bank, the SBA would provide no more than $1,000 at a time.[18] Under these conditions "black capitalism" was a hazardous enterprise. A potentially antagonistic administrative relationship had thus been built into loan program implementation. The EDA was interested in stimulating growth and creating jobs, while SBA viewed projects with a cautious banker's eye. Yet according to a Budget Bureau directive, EDA programs had to rely on SBA staff for working capital assistance.

Rainbow Car Wash produced twenty-five jobs at the bottom end

16. *Ibid.*
17. *Ibid.*, pp. 45–46.
18. Owen McShane interview with Bennie Smith, April 30, 1970.

of the economic ladder. Although these jobs were criticized as "dead end," they represented a reasonably successful investment for the EDA: the federal agency's cost per job was only $5,400.

Sierra Cotton Mills in 1968 was "in the position of imminent foreclosure by the Bank of America."[19] Soon it was bankrupt.

Berkeley Instruments met a similar fate, following a depletion of its working capital "as a result of one bad contract."[20]

National Plug Company, a firm to reprocess scrap paper, and *Value Engineering,* a pipe fabrication company, were both approved by OEDF but decided to withdraw their applications. A member of the Oakland EDA staff in 1966 remarked, "Value Engineering was turned down when it tried to get land in the Port's industrial park—the Port didn't think that a can-crusher was aesthetic enough."

The loan to *Hyatt Hotel Corporation* was approved in June 1968, but the hotel company had not yet made a final decision on locating in Oakland.

The gloomy record of business loans was summed up in an *Oakland Tribune* headline in March 1969: "U.S. INVESTS $1,085,000 TO CREATE 43 OAKLAND JOBS."[21] It is not difficult to understand why this program in Oakland has been substantially deactivated since that time. Let us now move from the depths of depression surrounding the outcome of business loans to consider an EDA project in Oakland that actually exceeded expectations—the West Oakland Health Center.

A PROJECT THAT WORKED: THE WEST OAKLAND HEALTH CENTER

In 1968, which was not in general a banner year for the EDA in Oakland, the federal agency embarked on a project that was directly tied to poor and black people. During the latter part of 1966 a dozen women residents of West Oakland had met with a graduate student in social work, a minister from the West Oakland parish, and an area physician in an effort to improve health services in the West Oakland ghetto. In early 1967 they were incorporated as a formal organization, the West Oakland Health Council, Inc. (WOHCI). Meetings with interested professionals and official agencies led the group to

19. EDA internal report, p. 43.
20. *Ibid.,* p. 41.
21. *Oakland Tribune,* March 16, 1969, p. 1.

concentrate initially on collecting statistics to document the needs of the community.[22]

Under a grant from the Office of Economic Opportunity, the Alameda County Health Department lent the services of a health statistician to the group to assist it in designing and carrying out a health survey for a random sample of the West Oakland population. The survey showed that, although the population of West Oakland comprised only 9 percent of the population under the jurisdiction of the county health department, the West Oakland area had: 20 percent of the measles cases, 30 percent of the tuberculosis cases, 50 percent of the gonorrhea cases, and 51 percent of the syphilis cases. In addition, the infant mortality rate was considerably higher (38 per 1,000 births) in West Oakland than for the county as a whole (19.2 per 1,000 births). There were few health care specialists in the area.[23]

The local community group determined to develop a health facility, and the WOHCI was encouraged by the United States Public Health Service to apply for funding for an outpatient program. For the land and construction of the building itself, WOHCI sought help from the Oakland Redevelopment Agency. Funds were also sought from outside sources like the National Medical Association Foundation, a black medical federation. The WOHCI also anticipated funding from the Model Cities program.

The EDA's Oakland representatives at that time, Charles Patterson and Fred Ricci, had followed these events and had given assistance to WOHCI. When it appeared that the original financing from both the NMA and Model Cities was in jeopardy, the EDA officials encouraged the community group to apply for EDA public works funding. The WOHCI and the Public Health Service formally requested that the EDA provide a 60 percent grant and 40 percent loan award for the center. The WOHCI would direct administration of the center and would contract with a group of physicians—the West

22. We are indebted to Douglas G. Montgomery, who was a postdoctoral fellow in the EDA during 1969–70, for the health center chronology. See his "The Federal Delivery System: Impact on the Community. A Case Study of EDA and the West Oakland Health Center" (paper delivered at the American Political Science Association annual meeting, 1970). Montgomery carried on the study as a temporary member of EDA's Office of Policy Coordination. Approval for the study was given by Richard Sinnott in the fall of 1969.

23. *Ibid.*, p. 19.

Oakland Health Group—to provide services there. The development of the project was estimated to create one hundred new jobs; furthermore, it would serve as a training facility for medical, paramedical, and subprofessional occupations.

Early in May 1968, the Oakland EDA office sent a memorandum to Washington recommending approval of the project. There was some concern in Washington about financing arrangements, since the EDA had had no previous experience with funding a health facility that operated on the basis of a recipient's ability to pay. Some doubted that the facility could produce revenues adequate to pay the loan.[24] Furthermore, the EDA's public works experience in Oakland thus far had not been pleasant at all; the hangar and terminal projects were both stalled at the time.

In spite of these doubts, the EDA agreed to fund the project early in June 1968. The promised EDA funding totaled $1.3 million to construct the 26,000-square-foot medical center; there was to be a $650,000 grant and a $650,000 loan. Participants interviewed credit George Karras, director of the Office of Public Works, with piloting this decision through the EDA bureaucracy. Thus, the project had for an ally a man who could offer sustained and effective help in the process of implementation that lay ahead.

With the project approved, those "technical details" began to crop up again. The Public Health Service and the WOHCI had entered into negotiations with a private contractor, Designed Facilities Corporation (DFC), to work on the building. This firm had assured the WOHCI that use of prefabricated structures would save time in building; it also wanted to operate both as the architect/engineer and general contractor under a negotiated contract with the WOHCI.

The EDA is normally opposed to a procedure that allows one firm to design and construct a project; competitive bidding is the agency's rule. Nevertheless, after some disagreement, the EDA agreed to let the WOHCI deviate from normal procedure in this case. The Public Health Service was firmly behind design-and-construct, and DFC had promised to complete the facility within ninety days after starting construction.[25] By acceding to design-and-construct, the EDA

24. *Ibid.,* p. 22.
25. *Ibid.,* p. 25.

had reduced the number of necessary clearances in program implementation.

Familiar troubles surfaced in July: the contractor notified its clients that cost overruns would occur. But the EDA was committed to building the center and showing results; besides, the overrun necessitated only a $200,000 increase. So in August 1968 the EDA increased the grant and loan by $100,000 each. Douglas G. Montgomery notes: "EDA continued to push the Center because of its direct benefits to the community although the special experience of the negotiated contract to fund this project was becoming less accommodative to the agency."[26]

Further delays were caused in fall 1968 when members of the WOHCI began to disagree "over what they desired and what they could afford."[27] In early December representatives of the EDA and PHS met to discuss the delayed construction. "Both federal agencies continued to agree," Montgomery reports, "that the self determination activity by WOHCI in managing its own program was an important part of the project's operation."[28]

While EDA officials were trying to decide what to do about the terminal and hangar projects throughout spring and summer 1969, the West Oakland Health Center was taking shape. In February a contract had been signed under which Designed Facilities Corporation was the prime contractor; that company in turn designated Trans-Bay Engineering and Builders (minority builders) as its principal contractor. The contract totaled $1,004,995 for the construction of the facility and the architect/engineering services.[29]

The financing arrangements for the project's construction were somewhat unusual. Because the borrower was unable to obtain interim financing, the EDA agreed to disburse funds on a cost-incurred basis during construction. (The federal agency wanted to avoid the cost escalation that inevitably followed undue delay.) Furthermore, instead of making loan and grant disbursements to the West Oakland Health Council, the EDA paid the contractors directly. An EDA public works staff member explains the reason for

26. *Ibid.*
27. *Ibid.*
28. *Ibid.*
29. *Ibid.*

this deviation from normal practice: "There was a lot of infighting within the West Oakland Health Council. They changed their top management, and the executive director who lost out in a power struggle sued the council. Pending the suit, we thought there might have been a judgment to freeze the Council's assets, so we paid the creditors directly to keep the project going."

Several delays prevented the center from being completed by the contractor's target date of June 15, 1969. The subcontractors had some trouble finding an adequate number of competent workmen and also made mistakes in scheduling. Then problems occurred with the assembly of fixtures in the facility. Although the primary contractor had intended to install plumbing fixtures in the modules at the factory, the city of Oakland Building Department ruled that fixtures had to be installed at the site. But these problems were finally resolved, and the center was completed on August 20, 1969.[30] By December 1970 the center had provided 160 jobs—including 150 for minorities.

30. *Ibid.*, p. 26.

5

The Complexity of Joint Action

INTRODUCTION

When we say that programs have failed, this suggests we are surprised. If we thought from the beginning that they were unlikely to be successful, their failure to achieve stated goals or to work at all would not cry out for any special explanation. If we believed that intense conflicts of interests were involved, if people who had to cooperate were expected to be at loggerheads, if necessary resources were far beyond those available, we might wonder rather more why the programs were attempted instead of expressing amazement at their shortcomings. The problem would dissolve, so to speak, in the statement of it. No explanatory ingenuity would be required. A trite and commonplace question would receive a self-evident answer. Even if the initiators of the programs failed to appreciate the bitter conflict they would set off, we should simply investigate their failures of perception, having thus explained the inevitable unhappy outcomes.

It is not surprising, for example, that the EDA business loans program in Oakland failed. Given contradictory legislative criteria, inherent administrative antagonisms between federal agencies, and the uncertainty of local action on the part of numerous businesses, it is no wonder that the program failed to achieve its aims. In public works, at least, the EDA had the advantage of dealing with one

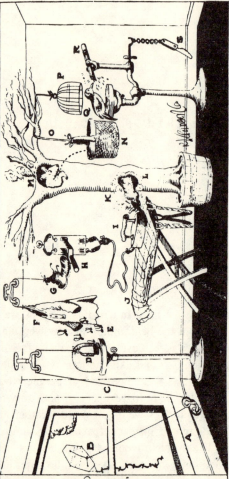

PROFESSOR BUTTS GETS HIS THINK-TANK WORKING AND EVOLVES THE SIMPLIFIED PENCIL-SHARPENER. OPEN WINDOW (A) AND FLY KITE (B). STRING (C) LIFTS SMALL DOOR (D) ALLOWING MOTHS (E) TO ESCAPE AND EAT RED FLANNEL SHIRT (F). AS WEIGHT OF SHIRT BECOMES LESS, SHOE (G) STEPS ON SWITCH (H) WHICH HEATS ELECTRIC IRON (I) AND BURNS HOLE IN PANTS (J). SMOKE (K) ENTERS HOLE IN TREE (L) SMOKING OUT OPOSSUM (M) WHICH JUMPS INTO BASKET (N) PULLING ROPE (O) AND LIFTING CAGE (P), ALLOWING WOODPECKER (Q) TO CHEW WOOD FROM PENCIL (R) EXPOSING LEAD. EMERGENCY KNIFE (S) IS ALWAYS HANDY IN CASE OPOSSUM OR THE WOODPECKER GETS SICK AND CAN'T WORK.

(Rube Goldberg cartoon from Rube Goldberg vs. the Machine Age, ed. Clark Kinnaird, New York: Hastings House, 1968, p. 18.)

DOES IT HAVE TO BE THIS COMPLICATED?

major recipient—the Port of Oakland—and that recipient was known to have excellent management and the best credit rating. There was no question of whether the port was qualified, only if it would make good on its promises. Business loans, on the other hand, had to work through a variety of local firms, a number of whom had management of doubtful quality. And the applications had to be approved by a board of local businessmen who were critical of the whole EDA effort. The statutory criteria for eligibility of borrowers, furthermore, were both stringent and incompatible. It was difficult for a potential borrower to demonstrate that his firm would provide new employment in the area that did not compete with existing business. It was more difficult for him to show that he could not finance his proposal through private lending facilities (which meant that he was considered a poor risk), while convincing the EDA and SBA that he would not default on his loan.

Yet EDA officials in Oakland took on an additional challenge by deciding to apply the employment plan to business loans projects. A former EDA loan official in Washington commented on the effects of this decision: "You start with poor borrowers. Then the poor borrower has to hire the world's poorest work force. Then we expect him to compete with rich businessmen with experienced work forces." When the EDA loan office tried to provide a struggling Oakland businessman (who had hired some unemployed minority workers) with enough management assistance to keep his firm afloat, an EDA technical assistance officer vetoed the project. After all, reasoned the official, if the man needs all that help, he couldn't be a good businessman. EDA can lend building capital, but not working capital. Under the watchful banker's eye of the Small Business Administration, which can loan working capital, the firm eventually went bankrupt.

Faced with a numerous and needful set of participants, compelled to relate to them through a series of complex criteria, EDA officials might well have begun to long for the relative simplicity of the public works projects. Who does this sort of thing to himself? In the full flood of enthusiasm, EDA officials may not have realized what they were getting into when they joined race and poverty with business management and employment. But they did have a long legislative history to warn them that loan programs involved deeply rooted conflicts of interests. The criteria for loans, which seemed to cry out for parody, are the product of accommodation to the conflicts that arose when the federal government first discovered that it wasn't always easy to help some people without hurting others. And a further conflict had been built into the program by the requirement that the EDA and SBA—agencies whose priorities differed markedly—should share responsibility for administering the loan program.

Because of pervasive conflicts within the business loans program, its decision rules were complex; competing interests had to be taken into account. The idea that employment for minorities is good in and of itself had to give way to the desirability of limiting competition with existing firms, to allowing the Small Business Administration to deal with applicants in its domain, to not taking over the role of the private market in funding companies able to use its facilities. The very complexity of the decision rules, however, militated against their successful use since so few applicants could satisfy them. The criteria, in fact, began to scare away applicants. The men in charge of moving the money had to simplify their lives. They ended up, quite reasonably in their own terms, deciding to pick a little of this and a little of that to see what would happen. They even made a concession in the direction of local opinion by insisting on the formation of a citizens group to help appraise proposals. But it did not help local citizens to be asked to make decisions that they were not competent to make. Moreover, there was little room for choice because not many proposals came up. There is a name for that, but rubber-stamping does not somehow equal citizen participation.

When a program is characterized by so many contradictory criteria, antagonistic relationships among participants, and a high level of uncertainty about even the possibility of success, it is not hard to predict or to explain the failure of the effort to reach its goals. "When, as in the case of ESEA," Bailey and Mosher write, "a law unprecedented in scope has to be administered through State and local instrumentalities, on an impossible time schedule, by an understaffed agency in structural turmoil, beset by a deluge of complaints and demands for clarification of the legislation at hand, as well as cognate legislation already on the books; the wonder is not that mistakes are made—the wonder is that the law is implemented at all."[1]

1. Stephen K. Bailey and Edith K. Mosher, *ESEA: The Office of Education Administers a Law* (Syracuse, N.Y.: Syracuse University Press, 1968), p. 99.

We are more surprised by program failure in a case in which there is apparent agreement at the beginning, but in which disagreements soon surface to block the program. Such a case was provided by the "new towns in-town" program, which is the subject of an excellent analysis by Martha Derthick.[2] Late in the summer of 1967, the Johnson administration started a program to build model new communities on surplus federally owned land in metropolitan areas. During the next year, the White House and the Department of Housing and Urban Development announced seven projects. They were to be located in Washington, D.C., San Antonio, Atlanta, Louisville, Clinton Township (Michigan), New Bedford, and San Francisco. Nearly three years later, the program had clearly failed. Three of the projects were dead, and the rest were in serious trouble. Almost no construction had been initiated.[3]

Why would anyone want to look a gift horse in the mouth? Why would anyone reject the benevolent efforts of President Johnson, the White House, and the Department of Housing and Urban Development to offer subsidies on federally owned surplus land in metropolitan areas for the laudable purpose of building new communities joining black and white, rich and poor, living together in harmony with the new technology? Although initial agreement appeared—at least to the federal officials—to be widespread, disagreements rapidly came to the surface. A number of local groups strongly opposed low cost public housing; local officials preferred kinds of development that would yield more tax revenue; and conservationists were opposed to plans for construction. As apparent agreement rapidly yielded to pervasive disagreement, the program ground to a halt.

We could justify our surprise at program failure still better (thereby enhancing the interest in asking why programs fail) by taking a case in which initial agreements dissolved slowly over time in unpredictable ways. Antagonisms would not be evident at the beginning, nor would they emerge rapidly. Rather, the conflicts would be covert and would become evident only after some time had passed. The interests and organizations involved would have thought they wanted to do something, but experience would teach them that they had been mistaken. Few programs could be undertaken if all par-

2. Martha Derthick, *New Towns In-Town* (Washington, D.C.: Urban Institute, 1972).
3. *Ibid.*, p. xiv.

ticipants had to be specified in advance, all future differences resolved at the outset, and future bargains made under yesterday's conditions. Something has to be left to the unfolding of events. Then as
latent conflicts become manifest, the original agreements have to be
renegotiated and a new and possibly more antagonistic situation
emerges. The federal agency may discover that its funding recipients
are not willing to abide by initial agreements, or the recipients may
interpret the agreements in ways that conflict with federal interpretations. An agency that appears to be a single organization with a
single will turns out to be several suborganizations with different
wills. The apparent solidity of original aims and understandings
gives way as people, organizations, and circumstances change. So far,
so good. But not good or far enough.

It could be said that the EDA public works program was characterized by the slow dissolution of agreement. As one delay succeeded
another, the major individual participants changed and so did the
understandings they had with one another. Agreements were reached,
eroded, and remade. The frequent calls for coordination, which we
shall subject to analysis in the next chapter, reflected the inability of
the machinery for implementation to move fast enough to capture
the agreements while they lasted. Allow enough time to elapse in a
rapidly changing external world and it is hard to imagine any set of
agreements remaining firm. We expect the national economy (and
the position of individual firms within it) to be subject to rapid fluc-
tuation. Why, then, should agreements made in what must seem like
a bygone era retain their original binding force? Anyone can understand why agreement is subject to modification over time; everyone
wants to know why it took so long to implement the public works
and employment program that everybody wanted in the beginning.
There is less of a challenge in explaining why agreements break
down years after they have been entered into than in discovering
why it is so difficult to implement them at the time they are made.

It is more interesting, we think, to maximize surprise. We have
chosen to analyze the EDA public works program in Oakland precisely because it lacks those elements that permit the easy explanations. Compared, say, with community action or urban redevelopment, the EDA's involvement in Oakland lacks both drama and conflict. Unlike business loans, there were no obvious conflicting inter-

ests and contradictory legislative criteria. And unlike "new towns in-town," there was no opposition on the local level. In EDA public works, all the major participants throughout the program's history insisted that they believed in the program and that there were no fundamental disagreements among them. The happenings we record are important to us for their everyday prosaic character. These are the kinds of things—changing actors, diverse perspectives, multiple clearances—that are found in any program.

Indeed, the EDA made special efforts to overcome obstacles that were known to have hampered other programs. The EDA's innovation, from its own point of view, consisted precisely in trying to avoid the institutional fragmentation, multiple and confusing goals, and inadequate funding that had characterized previous federal-city programs. The marine terminal and airline hangar projects, on which we shall concentrate for analytical purposes, deliberately included just one federal agency in one city; there would be only one major local recipient, the Port of Oakland, whose tenants' performance would be bound by a written and signed employment plan; and there would be an immediate commitment of $23 million. The straightforward construction of job-producing public works was the heart of the EDA program for Oakland. We are unlikely to get many programs that will be simpler in that they involve fewer participants or less complicated arrangements. Few programs would specify as clearly the benefits to the participants—cheap money, jobs, political credit—than this one. The difficulties that arose here, therefore, can be expected to afflict almost any new program. If we understand why this program ran into difficulty, we can hope to get at some of the underlying factors that make programs fail when there is no apparent reason why they should.

What we hope to show is that the apparently simple and straightforward is really complex and convoluted. We are initially surprised because we do not begin to appreciate the number of steps involved, the number of participants whose preferences have to be taken into account, the number of separate decisions that are part of what we think of as a single one. Least of all do we appreciate the geometric growth of interdependencies over time where each negotiation involves a number of participants with decisions to make, whose implications ramify over time. What is so hard about building a ter-

minal and airline hangar when the money is there, the plans are
signed, and the people agree that minorities are to get a share of the
jobs? We will show that what seemed to be a simple program turned
out to be a very complex one, involving numerous participants, a
host of differing perspectives, and a long and tortuous path of decision points that had to be cleared. Given these characteristics, the
chances of completing the program with the haste its designers had
hoped for—and even the chances of completing it at all—were
sharply reduced.

A MULTIPLICITY OF PARTICIPANTS AND PERSPECTIVES

Although the EDA had intended to carry out its program in a direct
and simple manner, without extensive participation by other government agencies, a large number of governmental and nongovernmen-
tal organizations and individuals eventually became involved in the
process of implementation. To list every participant who became
involved in some aspect of the EDA program would exhaust both us
and our readers. Let us agree, therefore, to oversimplify the situation. We shall restrict the participants to the EDA, the rest of the
federal government, and the city of Oakland, with their constituent
elements. For the EDA this would mean the initial Foley-Bradford
task force, EDA operating departments in Washington, the agency's
leadership after Foley, the regional office in Seattle, and the field
office in Oakland. Other federal agencies that became involved included the General Accounting Office; the Department of Health,
Education and Welfare; the Department of Labor; and the navy.
Participants in Oakland were the mayor, city administrators, the
Port of Oakland, World Airways, and several of the city's black
leaders, conservation groups, and tenants of the Port of Oakland.

Some of these participants (such as the departments of Labor and
Health, Education, and Welfare) became involved because they
possessed jurisdictional authority over important parts of the project; others (like the navy) entered the process when they felt their
interest being impinged on; and still others (such as black people
in Oakland) were intentionally brought into the program by the
EDA in order to build local support for the projects.

Each of the many participating groups, as Table 6 shows, had a

TABLE 6: Participants and Perspectives in the Oakland EDA Program

Participant	Connection with Program	Perspective and Major Objectives	Sense of Urgency
EDA—Foley, Bradford, Oakland task force	Designed program, set up project machinery in Oakland	Wanted to initiate, in a relatively short time, a program of economic development which would create jobs for unemployed minorities	Very high
EDA—Operating departments in Washington	Project implementation —construction, financial processing, etc.	Aimed for construction of facilities in an efficient and administratively proper manner	High (some resentment of special task force; insistence that process meet administrative standards)
EDA—Leadership after Foley	Exercised authority over projects after fall 1966	Sought to salvage original employment goals in Oakland project	Moderate (not personally identified with program; Secretary of Commerce Connor indicated lack of enthusiasm)
EDA—Seattle Regional Office	Unclear; processed paperwork, but no final authority to commit funds	Attempted to gain larger administrative role in project	Moderate
EDA—Oakland Office	Monitoring of projects at local level	Hoped to salvage initial employment goals and complete project	Varied with each man in office

TABLE 6: *(Continued)*

Participant	*Connection with Program*	*Perspective and Major Objectives*	*Sense of Urgency*
U.S. General Accounting Office	Questioned EDA policy regarding grant/loan ratio for Port projects	Concerned with standards for disbursement of federal funds	Low
U.S. Department of Health, Education, and Welfare	Joint control over manpower training funds for hangar project	Supported goal of job training in Oakland, but had commitment to established skills centers	Low (East Bay Skills Center bypassed by airline training program)
U.S. Department of Labor	Joint control over manpower training funds for hangar project	Main interest was in job training	Low
U.S. Navy	Objected to terminal construction because of effects on flight safety	Was chiefly concerned with effects of port construction on operations of Alameda Naval Air Station	Low
City of Oakland (mayor)	Represented city in dealings with EDA; tried to build support for program	Strongly supported EDA goals of economic development and job creation	High
City of Oakland (administration)	Drew up public works applications for EDA funding (coliseum access road approved)	Saw EDA funding as potential support for city public works projects	Low (access road completed early; no other city-sponsored projects approved)

Port of Oakland	Local recipient of major public works projects	Viewed EDA program as vital support for Port building program, but annoyed by multiplicity of federal guidelines	Moderate (Port is involved in building and operating numerous other facilities)
Oakland black leaders	Met by Foley and Bradford on early visits; some served on Employment Plan Review Board	Wanted job creation for minorities	High
Conservation groups	Protested Port of Oakland bay-fill activities	Strongly protested fill as damaging to bay and environs	Low
Port of Oakland tenants	If benefitted from EDA financing, had to sign employment agreement	Wanted to operate successful business	Low

distinctive perspective from which it viewed the EDA operation, and the groups differed widely in their sense of urgency about the program. Even within an organizational unit, there can be substantial differences in outlook. Thus, the special EDA Oakland task force was primarily interested in the agency's making a rapid and dramatic commitment to a job program for minorities, while the operating departments in the EDA Washington office concentrated their concern on the administrative and financial soundness of project construction. Within the city government in Oakland, Mayor Reading's focus on the job-producing aspects of the program was not shared by city administrators, who saw the EDA as a possible funding source for the city government's public works.

When perspectives differ, so also do measures of success. For the original EDA leadership, the major criterion of success was the number of jobs created for minority hard-core unemployed in Oakland. But other participants had competing success criteria: the Port of Oakland was mainly interested in the expansion of its facilities, while the Department of Health, Education, and Welfare was pressing for increased funding for its established skills centers.

None of the participants seriously disagreed with the policy of developing jobs for unemployed minorities in Oakland, nor did any of them question the advisability of creating jobs through grants for public works. Why, in view of this lack of opposition to the thrust of EDA policy, did the program run into so many obstacles?

When programs are not being implemented, it is tempting to conclude that the participants disagreed about the special ends they sought rather than the ordinary means for attaining them. Thinking about means and ends in isolation, however, imposes an artificial distinction, especially when more than one program is involved. One participant's ends, such as a training facility, may be another actor's means. Once innumerable programs are in operation, the stream of transactions among people who are simultaneously involved in them may evidence neither clear beginning nor end but only an ebb and flow. As the managers of each program try to impose their preferred sequence of events on the others, their priorities for the next step, which differs for each one and cannot be equally important to all, may conflict. The means loom larger all the time because they are what the action is about. Actually, it is easier to disagree about means because they are there to provoke quarrels, while ends are always around the corner. To make concrete an otherwise abstract notion we provide a list of reasons why participants may agree with the substantive ends of a proposal and still oppose (or merely fail to facilitate) the means for effectuating it.

(1) Direct incompatibility with other commitments.—Participants may agree with the merits of a proposal but find that it is incompatible with other organizational goals. HEW came to view the EDA's airline training proposal as competing for scarce funds with the East Bay Skills Center, which was on HEW's own list of approved institutions. And the Port of Oakland, while expressing its support of the EDA's employment goals, still stressed the need to "market its property." A port representative remarked that "the Port's methods and EDA methods are different, but . . . their principles are the same." The port spokesman said that his organization wanted to do something for minority unemployed, but that the EDA didn't understand what it is like to put together a project and make it work. Port officials felt that EDA restrictions—particularly the employment plan—were burdensome. This judgment was concurred with by Matson Navigation Company, which did not wish to use those port facilities that were subject to the EDA employment plan.

(2) No direct incompatibility, but a preference for other programs.—Many EDA employees, especially those who had served in the ARA, viewed rural areas and small towns as the proper focus of the agency. This view has also been held by the federal Office of Management and Budget. These participants did not oppose the idea of creating jobs in urban areas, but they did not feel this was the EDA's task.

(3) Simultaneous commitments to other projects.—Participants may agree with a proposal, have no contradictory commitments, and not prefer any alternative programs, but they may have other projects of their own that demand time and attention. The Port of Oakland's architect/engineer delayed his work on plans for the marine terminal, because his staff was busy on other port projects. And World Airways wanted to develop a general building program before it settled on specific criteria for the hangar. Such delays caused displeasure at the EDA, in much the same way that the federal agency's administrative delays caused disappointment at the port.

(4) Dependence on others who lack a sense of urgency in the project.—In the course of implementing a project, individuals or organizations may be called on because of their expertise or jurisdictional authority. Yet they may lack a sense of urgency about the overall program. Into this category would fall the consulting engineers, who designed plans for local recipients, and the Department of Labor, whose assent was necessary to carry out the airline training program under Section 241 of the MDTA.

(5) Differences of opinion on leadership and proper organizational roles.—Participants who agree about a program's goals may nevertheless disagree about which people or organizational units should be running the programs. Members of EDA operating divisions resented the special status accorded to Bradford's Oakland task force, and after the departure of Foley and Bradford the whole Oakland project was treated with less urgency. Both Secretary of Commerce Connor and Foley's successor, Ross Davis, felt that the Oakland project was Foley's personal project; they did not share Foley's enthusiasm for a dramatic EDA push in urban areas. And EDA regional officials, disturbed by the direct Oakland-Washington relationship, tried to convince Oakland representatives to route funding requests through the regional office in Seattle. Differences over program leadership constituted additional reasons for delay.

(6) Legal and procedural differences.—Discussing the frustrations of the early days of public works program implementation, an EDA task force member remarked that

There were all sorts of technical things that had to be decided. The job issue came later. There were a number of questions about EDA policy—how you process these things, how much meddling EDA would do in that. In September, October, November of 1966, there was hostility between the EDA and the Port on construction issues. The quality of land fill, for example. . . . At every point, the Port and EDA had their own engineering opinions. There was hardening, but not over the right issues. They were fighting about land fill, but they *should* have been worrying about employment.

Taking this viewpoint, however reasonable it may appear, depends on the intensity of one's concern with employment. Another man, differently situated, with responsibilities for protecting life in and navigation on the bay, would legitimately be concerned about the kinds of materials poured into it. The same is true for the navy's interest in reducing hazards to its planes. While it is easy to pooh-pooh these concerns, a plane crash or a scandal about additional pollution in the bay would lead to severe condemnation of the responsible officials. No one then would accept the argument that the main thing a few years earlier was to facilitate minority employment by building something. A parallel way of approaching the same problem is to say that the built-in conflict between overhead organizations, such as the government accountants concerned with legality of expenditure, and line organizations, who have direct operating responsibilities, had to be worked out in this case. Accommodations between the two perspectives are important and possible but there must be an ultimate residue of conflict. After all, the purpose of overhead organizations, whether they be personnel, accounting, or whatever, is precisely to establish a check on the behavior of line officials.

The technical issues of land fill and interim financing held up the marine terminal project. In the summer of 1969, the letting of bids for filling and dredging at the terminal project was delayed by the port's attorney because of legal complications. In none of these cases was there disagreement over the basic program goal of providing employment for minorities, but procedural and legal complications caused delay nevertheless.

Although some participants were peripheral in terms of interest in the project, expressing neither agreement nor disagreement with its substantive goals, they were nevertheless able to hold up implementation when they felt their interests being impinged on. Thus, the United States General Accounting Office questioned the EDA's grant/loan policies on port projects, while the navy lodged complaints about the terminal's effect on jet flights from the nearby naval air station. These agencies may have been peripheral in terms of their interest in the project, but their concerns had to be taken seriously by the EDA.

(7) Agreement coupled with lack of power.—Certain participants may agree enthusiastically with a proposal, but they may lack the resources to do much to help it. Mayor Reading strongly supported the EDA job-creation program, but he lacked the political and administrative power to force other participants to move the program along. Those members of Oakland's black community who had been

contacted by EDA officials also strongly supported the program, but they had no effective role. They were the recipients of the EDA's concern, but the port was designated to receive the project funding. Both the mayor and the black leaders were EDA supporters, but their lack of resources made them peripheral to the program. Although it had aimed for simplicity, the EDA program eventually involved a large group of diverse participants. And while none of these participants expressed disagreement with the goal of providing jobs for minorities through the building of public works, this does not mean that they were ready to make the decisions, provide the clearances, and come to the agreements necessary to speed the program on its way.

THE MULTIPLICITY OF DECISIONS AND THE DECREASING PROBABILITY OF PROGRAM SUCCESS

In tracing the path of decisions and clearance points in the EDA public works program, we will again oversimplify the situation. Instead of trying to isolate every decision in which a major participant had a discernible opportunity to make choices, we will concentrate on those major decision points that determined the course of the program or that had to be passed in order for the program to continue. (We shall also assume, but only for a moment, that each point of decision is independent of the others.) Table 7, which lists these decision points and identifies the participants involved in each of them, illustrates how the multiplicity of participants and perspectives combined to produce a formidable obstacle course for the program. When a program depends on so many actors, there are numerous possibilities for disagreement and delay.

We can see that, in starting the Oakland program and in determining its early course, the EDA had to make a number of important decisions: to enter the urban field in the first place; to select Oakland as the site for its urban experiment; to choose the port as the chief recipient agency within the city; and to tie construction to jobs by means of an employment plan. Some of these early decisions were hotly debated within the agency itself. There were those, for example, who felt that the EDA, as primarily a rural agency, had no business going into cities. And a number of agency officials expressed doubts about an employment plan, which they felt would be

TABLE 7: Points of Decision and Clearance Necessary for Completion of EDA Public Works Program

Decision Points	Participants Involved	Cumulative Total of Agreements
1. Decision to involve EDA in cities (fall 1965)	Eugene Foley	1
2. Selection of Oakland as the city for experimental effort (winter 1965)	Foley, EDA Washington	3
3. Bypassing mayor and seeking first contacts in Oakland Black community (December 1965)	Foley-Bradford, EDA Washington	5
4. Choice of special task force as organizational form for project (January 1966)	Foley	6
5. Selection of employment plan as mechanism for channeling jobs to unemployed (February 1966)	Bradford-Foley, EDA task force	8
6. Selection of local recipients of public works projects (spring 1966)	Foley, EDA task force, EDA Washington	11
7. Negotiation and approval of employment plans (April–November 1966)	EDA task force, EDA Washington, World Airways, other port tenants, Emp. Plan Rev. Board (representing poor)	16
8. Decision to set up training program (under Section 241 of Manpower Devel. and Training Act) at World Airways, rather than at Skills Center (summer-fall 1966)	EDA task force, EDA Washington, World Airways	19

TABLE 7 (*Continued*)

Decision Points	Participants Involved	Cumulative Total of Agreements
9. Agreements required for implementation of training program (1967–68)	Local MDTA Committee, mayor, State Dept. of Employment, State Dept. of Voc. Ed., Regional Office-DOL, Regional Office-HEW, Washington Office-DOL, Washington Office-HEW, Washington EDA	28
10. Agreement required on bay fill for construction of marine terminal (summer-fall 1966)	EDA Washington, EDA consultant, Port of Oakland	31
11. Agreement required on interim financing arrangement (summer-fall 1966)	EDA Washington, Port of Oakland	33
12. Negotiation of conditions for World Airways' lease of hangar (summer-fall 1966)	Port of Oakland, World Airways	35
13. Decision on port request to relocate terminal project (January-April 1967)	EDA Washington (Davis)	36
14. Approval of A/E contracts for terminal and hangar (March, June 1967)	EDA Washington	37
15. Approval of preliminary plans for terminal	EDA Washington	38
16. Decision on port request for terminal project changes and loan advance (January-February 1968)	EDA Oakland, EDA Seattle, EDA Washington	41

TABLE 7 (*Continued*)

Decision Points	Participants Involved	Cumulative Total of Agreements
17. Search for agreement with navy after complaint about port construction's effect on flight safety (April 1968–April 1969)	U.S. Navy, Port of Oakland, EDA Washington	44
18. Decision required on port request for additional financing for hangar (April 1968–February 1969)	Port of Oakland, World Airways, architect/engineers, EDA Oakland, EDA Seattle, EDA Washington	50
19. Decision required on port request for funds for revolving restaurant (April 1968–December 1969)	EDA Seattle, EDA Washington	52
20. Agreement required on grant/loan ratios for public works projects (April 1968)	General Acctg. Office, EDA Washington	54
21. Decision against hangar overrun; insistence on stricter employment conditions for port and World Airways (February 1969)	EDA Washington (Davis)	55
22. Letting of contracts for dredging and filling at terminal (June 1969)	Port of Oakland, EDA Washington	57
23. Agreement on Port of Oakland employment plan and equal employment officer (January–September 1969)	EDA Washington, Port of Oakland	59

TABLE 7 (Continued)

Decision Points	Participants Involved	Cumulative Total of Agreements
24. Decision to oppose terminal revolving restaurant and agreement to apply financing to construction overrun (fall 1969)	EDA Washington (Podesta-Sinnott), Port of Oakland	61
25. Selection of contractors for construction of terminal (December 1969)	Port of Oakland, EDA Oakland, EDA Washington	64
26. Veto of port's request that one firm both design and construct hangar (February 1969)	EDA Washington	65
27. Decision to go ahead with hangar project, but at reduced cost and with stricter employment guidelines (February 1970)	EDA Washington (Podesta-Sinnott)	66
28. Selection of alternative architect for hangar (April 1970)	Port of Oakland	67
29. Approval of preliminary plans and specifications for hangar (June 1970)	EDA Washington	68
30. Letting of contracts for construction of hangar (June 1971)	Port of Oakland, EDA Washington	70

difficult to enforce. Furthermore, Eugene Foley's administrative decision to expedite the program by means of a special task force was not received with complete joy by the EDA's operating departments.

Going beyond those initial difficult decisions, there were a number of points along the way at which clearance had to be received if the program was to continue. Some of these clearances were up to the EDA itself: approval of recipients' plans and architecture contracts, authorization for advances of funds, and ruling on changes in project design. Other decision points necessitated favorable clearances by numerous participants other than the EDA. The proposed training program for airline mechanics, for example, required approval by nine federal, state, and local organizational units.

In order to get by all the decision points, the program required dozens of clearance actions by a wide range of participants. In situations of high controversy and mutual antagonism, the probability that these actions would be favorable or taken in a reasonable time might be quite small. But we have ruled out this kind of drama. Instead, we shall assume the best. We shall deliberately err on the side of assuming more agreement and good will than might actually have been the case. We shall load the dice in favor of keeping the program going. Suppose, then, we take a spread of probabilities on the high side that each participant will take a favorable action at each decision point. We can try four: 80 percent, 90 percent, 95 percent, and 99 percent. (The computations for each of these probabilities are summarized in Table 8.) However you look at it, the ultimate probability of success is very low.

TABLE 8: Program Completion Doubtful Unless Level of Agreement Among Participants Is Terribly High

Probability of Agreement on Each Clearance Point (in percent)	Probability of Success After 70 Clearances	No. of Agreements that Reduce Probability Below 50 Percent
80	.000000125	4
90	.000644	7
95	.00395	14
99	.489	68

We conclude that the probability of agreement by every participant on each decision point must be exceedingly high for there to be any chance at all that a program will be brought to completion. On the assumption that the probability is 80 percent (see Table 8), the chances of completion are a little over one in a million after seventy agreements have been reached, and falls below the half-way mark after just four. By increasing the probability of agreement to a healthy 90 percent, we increase the ultimate likelihood of approval to something over six in ten thousand and allow seven agreements before dipping below the 50-50 mark. Moving to 95 percent increases the probability of completion to almost four in a thousand and permits fourteen moves before the chances it will fail are better than its opportunities for success. One must advance to the 99 percent level of concurrence, an extraordinary state of affairs by any calculation, to permit a healthier sixty-eight agreements to be reached before the probability of completion drops just below the half-way mark. Clearly the data here do not merely interpret themselves but require elucidation on our part.

There is no agreement among scholars on what constitutes a decision point and thus it would be difficult for us to demonstrate that there are any particular number in the case under study. We could, with no difficulty at all, double the number of decision points by shaving down our criteria of what constitutes a separable act. We have tried to err on the side of having fewer steps rather than more by reducing the number of decision points to thirty. But each one must be increased in size by the number of separate decision-makers involved. The best defense of our rough-and-ready procedure is that the results are largely insensitive to any but the most drastic (and hardly conceivable) change in the number of participants who are required to give their consent to various decisions. A glance at Table 8 will show that, until one passes beyond 95 percent probability of agreement on each issue, only fourteen separate clearances are required to reduce the probability of completion below equality. If there is 95 percent probability of favorable action at each point, and we assume only thirty clearance points—an unrealistically low number—the probability of overall program success is .215. If there are fifty such points, the overall probability of completion drops to barely 1 percent.

By emphasizing the conflicts within each of the major participants as well as among them, we can easily lower the probabilities of agreement. Or we could try to assess the degree of urgency and commitment manifested by each participant and raise or lower its probability of favorable action on that basis. But we have already decided to give the benefit of the doubt to program success.

The high probability of agreement at each step required to produce a modest probability of successful completion makes it unnecessary to know the precise probability for any particular one. No doubt the probabilities vary from one participant and organization to another, over time within the same organization, and between different levels of government and private *versus* governmental actors. But if one assumes the best—and 99 percent for each and every clearance point appears to be about as close as one can go without assuming away the problem entirely—the odds are still against program implementation.

The computational and political problems are similar. Do we consider each participant as a separate entity, so that the final probability is simply the product of the probabilities of favorable action by each participant? Or do we show that the probabilities are linked, so that a favorable response at an early time increases the likelihood of a similar response at a later time? In political (as well as statistical) language, we are asking whether each participant is independent. To what extent is it controlled by others and to what extent can it determine its own position? Turning the question around, we ask how powerful the participant is in relation to an issue. Does an action on its part increase the probability that others will agree where they might not have done so? The most reasonable assumption in the American context of fragmented power is certainly independence of the participants. In that case, the ultimate probability of success is terribly low. If we alter the assumption to say that the federal participants are expected to follow the leadership of the EDA, so that the probability of success within the federal camp is enhanced, we are still left with the obvious fact that it cannot control local bodies. The most likely outcome at the federal level is that, seeing no great reason to oppose the central EDA position, the other participants take out degrees of opposition by delay. If we postulate that there is not only conflict but common interest between the federal and local participants, as is manifestly the case, then we would expect delay and a mixed pattern of agreement depending on how they saw their interests from one period to the next. Consequently, we can argue that, while ultimate agreement is possible but by no means certain, considerable delay is probably inevitable.

Our normal expectation should be that new programs will fail to get off the ground and that, at best, they will take considerable time to get started. The cards in this world are stacked against things happening, as so much effort is required to make them move. The remarkable thing is that new programs work at all.

Program decisions, of course, do not always consist of clear-cut "yes" or "no" responses. Programs can be delayed, modified, scaled down, and otherwise adapted or distorted to fit their environment. The possibilities will be considered shortly. Now we wish to delve into the unexpected happenings that reduce the small prospects of program implementation still further.

We have seen that, given a large number of clearance points manned by diverse and independent participants, the probability of a program achieving its goals is low. But in the case of the EDA program, we cannot merely calculate overall probability of success by taking the product of individual decision probabilities. For this program should not be viewed as a single string of green lights, all of which had to go on for the program to achieve its objectives. The situation has been more complicated than that. Given multiple program goals, there were really two distinct strings of decisions involved. And within each of these strings, we should make a distinction between those decisions that moved the project in the direction of its goal and those that were unplanned diversions from that path.

TWO GOALS AND TWO DECISION PATHS

Rather than moving in a direct line to one goal, the EDA program aimed at achieving two major objectives: the construction of public works and the creation of jobs for the hard-core unemployed. In connection with the job-creating objective, the EDA proposed to implement a training program to prepare the hard-core unemployed to take the jobs that were opened for them. Figure 2 illustrates the two decisional sequences, as envisioned by the EDA, that would lead to the desired goals. Although the federal agency insisted initially that the two goals must be achieved together, there was always the possibility that one string of actions would be completed while the other was stalled. It is true that the employment plan tried to link construction of projects to job creation at the local level, but a crucial element of the employment strategy—the training program—was organizationally quite distinct from the rest of the program activity. The federal and state participants in that program—HEW, Labor Department, California Department of Employment—were not involved in other elements of the EDA Oakland effort, and they had no reason to share its urgency. When implementation of the training program proved impossible to effect in 1968, therefore, a key ele-

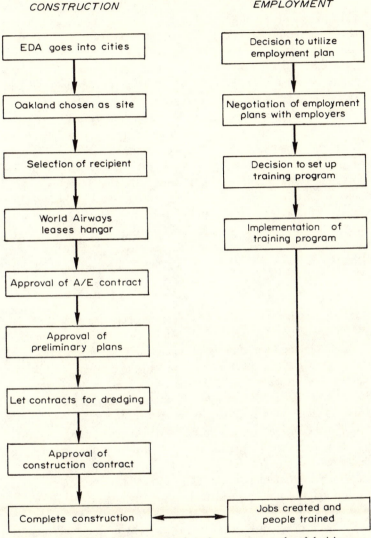

CONSTRUCTION

EMPLOYMENT

EDA goes into cities	Decision to utilize employment plan
Oakland chosen as site	Negotiation of employment plans with employers
Selection of recipient	Decision to set up training program
World Airways leases hangar	Implementation of training program
Approval of A/E contract	
Approval of preliminary plans	
Let contracts for dredging	
Approval of construction contract	
Complete construction	Jobs created and people trained

FIGURE 2. The EDA aims for two goals and sets up two paths of decisions

ment of the employment strategy was lost. Had the airline hangar been finished on schedule and had World Airways created jobs, there still would not have been the supply of trained mechanics that the EDA had counted on.

At the outset, the EDA had stated that the goals of construction and employment would go hand in hand. But as time passed and the training program became hopelessly stalled, there was pressure within the agency to concentrate on getting the construction completed. After all, a spending agency has to keep moving money and building projects or Congress will suspect that it is not doing its job. "As time goes on" an EDA official noted, "it gets harder and harder for EDA to take a tough line. We're under pressure to finish the project, and it begins to look bad for the agency if we don't. So there's great temptation to soften our demands." With frustration over mounting delays, there was always the possibility that goal displacement would occur and that the construction objective would stand alone at the EDA. But under Ross Davis and again under Robert Podesta, the agency forcibly reasserted its determination to meet both construction and employment goals. The two initial objectives were preserved, but so was the need to complete two separate strings of decisions that were each becoming longer all the time.

THE EMERGENCE OF UNEXPECTED DECISIONS

Not only was it necessary to complete two decision paths in order to achieve the EDA program goals; but within each path, the agency found that the number of decisions and clearances required was constantly growing. Figure 2, p. 111, showed the clusters of decisions that the EDA expected would lead to the completion of the program. But Figure 3 illustrates how a large number of unexpected decisions and clearance points eventually became part of project implementation. These decisions had not been part of the EDA's plans, and they did not advance the program directly toward the achievement of its objectives. Nevertheless, they were necessary to clear blockages and enable the program to move on. The result was the emergence in each decision path of numerous diversions not intended by the program sponsors.

The paths of required decisions, as we can see, were soon characterized by more unexpected elements than expected ones: they were anything but straight lines leading directly to goals. And in one case —the failure to implement the airline training program—a decision path had been broken at a crucial point. Furthermore, the diagram in Figure 3 does not—and cannot—show a completed program. For as this is written, total project construction has not yet been completed and the job-creation process lies in the future. There will doubtless be more surprises to come.

What had looked like a relatively simple, urgent, and direct program—involving one federal agency, one city, and a substantial and immediate funding commitment—eventually involved numerous diverse participants and a much longer series of decisions than was planned. None of the participants actually disagreed with the goal of providing jobs for minority unemployed, but their differing perspectives and senses of urgency made it difficult to translate broad substantive agreement into effective policy implementation. It was not merely the direction of their decisions—favorable or unfavorable—but the time orientation of the participants—fast or slow, urgent or indolent—that determined the prospects of completion. When so many future decisions depend on past actions, delay in time may be equivalent to defeat in substance.

THE ANATOMY OF DELAY

Expectations about new governmental programs violate common, everyday experience. People who regularly deal with inanimate objects such as computer programs would never expect a new one to run the first time. "Debugging" is not something done on the rare occasion when things go wrong but is an expected part of making a program work. Numerous iterations, extending over long periods of time, may be required before the new program performs adequately. The wise man, who knows that implementing the program will require a substantial investment though he cannot quite predict how much, will at least make an informal calculation that the likely benefits are worth the effort. Failure to implement the program in a short time, working under imposed deadlines, would not surprise him. He is merely fortunate that, hidden from public view, he is less likely to be taken to task for lack of results. And the machine will not make speeches about how he has abused it.

Appearances are deceiving. Looking back at the very array of governmental programs that are in operation, we conclude that they must have been implemented. Why, then, should our new program fail in implementation when so many others that fill the landscape have evidently succeeded? It is easy to forget (perhaps be-

CONSTRUCTION   EMPLOYMENT

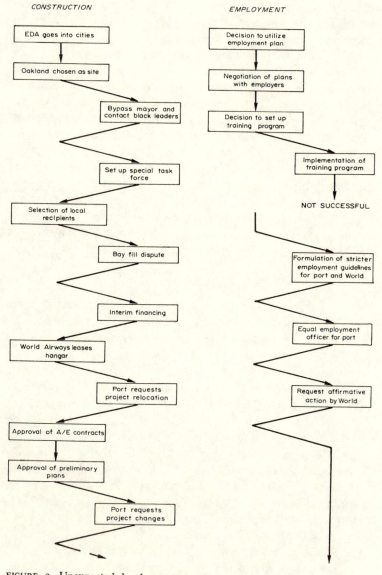

FIGURE 3. Unexpected developments cause divergences in decision paths

CONSTRUCTION   EMPLOYMENT

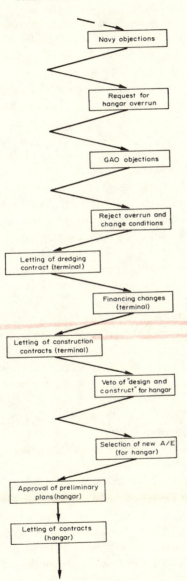

Navy objections

Request for
hangar overrun

GAO objections

Reject overrun and
change conditions

Letting of dredging
contract (terminal)

Financing changes
(terminal)

Letting of construction
contracts (terminal)

Veto of "design and
construct" for hangar

Selection of new A/E
(for hangar)

Approval of preliminary
plans (hangar)

Letting of contracts
(hangar)

cause we never knew) about their initial difficulties. The years of trial and error that led to the present state of operation are lost from view. The huge amount of resources that may have been poured into different alternatives before one caught on is conveniently part of past history for which we are not responsible. Programs that started out to accomplish one set of objectives end up accomplishing another for which, long after the fact, we give undue credit for implementation. Everything that exists must have some consequences, even if they are not the ones anticipated or if no one is quite certain what they are. Every program is likely to affect someone, somewhere, sometime. Adaptation to the environment must have been achieved; otherwise, by definition, programs would not exist. No genius is required to make programs operative if we don't care how long they take, how much money they require, how often the objectives are altered or the means for obtaining them are changed. Indeed, the law of averages would suggest that, given sufficient new initiatives, some of them must grow and prosper in the world, though the flawed adult may bear scant resemblance to the promising child. Our task is not to romanticize the past but to learn from its errors how to improve the future.

A basic reason programs survive is that they adapt themselves to their environment over a long period of time. In considering the sequence of events necessary to implement a program, we assumed that at each decision point the various participants would give a simple "yes" or "no." While this assumption may be met by some participants part of the time, it would rarely hold for all participants all of the time. However useful an all-or-nothing assumption may be to begin analysis, it is clearly insufficient to end our discussion. We know that a negative act by a participant at a decision point need not signify that the program is dead; it can be revived by going back later on and seeking a favorable verdict. Vetoes are not permanent but conditional. Accommodations may be made, bargains entered into, resistances weakened. The price of ultimate agreement is delay or modification of the existing program. Let us see what happens to our original analysis when we alter our assumption to include the possibility that numerous attempts may be made to secure clearances from participants whose agreement is required to further the program.

For present purposes, each actor's relationship to a program may be characterized along three dimensions. What is the direction of his preference on the matter at issue? Is he for or against? What is his intensity of preference? Does he care a lot about it, or is he relatively indifferent? What resources can he bring to bear to affect the outcome? Is he strong or weak? In regard to resources, we really want to know not how strong a participant is in general, but how much of his available resources he is willing to commit to influence a particular program. We can, therefore, without prejudicing the analysis, make the simplifying assumption that use of resources is a direct function of intensity of preference. Those who manifest high intensity will use up resources to control outcomes, and those with low intensity will not. Table 9 shows how the differing types of relationships among these participants would lead to varying amounts of delay.

TABLE 9: Delay

| Direction | Intensity | |
	High	Low
Positive	1. minimal delay, no bargaining	2. minor delay, no bargaining
Negative	4. maximal delay, bargaining over essentials	3. moderate delay, bargaining over peripherals

Participant 1 shows a positive direction and high intensity. He gives his consent immediately if not sooner. Participant 2 likes the program, but it does not matter much to him. It will have to wait its turn on his desk, but he will act affirmatively after a minor delay for processing. Although participant 3 evaluates the program (or the part that affects him) negatively, he is not terribly interested in it. A moderate delay can be expected during which time he bargains with the directors over peripheral aspects of the program. When he is satisfied or bought off in some other way, the program can continue to the next step. Maximal delay occurs when a participant is negative and feels strongly about his opinion. Depending on the amount of resources at his disposal, he will try to block the program unless basic concessions are made. Participant 4 may be capable of extending maximal delay into a permanent end.

Delay, then, is a function of the number of decision points, the number of participants at each point, and the intensity of their preferences. The EDA employment program was not characterized by the presence of participants with intensely negative views. Hence, it was not forced back to the beginning. But it was noteworthy for the presence of substantial numbers of minor and moderate delay types. While no one delay stands out from the others as excessive, the combination of delays has kept the program from realizing its potential.

Suppose we were to say that during the years covered by our study, 1966 through 1970, there were no maximal delay participants and that the other three types were equally divided among the actors who at one time or another were required to give their assent. How much delay would take place? Each clearance represents a potential for delay. We must, therefore, count each participant not once but every time his consent is required. Thus we begin with 70 clearances. Arbitrarily assigning a value of one week for minimal delay, three weeks for minor delay, and six weeks for moderate delay, we come up with a total of 233-1/3 weeks. (One week for each minimal delay equals 23-1/3, three weeks for each minor delay equals 70, and six for each moderate delay equals 140.) Under these assumptions the delay thus far would come out to approximately four and a half years, which is not far off the mark.

Now wait a minute. We still have not taken into account two aspects of real-life situations that affect the amount of delay. It is possible for several clearances to be sought during the same time period, thus reducing the total delay involved. At each decision point several clearances can be received simultaneously. Thus the appropriate number, given this assumption, would not be the 70 clearances but the 30 decision points. Yet it is also the case that failure to reach agreement the first time need not necessarily be fatal to a program because the parties can and do try again. We must consider the necessity of engaging in several rounds of negotiations, if not with all participants, at least with those inclined to moderate delay.

Here's how our calculations would look when we take these two new factors—simultaneous clearances and multiple, repeated negotiations—into account. Our starting number is made up of the 30 decision points. Again we allot one week for minimal delay, three weeks for minor delay, and six weeks for moderate delay. Hence there would be ten weeks taken up by the minimal and thirty by the minor delay types, as the assent of numerous participants was sought and achieved at the same time. But we must now consider that, say, three negotiating sessions will be required for each of the 10 moderate delay participants, leading to a delay on their part of 180 weeks (10 participants times six weeks delay times three rounds of negotiations apiece). Total delay is 220 weeks, which is a few months over four years.

Anyone can play this numbers game and make the totals come out as he wishes. We do not (and the reader should not) place any credence in these specific numbers. We have set aside, we believe, too little time for each type of delay, but we would rather err on the conservative side. The total delay of some four years is too low, possibly because no one, however favorably inclined, can really make a decision in a single week. Or perhaps we have discovered something about the dedication that characterized EDA officials in expediting this program as best they could. We hope to have illustrated, however, the kinds of variables that should go into theories that intend to explain delay in governmental programs.

Now we are in a position to make the analysis more complicated by reintroducing the resource variable. We can omit most of the relationships from Figure 4 because we have previously considered them. Those participants, for instance, who are positive in direction,

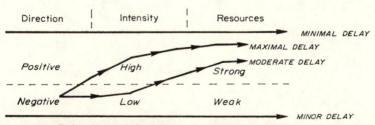

FIGURE 4. Delay (expanded version)

high in intensity, and strong in resources, lead to minimal delay; and those with the opposite characteristics to maximal obstruction. The participants characterized by the negative direction, high intensity, and weak resources might be interesting, but none appeared in our study. We wish, therefore, to concentrate on those who are positive in feeling about the program, strong in resources that might be committed or opposed to it, but low in intensity. Several of the potential employers of minorities may have fallen into this category. They liked the idea of minority employment—or at least they appreciated the prospect of low-cost financing—but they were not intensely committed. Had they been opposed from the start, to be sure, they would not have gotten involved in the first place. Once they decided to take part, however, their enthusiasm waned. Another way of putting it would be to say that we have located the essential policy problem: how to provide incentives to change low to high intensity or, more accurately, how to maintain high positive intensity through lengthy delays. We have treated intensity as a constant. For all but the most devoted participants, however, it is a variable. The longer the delays, the more time for intensity to decay.

The argument can be displayed graphically. Delay, as we have conceived it, as a function of resources, intensity, and direction of interest. Since "direction," that is, support or opposition, is a dichotomous variable, we can draw two sets of curves to illustrate its relationships with the other forces in the field. We would expect, from the nature of our argument, the form of the curves and the spread among them to appear as indicated in Figure 5. When resources are held constant, for instance, delay decreases with positive intensity of interest; when intensity is held constant, delay decreases with a greater commitment of resources. The shape of the curves suggests that there are diminishing returns to the application of either in-

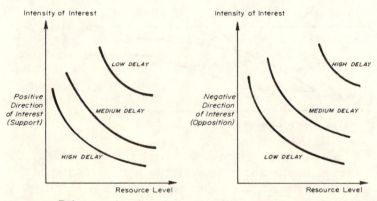

FIGURE 5. Delay as a function of direction of interest, intensity of interest, and commitment of resources

tensity or level of resources. There are also diminishing returns to scale in the sense that expanding each variable in proportion (doubling, say, resources and intensity) will not affect the amount of delay.

"Time is money," the old saw goes. "Delays are lost opportunities" might be a modern equivalent. It is worth spending a little time applying our model of delay more closely to the EDA experience in Oakland. Time is a scarce resource for men and for organizations. If you want to know what a man loves, observe how he spends his time. If you want to know what matters most to an organization, chart the activities on which its members spend their precious allotment of hours. The allocation of time deserves, though it does not receive, the same attention that we give to the allocation of financial resources.

By focusing on the policy that interests us most at a given moment, we tend to gloss over the temporal dimensions of the problem that produce so many of the difficulties that we experience. As years pass, we fail to recall the sense of time that motivated the policy in which we are interested. We would not, for instance, question the lack of a developed experimental design if we recalled that the policy was created in a few weeks and the decisions made in less than nineteen days. Care in formulation and speed in execution may be incompatible if the two are telescoped together. It is easy to ignore the fact that the sense of urgency manifested by the observer may differ from that of the participant and that, indeed, the participants may differ widely in the time and hence importance that they allocate to the program in question. We must ask whether the problem was central or peripheral. If it was central, we must also know how many other things of major importance the participant had to do at the same time. If it was peripheral, we want to know how far down in his time priorities it actually went. Even where participants agree about the merits of a program, they may still conflict over the time priority each one is to give to it. Multiply the number of participants, give them varying degrees of centrality, arrange their time budgets differently, and you have set up a typical pattern of stop and start characterized by a little forward movement and a lot of delay. We can make this analysis more concrete by illustrating the various causes of the innumerable delays that afflicted the EDA employment program in Oakland.

Not all the delays were unplanned, accidental occurrences; some were caused intentionally by participants who wanted to stop an undesired action or to step back and reassess the development of the program. Blocking delays, or purposeful halts in the process, occurred when the EDA objected to the port's bay fill in 1966 and when the agency turned down the port's request to have one firm design and construct the hangar in 1970. Delays for reassessment were ordered by the EDA in considering the port's request for the hangar overrun in 1968–69 and by the new Republican administration in order to reevaluate the entire Oakland program in 1969. In addition, procedural delays were caused by the routing of plans and funding requests through the regional office; by 1968 the EDA was searching for a useful role for its field representatives.

A number of delays resulted from alternative time priorities. No one specifically ordered these delays; they were caused by the fact that participants had other things to do at the time. The EDA's eleven-month delay in giving the port an answer on the hangar overrun request reflected the lowered priority of the Oakland project within the agency. There was a flurry of activity in 1966, followed by lengthy periods of inactivity. Participants did not turn flatly against the project, but they had other things to do. The port and World Airways had other commercial ventures to draw their attention; the EDA had hundreds of public works projects to supervise; and other federal agencies had numerous manpower projects to approve and to fund. After the departure of Foley and Bradford, the EDA cared less intensely about riding constant herd on the Oakland program. No one planned these delays, but they occurred anyway.

Program delay is often difficult to distinguish from program failure. If a favorable decision is made but it is made after a delay of years, does this count as success or failure? The answer to this question depends in large measure on the criteria that the sponsors of a program set for themselves. In the case of the EDA program in Oakland, speed was felt to be essential. Eugene Foley argued eloquently that the need for creating jobs was urgent and that immediate action was needed. In a 1966 speech Foley said,

Good grief! How many riots do we need in how many cities in this country to sink the point home that our programs for the ghetto cannot all be aimed in the long run? . . . The Negro's sounds of "NOW!" are not irrational demands or threats; they are a cry of desperation, a plea for help. . . . The heart of the problem is Negro unemployment. Jobs are the great need in a land where people are judged by what they do. . . . Unless jobs are provided, . . . jobs of dignity, jobs with career possibilities, . . . all (other) programs are practically futile.[4]

In the light of this high standard—the creation of jobs for black people *now*—delay constitutes failure. But others may reasonably argue the maxim "Better late than never."

The same problem emerges in a different form in attempting to determine the probability that a program will succeed. If decisions are not taken as rapidly as planned, if a program takes five or ten years to implement, how can we determine whether the program has succeeded? If we don't know whether or to what degree success has been achieved, we certainly cannot estimate the probability of achieving that nonexistent status. For many reasons—the existence of separate decision paths, the constant diversion of unexpected decisions that branched from each path, and the difficulty of saying whether delay constitutes failure—it would be very difficult to calculate in advance the probability of a program's success, even if we knew the probability of a favorable decision at each individual point. We are like travelers who are asked to meet people we do not know at times we cannot say and in places where the road maps take the form of mazes.

To what degree are our findings about the problems of implementation applicable to other federal programs involving localities? The EDA public works program is a bedrock example: almost any other one we could think of would involve a greater conflict over ultimate ends or more public dispute, less adequate resources in view of the end contemplated, and other features that make it evident why programs fail. We have argued, therefore, that the problems of implementation found in the Oakland program are likely to be found in other cases that occur under less favorable circumstances. An empirical demonstration would, of course, be preferable to a hypothetical one. We are hampered in this respect because we have been unable to locate relevant research. None that we know of attempts to deal with the problems posed by long sequences of decisions involving multiple participants, each dependent on what has gone before

4. Quoted in Amory Bradford, *Oakland's Not for Burning*, pp. 2–3.

and unable either to control the others or to predict the probability of successful outcomes at succeeding points, or even to be certain what those points will be or where their branches will lead.

But the EDA public works program did not spring ready-made out of the void. It was part of the spirit of its times. It emerged against a background of structural features—separate institutions (the federal government and the cities), each fragmented internally, seeking to cooperate in pursuit of immediate social objectives. There are relevant comparisons, both domestic and foreign, to the huge gulf between the syndrome of glorious aims and ignoble results that flow from these conditions.

6

Learning from Experience

The individual who fails to learn from experience is forever lost in a chaotic world. He repeats his errors. Worse still, he has no way of navigating among the rocks and shoals of life. One direction is as good or as bad as another. He can make no sense out of his world because he is unable to use his past experience to do better in the future.

Organizations, which deal with the collective efforts of men, are devoted to the processing of information and the generation of knowledge. Their ability to test the environment so as to correct error and reinforce truth makes them effective. Inability to learn is fatal. Yet learning is more difficult because so many men must do it together. A major criticism that can be made of the EDA public works program in Oakland is that it closed off the possibilities of learning. Far from being a model from which the organization could learn success, it was not even an experiment from which the organization could learn from failure.

WHEN AN EXPERIMENT ISN'T

Our assumptions about new public programs are far removed from reality. We assume that the people ostensibly in charge can predict the consequences of their actions, and that is often not the case. Since a problem exists, we assume that there must be a solution and that it is embodied in the program. Knowledge connecting the activities of government with desirable results in society must exist, we reason, for a program to be established. Hopes and prayers, the general desire to do good without knowing how, would seem to us frail reeds on which to lean, though these are the bases on which many programs are begun. When there is a clamor for action that must be satisfied, however, any plausible course of action must do.

Should lack of knowledge be admitted and the program emerge as a so-called experiment, we like to think that the activities involved must be so arranged that the people who run them can learn from their errors. But learning from experience is not easy. Experimental design requires a high level of sophistication and attention to detail, factors often in short supply. One would need to know what the world would have been like without the intervention and one would need to gauge its precise impact on the world apart from the other multitudinous influences working at the same moment. The very notion of discovering whether a new venture will work suggests, albeit falsely, that there is time to work out an experimental design for interpreting events in the world.

A major reason for the shortcomings of the EDA Oakland operation was its false characterization as an urban experiment. The EDA's ability to address the problems of the core cities was to be demonstrated to the world in a brief, dramatic, and highly publicized venture. The idea of a social experiment has considerable appeal, but no worthwhile experiment can be carried out in an environment where all decisions and procedures are determined by a rule of "minimum delay." The most powerful single decision rule was: "Given that there is a requirement to spend $23,000,000 in four months, select those projects which can be processed in the least time." Very little research and no experimentation could be carried on in the short time available. The decision rules actually followed (see Figures 6 and 7) are of the simplest sort imaginable.

The dictation of action by urgency means that little can be learned from analyzing the rules that led to these decisions being made. If we learn that the agency chose to fund project X simply because it had no time to search for or evaluate projects Y and Z, then we have learned little about how one might better choose between projects X, Y, and Z in the future. This is no way of turning bad experience to good use.

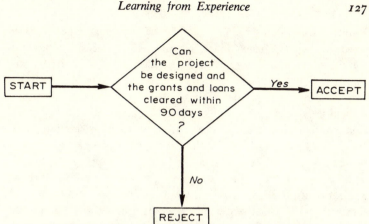

FIGURE 6. The public works decision tree (during initial phase)
(figure by Owen McShane)

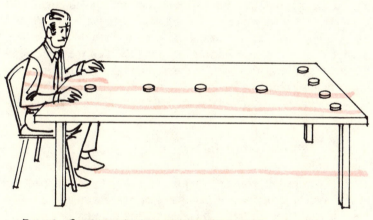

RULES: SELECT THE TWO BEST CHECKERS.
(THERE ARE NO AVAILABLE CRITERIA AS TO WHAT
MAKES ONE CHECKER "BETTER" THAN ANOTHER.)
TIME TO COMPLETE SELECTION — 0.5 SECONDS

FIGURE 7. An analogue of the EDA selection game, initial phase
(figure by Owen McShane)

Here we have touched a sensitive nerve. Our concern with the difficulties encountered by numerous programs aimed at alleviating poverty in recent years is not merely that they are often unsuccessful. We expect that there will be a degree of initial disappointment.

Public unease stems rather from the feeling that, collectively, we have not learned from failure, leaving us not only as poor but as puzzled as we were before. Even if the nature of EDA's "experiment" makes it difficult for us to learn how to choose new public works projects, one might hope that a study of the program's administrative difficulties would provide clues to the creation of better organizational designs in the future. The conditions we described in the EDA public works program are familiar to the most casual student of administration—obstruction, delay, red tape, overlapping, duplication, vacillation, hesitation. Before exploring further the nature of the organizational problems involved, we must first deal with two widely espoused administrative remedies: going outside the bureaucracy and coordination. The first remedy was actually attempted by the EDA in this case, and the second is often suggested as a cure for the kind of institutional fragmentation and competition that has characterized the program. But we will show that attempts to circumvent the bureaucracy often create more problems than they solve. And as for coordination, on closer examination we will see that it is a term not for solving problems but for renaming them so they emerge at the end the same as they were at the beginning. These nostrums are not only misleading, but their quick espousal tends to block deeper consideration of the nature of organizational difficulties, thus impairing the learning process.

GOING OUTSIDE THE BUREAUCRACY

The first temptation is to establish a new organization. This way you can hire new people, establish your own rules, and work out patterns of operation you believe will facilitate the new activities. Since the point is to get special treatment, establishing the new organization in the White House or the Executive Office of the president is often considered. The number of outfits that can be located in this high station, however, is limited by the time and attention the president and his staff are able to devote to them. In order to conserve their time and energy, the president and his aides must normally limit severely the number of agencies reporting directly to the chief executive. Unless the president has a very special interest in an organization (including the willingness to be blamed for its errors), he will ordinarily resist taking it on. Besides, the sponsors of the new agency may not always welcome close White House scrutiny.

The next alternative in the search for organizational freedom is existence as an independent commission or semi-independent board. Such agencies report to Congress (meaning a subcommittee or two or no one at all). Their terms of office and appointment are circumscribed by numerous qualifications. The price for this sort of independence usually includes a plural form of executive, which is an open invitation for a diversity of interested parties to demand representation. The result may be watering down of the original ideas, internal conflicts, and worst of all the very delays that independence sought to avoid. The popularity of boards and commissions, moreover, has begun to wane because existing bodies are often not in high repute. The boards tend to insist on judicializing their procedures, leading to endless hearings and interminable delays, followed in important cases by long drawn-out legal battles. The affected interests, it also appears, have a way of capturing commissions largely because, over time, they are the ones who care the most. The cost of independence from ordinary bureaucratic constraints turns out to be loss of contact with the very political forces necessary to preserve the thrust of the organization.

If formal independence is rejected, it is still possible for a would-be organization to be born as a new bureau rather than as part of an established agency. A new bureau in an old department is, it appears, something of a mixed bag. A new bureau may have more autonomy in selecting personnel and establishing procedures than it would as part of an existing organization, but it is also subject to departmental regulations on all these matters. Life for departmental officials is easier if they can treat all their agencies in similar fashion; each exception is a headache increasing workload and decreasing the ability to rely on past experience. The question must also arise concerning why the new bureau should be able to circumvent civil service regulations for hiring, Budget Bureau rules for spending, comptroller general specifications for accounting, and on and on. Since the new bureau must deal with its department and possibly other bureaus, it will be under pressure to conform to their ways of doing business. The very act of repeatedly asking for exceptions may exhaust the élan of the new bureau and wear out the patience of other agencies with whom it must deal. Each exception has to be justified; each concession represents a favor that may have to be returned, a claim on future resources. Following routine procedure is just doing your job; acting outside its boundaries means doing a favor. Unless one believes the flow of favors can continuously move in a single direction they must be returned and not always in ways the new bureau would like.

The creation of new bureaus is also beset with difficulties similar to those encountered in getting started within the White House. Department heads may wish to cut back on the proliferation of new organizations. The scheduling of their work is made more difficult and the demands on their time rise with the increase in the number of organizations that account to them, whose special problems they must become aware of and whose personnel they must come to know. They fight new organizations, if only because they prefer known evils. They have a stake in existing patterns because they have learned about them. The time for change is when they arrive. But department heads rarely know enough to initiate change at the outset. After they have come, each new arrangement takes its toll in time, energy, knowledge, and adaptability.

The advantages of being new are exactly that: being new. They dissipate quickly over time. The organization ages rapidly. Little by little the regulations that apply to everyone else apply also to it. Accommodations are made with the other organizations in its environment. Territory is divided, divisions of labor are established, favors are traded, agreements are reached. All this means that the new organization now has settled into patterns of its own which it defends against interruption. Youth has gone and middle age has come, hopefully more powerful, certainly more experienced, inevitably less innovative.

The category of greatest empirical interest to us—the establishment of special arrangements, special preferences, special personnel to free an operation from the usual internal bureaucratic constraints —we have left for last. One way of establishing priority among programs is to give one of them preference in time and attention up and down the line. The head of the organization sets up a special unit in his office. He hires the people himself or at least the subordinate in charge of its operations. He gives its personnel and activities privileged access to him; it has first call on his time. Normal rules for hiring, clearing, and consulting are suspended for this program.

Immediately problems arise. If the special arrangements are so good, the other members of the organization say, they would like to share in them. They could do a few things too, they observe, if released from the ordinary constraints. They can think of some interesting ventures they might engage in so long as they too are not held strictly accountable (or held as little accountable as the privileged unit). They resent special treatment for others. Consequently, they are not enthusiastic about the privileged operation, and its success is not high on the priority list of other organizational actors. There was evidence of considerable resentment of the EDA Oakland task force on the part of other agency members in public works.

Efforts to circumvent the bureaucracy are often, in current public discussion, linked to decentralization. Whereas bureaucracy connotes red tape, decentralization bespeaks getting things done. Where bureaucracy suggests the verb "to stultify," decentralization bespeaks more admirable action words: to energize, to liberate from rigidity. To decentralize is apparently to debureaucratize.

But what happens when rival orthodoxies conflict? As we have met them in our tale of woe in Oakland, the decentralization and debureaucratization movements were at loggerheads. The Western Area Office, a decentralized field unit which officially opened in July 1966, wanted a voice in what happened in Oakland—which was in its territory. After all, the field offices were supposed to be closest to the people in a given region. But the nonbureaucratic Oakland task force did not take kindly to the initiative of the area office. Members of the task force were impatient with questions raised—and demands for authority made—by a regional office that had not been involved in the initial development of the project and that lacked any special expertise connected with it. For the task force, which was linked directly to the head of the organization, the regional office was not a manifestation of a noble principle; rather, it represented another irritating delay of the sort they once thought they had a mandate to avoid, undercut, or circumvent.

The idea of creating a nonbureaucracy within a bureaucracy was strictly a one-time short-run theory. No one expected it to last. It was designed to get something done in a hurry, after which it would presumably be all right for events to take their usual course. But that very short-run orientation—get in fast, get the job done, move out, turn it over to the bureaucrats—suggests an orientation to time that is unlikely to coincide with the requirements of a program designed to make a permanent and significant decrease in minority employment. The in-and-out perspective also speaks to the personal orientation of the key men involved: antibureaucratic men are unlikely to stick around long enough to shepherd the implementation of their program after it is started.

Racial discrimination has existed in America for over three hundred years, and the consequences of racism have left their indelible mark on the differing life chances of black and white in this country. Whatever their proximate causes, the race revolts that began with Watts are rooted squarely in history. All this suggests that it will take a lot of concentrated effort and a long time to eradicate poverty and racism. "Turning around Oakland," or turning around any American city, is something that cannot be accomplished overnight, no matter how dramatic the program. Imagination is needed, but so is perseverance.

Participants in the initial EDA Oakland effort talk about the early days in 1966 as exciting and exhilarating. Task force members worked hard to get the money to Oakland. They were diligent in setting up the employment plan and negotiating with employers. Whatever else can be said, they got the program going. Agreements were signed, public proclamations made, and intentions of future cooperation expressed. But that stage—the point at which Foley and Bradford left—was just the beginning of the story we have chronicled here.

When one lists the steps involved in setting up federal programs, one usually starts with the administration's proposal of a measure, followed by congressional approval and then commitment of funds. But the EDA Oakland experience suggests that these steps constitute only the tip of the iceberg and that a tortuous and frustrating path of implementation may lie below the surface. The creation of an antibureaucratic unit and the concerted efforts of nonbureaucratic men may be able to get a program launched; but as we have seen, launching is not enough.

If one wishes to assure a reasonable prospect of program implementation, he had better begin with a high probability that each and every actor will cooperate. The purpose of bureaucracy is precisely to secure this degree of predictability. Many of its most criticized features, such as the requirement for multiple and advance clearances and standard operating procedures, serve to increase the ability of each participant to predict what the others will do and to smooth over differences. The costs of bureaucracy—a preference for procedure over purpose or seeking the lowest common denominator—may emerge in a different light when they are viewed as part of the price paid for predictability of agreement over time among diverse participants. The price may be too high, but the cost of accomplishing little or nothing otherwise must be placed against it.

COORDINATION

If we agree that merely circumventing the bureaucracy is not a panacea for program woes, then we must look elsewhere for organizational solutions. No phrase expresses as frequent a complaint about the federal government as does "lack of coordination." No suggestion for reform is more common than "what we need is more coordination." The EDA's traumatic experience in Oakland has certainly had its share of obstruction and delay. Yet when an evil is recognized and a remedy proposed for as long and as insistently as this one has been, the analyst may wonder whether there is not more to it.[1]

The word "coordination" has a deceptively simple appearance. Policies should be mutually supportive rather than contradictory. People should not work at cross-purposes. The participants in any particular activity should contribute to a common purpose at the right time and in the right amount to achieve coordination. A should facilitate B in order to achieve C. From this intuitive sense of coordination, however, two important and possibly contradictory meanings emerge. Participants in a common enterprise may act in a contradictory fashion because of ignorance; when informed of their place in the scheme of things, they may be expected to behave obediently. If we relax the assumption that a common purpose is involved, however, and admit the possibility (indeed, the likelihood) of conflict over goals, then coordination becomes another term for coercion. Since actors A and B disagree with goal C, they can only be "coordi-

1. For a more extended discussion of coordination see Naomi Caiden and Aaron Wildavsky, *Planning and Budgeting in Poor Countries* (New York: John Wiley & Sons, 1974).

nated" by being told what to do and doing it. Coordination thus becomes a form of power.

When one bureaucrat tells another to coordinate a policy, he means that it should be cleared with other official participants who have some stake in the matter. This is a way of sharing the blame in case things go wrong (each initial on the documents being another hostage against retribution) and of increasing the predictability of securing each agreement needed for further action. Since other actors cannot be coerced, their consent must be obtained. Bargaining must take place to reconcile the differences, with the result that the policy may be modified, even to the point of compromising its original purpose. Coordination in this sense is another word for consent.

Telling another person to coordinate, therefore, does not tell him what to do. He does not know whether to coerce or bargain, to exert power or secure consent. Here we have one aspect of an apparently desirable trait of antibureaucratic administration that covers up the very problems—conflict *versus* cooperation, coercion *versus* consent —its invocation is supposed to resolve.

Everyone wants coordination—on his own terms. Invocation of coordination does not necessarily provide either a statement of or a solution to the problem, but it may be a way of avoiding both when accurate prescription would be too painful.

Coordination means getting what you do not have. It means creating unity in a city that is not unified. It means the ability to enforce agreements on employers when you are unable to do so. It means compelling federal agencies and their component parts to act in a desired manner at the right time, when achieving this purpose is precisely what you cannot do. Even when participants appear to agree with the substantive merits of a proposal, they can still oppose it or, at least, not do very much to help carry it out. One can believe that a program has merit but still think that others are more desirable. Rural areas, for example, may appear more deserving than urban ones or results there may seem more promising. One can agree with the program but believe that the wrong people are controlling the decisions or that faulty procedures have been followed. The regional organization may think that it should make critical decisions, though these might be no different from those made by its local or national affiliate. Guardians of the larger organization's integrity may believe that it will suffer if its existing procedures are violated. Full of agreement, bursting with goodwill, they may yet not take the actions required to expedite the program. Still other participants might agree on the program if they were interested in it, but they are not; for them the issue has to do with legality or compatibility with their programs and not with what the initiators think is at stake. Obtaining agreement, therefore, means first securing a meeting of the minds that the issue is what the main proponents say it is. Yet it took years for the prime movers of the EDA public works program to create mechanisms for imposing their own definition of the situation on other actors, and it is still uncertain whether they have succeeded.

Achieving coordination, again, means getting your own way. You can't learn how to do it from a slogan that tells you the way to get what you want is to already have it. Coordination has become a tautology. No one can find a solution to a problem that he is unwilling to state even to himself. No one can learn when his answers are constituted entirely by reiteration of his questions.

We began this chapter by relating the lack of organizational learning to the deficiencies of the EDA public works program in Oakland as an experiment. We then dealt with the false messiahs—bureaucracy and coordination—whose invocation only serves to obscure problems. Now it is time to bring in a real devil—the divorce of implementation from policy. Learning fails because events are caused and consequences are felt by different organizations.

Obstacles to learning have become part of the contemporary American scene in which demands for instant action interact with the federal system so as to produce separation of ideas from execution. These features render the specific events we have been discussing more familiar. Déjà vu: we have met them before. Particular facts may vary but the general story is the same: a sensational announcement from Washington on page 1, temporary local jubilation, permanent difficulties, and, perhaps years later, a small blurb on the back page signaling the end. In fact, a similar pattern of events occurs around the world when aid is dispensed by one nation to another. By bringing in an extended analogy to foreign aid, certain structural features affecting federal assistance to cities—the rival needs and circumstances of donors and recipients—stand out in bold relief.

FOREIGN AID IN AMERICA

We can deepen our insight into the gap between the announcement of a desirable objective and its fulfillment that generates the demand for coordination by looking at the EDA's employment efforts in Oakland as analogous to problems of foreign aid. By thinking about it in this way, instead of assuming a unity of interests, we shall become aware of differences of opinion, emphasis, and timing between federal donor, host city, and the numerous organizations through which they do business. One side has limited resources to allocate; the other, limited ability to spend. They could take account of each other's limitations by designing programs geared to implementation. They might then manage to make good on their promises. Instead, both succumb to the temptation to juxtapose grand schemes for which their resources, both in terms of money and administrative capacity, are inadequate.

Failure to implement may result either from overestimation of what can be accomplished or from underestimation of ability to implement. Each error can be explained by structural features of relations between aid givers and recipients under conditions of stress.

The aid process begins in an aura of emergency: Do something! Do anything! Do it right away! Poor cities, like poor countries, are in trouble. They need so much so fast. They are always conscious that time is running out on them; hence, they are tempted to engage in short-run expedients to overcome long-run problems. Perhaps one major project, absorbing all their resources, will enable them to catch up and move ahead. Donors of aid also are caught up in the "great-leap-forward" psychology combining undue pessimism about the past with wild optimism about the future: if only they could contribute to the one big project that would turn the tide! The recipient wishes to escape the vicious cycle of poverty, the donor to be the one who helps bring this miracle about. But the ability of the donor to provide huge infusions of funds is severely limited, as is the capacity of the recipient to absorb them. Finally, they hit upon, in America, the idea of the experiment or, abroad, the demonstration project. Here is a way to join a paucity of actual resources with a maximum amount of imagination.

The view from the top is exhilarating. Divorced from problems of implementation, federal bureau heads, leaders of international agencies, and prime ministers in poor countries think great thoughts together. But they have trouble imagining the sequence of events that will bring their ideas to fruition. Other men, they believe, will tread the path once they have so brightly lit the way. Few officials down below where the action is feel able to ask whether there is more than a rhetorical connection between the word and the deed. They need money and they must get what advantage they can out of the situation. The behavior of program participants is strongly influenced by their organizational problems with giving and receiving money. The donor nation or international organization is set up to grant funds to a variety of recipients. Whether it has a lot to give or just a little, the granting organization must get rid of what it has. It is a mover of money.[2] Its task is to remove a certain amount of money from its coffers in the time period allotted. Spending, to be sure, is not the prime goal of the granting organization. It may wish to further economic growth, to see that the money is used efficiently, to reduce population. But it is difficult to determine whether these goals have been achieved, and in any event the results would not be in for a number of years. The one major criterion of success that is immediately available, accordingly, is ability to spend the allotted amount.

An important internal goal for any organization is the rationalization of its work schedule. It must secure for itself a stable flow of business so that it can allocate its time and resources. Applied to the field of foreign aid, where many of the recipient nations are disorderly and unstable, this means that the foreign donor has an interest in establishing a steady flow of projects requesting funds. Should the recipient nation be unable to supply this flow, the donor organization will stimulate it by engaging in a form of vertical integration. It sends out teams that suggest the kind of projects desired and that may even help draw them up. It seeks oases of calm and stability in the form of autonomous organizations that do not have to follow civil service regulations and that control their own funds. The donor establishes genial relationships with subunits in the recipient nation. They have a supportive relationship: one spends and the other supplies the money.

For the host country, foreign aid is both an opportunity and a problem. It is an opportunity to overcome the perennial shortage of

2. See Judith Tendler, "The Abundance of Foreign Assistance" (unpublished paper, Dept. of Economics, U.C., Irvine, 1970); and Caiden and Wildavsky, *op. cit.*

funds for investment; it is a problem because it is not easy to determine which projects should be supported and because the expenditures always include local funds that are in perpetually short supply. To the degree that the recipient nation is not subject to powerful central direction, various autonomous organizations and ministries may make separate arrangements with the granting organization. The money goes to those agencies able to produce the largest number of projects with the appropriate glossy brochures, and it is worthwhile for them to keep a shelf of projects on hand. Where this nation is internally divided, as is often the case, it is not possible to give foreign aid to any one segment without alienating others. Nor is it possible to guarantee that the government in power at the time the arrangement was made will still be there when the money is spent, or that the new government will honor the arrangements of the old.

The EDA experience in Oakland began with two features familiar to observers of foreign aid programs—the atmosphere of crisis and the need to spend money in a hurry. Just as it is often alleged that a certain country will undergo revolution, flood, or famine unless foreign aid is immediately forthcoming, so was it believed that Oakland would face race riots unless something was done. The post-Watts atmosphere in America was heavy with foreboding. Although no one really understood or understands today the origins of the race riots that swept across America, speculations about the next places likely to blow up invariably included the city of Oakland. Many people who lived or visited there were convinced it was ripe for destruction. One cannot understand the actions of Foley, Bradford, and the other people in the EDA unless one shares with them their feeling that unless they did something immediately terrible consequences would ensue.

The supercharged emotional atmosphere favorable to immediate action was greatly enhanced by the prevailing budgetary situation. Funds were available in that year's budget and they would lapse unless they were committed within four months. The money had to be moved or the opportunity to do good with it would be lost. So the question of whether they really understood how to increase minority employment was beside the point: they had one idea, and it was that or nothing. The money movers did not face a choice between good and bad actions or better and worse actions, but between some action and none. Oakland would burn, they thought, and they would make no impact, they were certain, if they stood around and waited for better ideas. Public concern and private interest combined to force action. Their indicators of success—visible activity to reassure Oakland's black citizens and movement of money—pointed in the same direction: Action.

Faced with the necessity of moving at once, the EDA jumped at the chance of developing a relationship with the Port of Oakland. As an autonomous organization it controlled its own sources of funds and could enter into arrangements without the approval of other organizations such as the city. Besides, the port was a going concern with a competent staff and, best of all, a shelf of projects ready to go. Those already advantaged are in a position to spend money and, therefore, to receive more. By the same token, they can resist pressure to make them act in ways they deem undesirable.

Building agreement into a foreign aid situation is difficult. The donor agency must enter into working relationships with officials of the recipient polity, but it must also maintain enough distance from those officials to avoid being captured. Somehow, the distant donor must encourage diverse local institutions to work together for a common purpose. And the donor is by no means a monolithic organization; not only is the principal donor agency typically required to work with other aid-giving units, but the principal agency itself may be fragmented by differing perspectives.

The EDA was far from being the only federal organization interested in establishing connections with local bodies that would agree to spend its money. The Office of Economic Opportunity had its poverty programs (OEDCI); the Department of Housing and Urban Development (HUD) supported the local redevelopment authority; Health, Education and Welfare (HEW) dealt with the skills center; and the Department of Labor was in constant touch with the subdivisions of the State Employment Service (SES). These federal organizations all had an interest in assuring a flow of proposals they can support to whatever amount they have available. (They can also point to the flow of projects as a basis of enlarging support.) These relationships, however, were long established compared with the EDA in Oakland. It could not poach, so to speak, on the territory of these other federal organizations. Nor could it deal with the city as a whole, because the municipality was not organized to submit projects to create employment. The city was interested in saving capital expen-

ditures[3] and was appeased rather cheaply with the Hegenberger over-
pass to the coliseum.

The struggle of EDA officials to comprehend the divided city of
Oakland reads like a replay of the dilemmas of foreign aid officials
almost any place around the world. They need official contact and
approval to get their projects ratified; but they fear being labeled with
the stigma of status quo, so they point first in the direction of the
powers that be and then to their opponents and end up, naturally,
satisfying neither one. No one knows for certain whether the city is
as explosive as is claimed. No one knows who, if anyone, can really
speak for the black people of the city. Amory Bradford sought out
certain local militants only to be told by others that the first were
not to be taken seriously. Visitors to EDA headquarters in Washington report always being asked for information on what Oakland was
really like, questions that did not vary from the first visit to the last.
It is not easy to grab hold of a shifting and volatile environment,
particularly when the people in it do not agree on what is there, who
is responsible for it, how it might be remedied, or who speaks for
them.

Time and again various officials connected with the EDA bemoan
the fact that there was no comprehensive economic development
plan for the city. Hiring the Floyd Hunter organization was a desper-
ate effort to produce some economic studies they could actually use.
Once more we note the parallel to the insistence of donor nations
(including the so-called capitalistic United States) on seeing national
plans before they will spend money. Apparently there is something
reassuring about seeing numbers and figures and words in a multi-
volumed document. Part of the insistence on an economic plan undoubtedly stems from a belief that it would do Oakland good to have
it. But what the EDA people really wanted, though they were only
occasionally able to verbalize it, was the political control and agreement symbolized by the plan. They were too far away and too busy
with other things to dream of running the city of Oakland. They
could not even imagine intervening on a constant and effective basis.
No, their one devout wish was that the city would organize itself and
present the EDA with a list of priorities that would include a series

3. See Frank Levy, Arnold Meltsner, and Aaron Wildavsky, "Urban Outcomes" (Oakland Project paper, 1972), chapter 3.

of well-worked-out projects that it could implement. That is why some officials spoke longingly of Mayor Daley of Chicago, who, although not exactly their favorite person, was able to impose sufficient agreement on a committee made up of minority representatives, city officials, and businessmen to produce projects that the EDA could then support, and then help the agency follow through on enforcing employment agreements. Their conclusion, expressed by a high-level EDA official, was that, "if a community can't plan for its own development and its own growth, we can't do a damn thing for them."

The complaints of federal officials about the fragmented form of government in Oakland are the equivalent of those made by foreign aid officials about the instability of regimes in developing countries. The consequences are much the same; the donor nation finds it difficult to deal with existing authorities or to know who is in authority. Just as there is more than one potential recipient within the city, however, there is also more than one potential donor whose interests may have to be reconciled. Given the institutional fragmentation of both donors and recipients, it is hard to make "agreement" or "coordination" operational.

Evidence that America has not yet lost its taste for internal foreign aid comes from Martha Derthick's study of President Johnson's "new towns" program. Like the EDA Oakland effort, the new towns program was part of an ambitious and exciting federal design. Derthick states that HUD's planners wanted

to create a community that would be a model for urban society in the second half of the twentieth century. They assumed that different social classes and races could be integrated through a shared attachment to a place and the symbols, lifestyle, and activities associated with it. With an emphasis on "participation" and "decentralization," they also sought to set new styles in social action. And they sought innovation in every aspect of planning, design, and development.[4]

The federal design was stirring, but those who drew it up did not adequately appreciate how great the difficulties of implementation would be. Federal officials were too remote from the urban scene to appreciate the mixed reception that low-income housing generates in cities or the reluctance of city councils to mix problems of race

4. Martha Derthick, *New Towns In-Town*, p. 92.

and class in view of substantial local opposition and little visible
local support. The federal government's planners had thought that
they could encourage local construction of public housing by offering
the incentive of cheap land. But this incentive proved illusory; it
was learned that there were laws on the books prohibiting disposal
of land at less than fair market value. Derthick observes that "separation from local politics and administration gives policy-makers in
the federal government a license to formulate ideal objectives; it may
also give them a license to formulate innovative ones, for the political
and administrative burdens of the innovations they conceive will be
borne locally. They are free, much freer than local officials, to stand
publicly for progress and high principle."[5] But after formulating high
principles, federal authors have to depend on local actors for implementation; and local resistance finally made implementation of the
"new towns" program impossible.

It is easy to say that federal policy makers should not overestimate
the amount of support local officials can and will bring to their cause.
EDA officials in Oakland felt that the employment plan would represent a commitment on the part of the port and World Airways to
hire minority unemployed, but that "pressure" on the part of local
officials would be forthcoming to hold these institutions to their word.
(Foley and Bradford had expected that the EDA itself would enforce
employment plan agreements, but subsequently the "local pressure"
view became dominant at the EDA). Given the lack of power in City
Hall, however, local officials had no way to exert influence on the
port. Nor was the Black Caucus sufficiently organized at that time to
bring the influence of potential job holders to bear. Derthick comments that when federal programs are dependent on local political
actors, "whatever flaws there are in the local officials' ability to act
effectively—to gather public support, to overcome opposition, to
assemble an administrative organization—were liabilities for the
federal government as well."[6]

In both the new towns and the Oakland EDA programs, we find
similar phenomena: federal grandeur, inadequate local support, and
a divorce of implementation from policy.

5. *Ibid.*, p. 94.
6. *Ibid.*, p. 88.

TOWARD IMPLEMENTATION

We have learned one important lesson from the EDA experience in Oakland: implementation should not be divorced from policy. There is no point in having good ideas if they cannot be carried out. Stated in the form of this homily, everyone would agree. But in the EDA Oakland program, the formulation of policy was divorced from its eventual attempt at execution. From the outset the emphasis was on designing the program, obtaining initial agreement at the local level, and committing the funds. All this was done quickly, with fanfare and enthusiasm, by EDA leaders and by the agency's special Oakland task force. The later steps of implementation were felt to be "technical questions" that would resolve themselves if the initial agreements were negotiated and commitments were made. But the years have shown how those seemingly routine questions of implementation were the rocks on which the program eventually foundered.

The great problem, as we understand it, is to make the difficulties of implementation a part of the initial formulation of policy. Implementation must not be conceived as a process that takes place after, and independent of, the design of policy. Means and ends can be brought into somewhat closer correspondence only by making each partially dependent on the other.

Having observed one project that fulfilled original expectations (the health center) and two that did not (public works and business loans), we would like to suggest some ways in which policy might be designed to facilitate implementation. If policy makers were to close the gap between design and implementation by gearing programs more directly to the demands of executing them, what sorts of actions might they undertake?

First of all, an appreciation of the length and unpredictability of necessary decision sequences in implementation should lead the designers of policy to consider more direct means for accomplishing their desired ends. Since each required clearance point adds to the probability of stoppage or delay, the number of these points should be minimized wherever possible. The fact that the training program considered for Oakland required approval by nine separate organizations made it unlikely that the program would move along as quickly as its sponsors would have liked; in fact, it never did survive the hazardous round of clearances. Compared to business loans and the other public works programs, the West Oakland Health Center (see Table 10 and Figure 8) was notable for its directness. Instead of providing money to white-owned businesses who would then be required to find and hire unemployed minorities, the health center was to be run by people from the black community. By its very nature and location, this community health institution would be strongly inclined to hire minorities.

A second way of joining policy more closely to implementation would be to pay as much attention to the creation of organizational

TABLE 10: Points of Decision and Clearance Necessary for Completion of West Oakland Health Center

Decision Points	Participants Involved	Cumulative Total of Agreements
1. Submission and approval of application for funding (spring 1968)	West Oakland Health Council, Inc., EDA Oakland, EDA Washington	3
2. Decision to allow one firm to design and construct project (June 1968)	West Oakland Health Council, Inc., US Public Health Service, EDA Washington	6
3. Decision to approve cost overrun of $200,000 (August 1968)	EDA Washington	7
4. Agreement on interim financing and method of paying contractors (February 1969)	West Oakland Health Council, Inc., EDA Washington	9
5. Letting of construction contracts (February 1969)	West Oakland Health Council, Inc., Designed Facilities Corporation, EDA Washington	12
6. Agreement on assembly of plumbing fixtures (summer 1969)	Designed Facilities Corporation, Oakland Building Department	14
Project completed:	August 20, 1969	

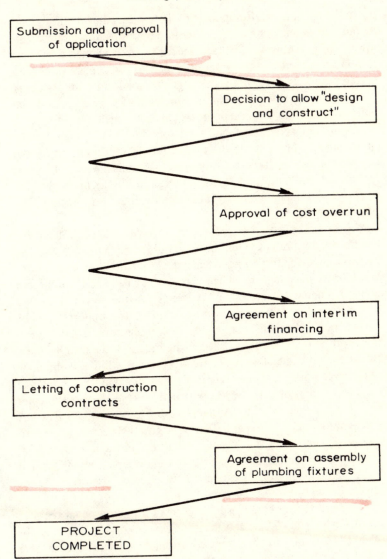

FIGURE 8. The decision path: the West Oakland Health Center

machinery for executing a program as for launching one. EDA
leaders took great pains to design the best organization they could
think of for approving applications, committing funds, and negotiat-

ing initial agreements. But in most of the projects they did not spend as much time ensuring that the initial commitment would be followed up by the agency; in fact, the EDA itself seemed to lose its own intense interest in the program after 1966. Although those who design programs might not generally enjoy the less exciting work of directing their implementation, a realization of the extent to which policy depends on implementation could lead such people to alter their own time perspectives and stay around for the technical details of executing a program. In the case of the health center, one of the project's most enthusiastic supporters—Public Works Director George Karras—was also in charge of much of the machinery for day-to-day implementation. Thus formulation and execution of policy were joined.

We recognize, however, that in some respects the history of the health center represents a limiting case rather than a typical one. The neighborhood supporting group managed to maintain a united front in facing the outside world. Their project was small and their purpose noble. No one wanted to oppose it; everyone—the mayor, a number of local doctors, the congressmen—wanted to support it. EDA bureaucrats dedicated themselves to making it work. Their frustrations with other programs worked to the benefit of the health center. By the time it came along, the bureaucrats were willing to eliminate obstacles that had held up earlier projects—for example, the demand for a separation of design and construction. Had the health center been much larger or subject to more visible internal conflicts, EDA bureaucrats might not have been able to use their extensive experience to provide shortcuts around, under, and through the usual obstacle course. The EDA was anxious to achieve a success in Oakland and it had enough money to construct the center. Performance, for once, equaled or exceeded promise.

Local unity, federal modesty, an excess of resources over requirements—it all sounds like too much to expect. And it is. No doubt other EDA public works programs are more typical. What advice might have been given under the actual circumstances prevailing at the time to bring policy and implementation closer together? We shall conclude by suggesting how the economic theory that lay behind the public works program could have been modified to enhance the prospects of implementation.

7

Economic Theory and
Program Implementation

Experience with the innumerable steps involved in program implementation suggests that simplicity in policies is much to be desired. The fewer the steps involved in carrying out the program, the fewer the opportunities for a disaster to overtake it. The more directly the policy aims at its target, the fewer the decisions involved in its ultimate realization and the greater the likelihood it will be implemented. Simplicity is, of course, not an end in itself; a fast train is worse than a slow one if it takes you in the wrong direction. Simplicity can be ignored, however, only at the peril of breakdown.

Behind the seemingly endless number of roadblocks in the path of the EDA employment program in Oakland lay deficiencies in concept. The economic theory was faulty because it aimed at the wrong target—subsidizing the capital of business enterprises rather than their wage bill. Instead of taking the direct path of paying the employers a subsidy on wages after they had hired minority personnel, the EDA program expanded their capital on the promise that they would later hire the right people. Theoretical defects exacerbated bureaucratic problems. Numerous activities had to be carried on—assessing the viability of marginal enterprises, negotiating loan agreements, devising and monitoring employment plans—that would have been unnecessary if a more direct approach had been taken.

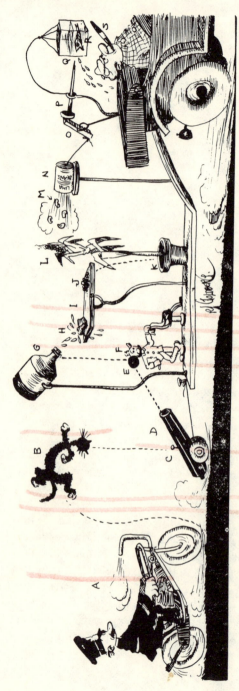

WHEN AUTOMOBILE SPEEDS AT FIFTY MILES AN HOUR MOTORCYCLE COP (A) STARTS IN PERSUIT-MOTORCYCLE HITS CAT (B) CAUSING IT TO FALL ON BUTTON (C) WHICH SETS OFF CANNON (D) - CANNON BALL (E) HITS IVORY DOME OF BARBER (F), BOUNCING OFF AND KNOCKING NECK OFF BOTTLE OF STRONG ACID (G) - ACID DROPS ON GOLD NUGGET (H) DISOLVING IT - WEIGHT OF KERNELS OF CORN (J) LOWER BOARD (I) AND FALL INTO FLOWER POT (K) - CORN GROWS TILL IT REACHES HEIGHT (L) - CAN (M) OF LIMA BEANS (M) JUMPS AT CORN ON ACCOUNT OF THE NATURAL AFFINITY FOR SUCCOTASH - STRING ON END OF CAN PULLS LEVER (O) WHICH RUSHES POINTER (P) INTO PAPER TANK (Q) HALF FILLED WITH WATER IN WHICH SARDINE (R) IS SWIMMING - POINTER PUNCTURES PAPER TANK, WATER RUNS OUT AND SARDINE CATCHES SEVERE COLD FROM EXPOSURE-SARDINE CONTRACTS A VERY HIGH FEVER THAT FINALLY SETS FIRE TO PAPER TANK AND LIGHTS CIGAR (S).

(Rube Goldberg cartoon, courtesy of the Bancroft Library.)

THERE MUST BE A BETTER WAY.

SUBSIDIZING CAPITAL VERSUS LABOR

The difficulties were rooted in reliance on organizational tradition. The EDA, which had been created to deal with economically depressed regions such as Appalachia, could hardly be expected to realize that Oakland, though suffering from heavy unemployment, nevertheless lay in the midst of a prosperous region. The desire of Eugene Foley and his associates to act quickly led them to overlook ways in which cities like Oakland differ from the pattern of depressed areas. They did understand that it was insufficient merely to create economic growth; they knew they had to seek assurances that new jobs would go to the minority people in whose interest the federal money was presumably being expended. But their desire to move with the greatest possible speed persuaded them to devise a program based on promises rather than performance. Their innovation, they thought, was funneling money into a city rapidly on condition that it be used to generate the right kind of employment. Their creativity consisted in moving money and devising mechanisms of compliance after it had been spent. No one asked them whether it might have been better to give firms incentives to hire minority personnel by paying part of the cost after the men had been hired. No one asked whether Oakland fit the mold of the depressed region on which the EDA's previous public works-employment projects had been modeled.

Oakland is undergoing a transition from a manufacturing to a service center.[1] A study conducted by the city Planning Department shows that

beginning in the late 1940's and throughout the 1950's [Oakland] experienced a continued net loss of jobs in the manufacturing sector at the very same time southern Alameda County [the county in which Oakland is located] registered continued growth in these industries. . . .

But manufacturing was not the only economic activity breaking out of its traditional locational framework. The vast outlying residential development and consequent population shifts caused significant changes in the locational pattern of retail establishments. The postwar housing boom caused a major drop in the old downtown's share of retail sales. . . .

Certain elements of the "service" sector—finance, insurance, and real

1. Pp. 149–158 have been adapted from Owen McShane, "Towards a Transitional Economics: A Reappraisal of Urban Development Administration in Oakland, California," M.C.P. thesis, University of California at Berkeley, June 1970.

estate (FIRE) services, and government—never migrated to the developing outer areas as manufacturing and retailing did.[2]

Manufacturing jobs are increasingly available in Alameda County, while the nonmanufacturing jobs are available in the Oakland city core itself.

Oakland is *not* the core city for a depressed hinterland. The East Bay is a flourishing region, and even within that larger entity Alameda County is enjoying a boom when compared to most of the nation. For Alameda County, for example, "the 15 percent rate of growth anticipated in wage and salary employment over the five years to 1971 is greater than the projected rate for the United States."[3] But this boom is not evenly distributed geographically within the county:

Between 1958 and 1966, total employment in Alameda County increased by 90,800 jobs, a growth of 28 percent over the eight year period. This rate of growth was faster than that for the five county San Francisco-Oakland Standard Metropolitan Statistical Area. However, while parts of Alameda County experienced considerable economic growth, employment in the core city, Oakland, increased by only 8,900 jobs, for a rate of 5 percent over the eight years. Only one in ten of all jobs added in the county were located in Oakland. As a consequence, the proportion of County employment located in Oakland fell from 53 percent in 1958 to 44 percent in 1966.[4]

Postwar housing expansion redistributed the population away from the dense cores, a move both accommodated and encouraged by the increase in car ownership and freeway development. Many industries followed the labor force.[5]

The result was that

In each of the four major industries that together provide 80 percent of all jobs both in the County and in Oakland (manufacturing, trade, service and government), jobs were added at a much faster rate outside Oakland than in the central city. The sharpest discrepancy in employment trends occurred in manufacturing, where Oakland lost over 9,000 jobs since 1958 (mostly to industrial areas in South County) while the County had a net gain of 13,900 manufacturing employees.[6]

2. City Planning Department, Oakland, *Options for Oakland,* p. 61.
3. California Department of Employment in cooperation with the city of Oakland 701 Project, *East Bay Manpower Survey, Alameda County, 1966–1971* (San Francisco, July 1967), p. 1.
4. *Ibid.*
5. City Planning Department, Oakland, p. 61.
6. *East Bay Manpower Survey, Alameda County,* p. 1.

Thus, the East Bay enjoys a flourishing economy, within which Alameda County is growing even more rapidly than most. The suburban areas, however, are growing more rapidly than the core and are attracting a greater share of manufacturing and retail industry as they do so. Central Oakland is increasingly having to adapt to serving the role of service center to the East Bay region.

A population that is well trained, with good access to public and private transportation, will have little difficulty in adapting to the shifts in job locations. The characteristics of a large section of Oakland's population, however, makes it peculiarly susceptible to unemployment under these circumstances. Oakland has a disproportionate share of the poor, the low skilled, and the minorities. The white suburban middle-class resident has no difficulty in learning of a job in central Oakland in its expanding service sector; he has no problem in getting into the job for interviews; and finally, he has no difficulty in commuting to the job each day, be it by car, bus, or the forthcoming rapid transit. For the poor, unskilled minority member trying to find employment after his previous manufacturing job has been relocated to the suburbs, the situation is markedly different. His informal connection with the manufacturing job market has been atrophied, for his friends and neighbors are in no better position than he. Even if he finds a job, he may not be able to commute daily, for he is either too poor to own a reliable car or the public transport system does not serve the new plant. When he turns to the expanding nonmanufacturing job market near at hand, he finds his skills are no longer in demand, his poor educational background ill fits him to learn new skills, and he faces anew the problem of overcoming racial discrimination.

The redistribution of people and jobs has left city residents at a disadvantage. According to the city Planning Department, "Almost 40 percent of all employed persons residing in Oakland were commuting to jobs outside the city. The net result of total commuter movement into and out of the city was that less than half of all Oakland jobs were filled by its residents. . . . In-commuters are disproportionately *white*. By contrast, a larger proportion of blacks than *whites* leave the city for employment. Thus, the overall relationship between commuter patterns and ethnicity indicates that Oakland is increasingly providing a home for blacks and a place of employment for *whites*."[7]

Unemployment may occur in the "depressed region" or the "distressed neighborhood." Recognition of these two types is critical to the kind of policy likely to be successful in one environment as compared with the other. Appalachia is the epitome of the depressed region. As Franklin D. Roosevelt, Jr., observed,

The problem behind Appalachia's unemployment problem is not simply that the resource potential is underdeveloped and that it lacks an industrial complex which might be diversified or amplified to make use of the unemployed. The problem is even more basic and more grave: It is that in Appalachia there exists no standard American labor force, with ready aptitudes or a diversity of basic skills; there is a deficit in the educational resources needed to raise even the level of functional literacy—let alone the level of vocational ability; and finally the region lacks the financial or physical mobility necessary for resettlement or retraining in areas of more opportunity.[8]

Appalachia is ten times the size of Switzerland, comprising 362 counties in ten states. Thousands of people live in this region and yet there is no "town"—and hence no water supply, no firehouse, no library, and no police station and hardly any beauty parlors, soda fountains, or offices where women, boys, and girls might find even part-time jobs. The weakness of the economic base of the region depresses the wealth—fiscal, social, and cultural—of all who live there. Most everyone stands to gain from any program that brings money and jobs to Appalachia. Any project that creates jobs is bound to draw on those who need them; there is no alternative, unless the project attracts skilled people to the area from outside. But the depressed region needs them, too.

In contrast to the depressed region, the distressed neighborhood exists, not separate and distant from the nation's wealth, but completely within and surrounded by it. The urban ghetto is often within two blocks of some of the highest value real estate in the nation. Industry and commerce thrive around it so that the unemployed can sit in their doors and watch the "fat cats" go to work. Typically, this distressed neighborhood lies in the heart of a growing, diversifying region that is by no means "outside the mainstream of the Nation's

7. City Planning Department, Oakland, pp. 71–72.

8. Franklin D. Roosevelt, Jr., "Appalachia: Case Study for Regional Development," in *The Manpower Revolution: Its Policy Consequences,* ed. Garth L. Mangum (New York: Doubleday, 1965), p. 397.

prosperity" but is at its very heart. Creating employment in the larger Oakland area, therefore, may bring jobs to those who can get them rather than those who need them.

According to EDA criteria, the city government jurisdiction known as Oakland qualifies as a depressed region. But former Senator Knowland disagrees,[9] and one's own common sense suggests that the East Bay region or metropolitan Oakland[10] by no means qualifies. But it is this "economic region" that must be considered when dealing with problems of unemployment and the local labor market. Under this model an appropriate observation would be that the East Bay is an area of rapid growth with a diverse economic base, a high per capita income, and so forth but in which, because of certain characteristics of the postindustrial economy and deficiencies in the labor market, many residents remain chronically unemployed, even during periods of high aggregate demand. These people are mainly found in the inner city ghettoes of Richmond and Oakland. These characteristics reduce the efficacy and leverage of many of the techniques developed by the ARA in its rural experience when they are applied to the problems of the distressed neighborhood. The problem is not one of bringing a regional economy up to the strength required to employ an underemployed population, but one of rigging a strong and well-developed metropolitan economy so as to reduce the disparity between the location and characteristics of jobs available and the location and skills of the distressed population.

As one would expect with Appalachia in mind, the Public Works and Economic Development Act outlines a program designed to develop the economy of a depressed region. The act says, "Project criteria: Projects must contribute (directly or indirectly) either to the creation of new jobs or to the alleviation of poverty. . . . Example of eligible projects: Waterworks and lines, sanitation facilities, access roads for industrial areas or potential industrial areas, public tourism facilities, and vocational schools, airports, or flood control projects for which there is a serious need but for which other federal

9. See letter from William F. Knowland to the *New York Times Magazine,* Sept. 4, 1966, p. 12.

10. For statistical evidence see "Metropolitan Oakland, Bright Spot, '66–'67" (published by the *Oakland Tribune,* n.d.).

financing is not available.""[11] These examples all refer to building up
infrastructure—services and capacities—to support development in
a large area. The fact that this section of the act is directed toward
the economies of rural areas and small towns is evident from statements by the legislators responsible for the bill. None of the presentations, submissions, hearings, and debates leading to the passing of
the Public Works and Economic Development Act of 1965 ever
suggests that the legislation was intended to operate in the distressed
neighborhoods of flourishing regions.

When the EDA came to Oakland and funded an access road to the
Oakland coliseum complex with the aim of opening up new industrial land, it was working within the intent of the act. The building
of such access roads has been a major part of expenditure in depressed region programs. It was expected that hotels, motels, and
restaurants providing approximately six hundred jobs would be
developed along this road.[12] The emphasis on jobs per se can be
explained by the tradition of evaluating infrastructure projects in
depressed regions where "any job is the right job," whereas in Oakland a motel can draw its staff from the whole East Bay region. As
of October 1969, the coliseum access road had created no new jobs
for the hard-core unemployed.[13]

EDA policy not only favored industrial infrastructure, but also
stated a clear preference for manufacturing rather than the service
industry. In response to an inquiry about the possibility of the EDA
lending money to hotels, Foley replied, "It is difficult to see how such
enterprises create a net increase in employment and do not simply
transfer employment from one part of the community to another.
We're not writing off the idea. At the Small Business Administration,
we funded a shopping center in South Chicago. Usually, though,
we're interested in manufacturing."[14]

Again, in the industrial, or even preindustrial, economy of the
depressed region, a policy favoring manufacturing makes some sense
as an array of subsidiary service activities can be expected to develop
around initial prime employers. But in the East Bay, such prime em-

11. U.S. Department of Commerce, E.D.A., *Facts About EDA,* Public
Works and Economic Development Act, 1965. Public Law 89–136, pp. 1–2.
12. EDA internal report, p. 20.
13. McShane, p. 83.
14. From Dunsmuir meeting minutes, quoted in McShane, p. 84.

ployers already exist, and the core city locations are attractive mainly for the service sector.

If one is providing money to develop industry in a depressed region of, say, a hundred-mile diameter, one of the comforts is that for every job created directly by funding—either in the public or private sector—there will be other jobs ("spinoffs") resulting from the need to service the initial jobs. If a factory makes water pumps, extra trucks will be needed to transport the pumps, extra service stations will be needed to service the trucks, and so on. In the depressed region, all these jobs benefit the target population. There is little need to be concerned with identifying a target population and ensuring that they are the recipients of the jobs. Drawing attention to the benefits of spinoff, Senator Douglas, in a hearing before the Banking and Currency Committee in 1965, argued that a 70,000 increase in direct jobs could represent a total increase of 140,000 jobs.[15] Building a road to open up land for industrial development is sufficient. Unless potential employees are prepared to drive fifty miles from an adjoining rich region, there is little chance of the project benefiting the wrong population. Yet the problem in Oakland is precisely to assure that the jobs go to the right people.

Increased economic prosperity for a firm can lead to a significant increase in jobs if the firm is labor intensive and if the aid offered subsidizes the cost of labor—an employment subsidy. The EDA offered cheap capital. Such a program would tend to attract capital-intensive industries which, on receipt of low cost capital, would become even more capital intensive. "It seems reasonable to suppose," Clopper Almon wrote, "that a spurt in an industry's expansion, bringing with it an influx of new equipment, would quicken the rate of its [labor] productivity growth."[16] The two major recipients in the business loans program were in food processing, a highly capital-intensive industry. Both increased their employment much less than anticipated.

Any incentive to industrial growth and development, whether at the national level in the form of tax cuts or increased depreciation

15. U.S. Senate, *Public Works and Economic Development Hearings* before a subcommittee of the Committee on Banking and Currency, 89th Congress, 1st Session, on Titles II and IV of S 1648, May 4–7, 1965, p. 73.

16. Clopper Almon, Jr., *The American Economy to 1975* (New York: Harper and Row, 1966), p. 128.

rates or at the local level in the form of low cost loans or capital grants, is likely to reduce the labor intensiveness of industry unless countervailing pressures are brought to bear. In explaining the hostility of other bakers to the EDA loan to Colombo Bakery, Mr. Mueller said, "After all, as far as they were concerned, EDA was providing cheap money for Colombo to fully automate its plant . . . !"[17]

Offering low cost capital to attract firms to depressed regions makes more sense in that labor costs tend to be low in such areas anyway; the firm is offered both cheap capital and cheap labor. This combination is unlikely to exist in the union-controlled metropolitan areas. The capital subsidy program makes sense in the depressed region where there is a surplus of semiskilled labor left behind by the departure of another industry and where it is a shortage of capital that prevents firms setting up in the area. In the flourishing regions such as the East Bay, finance is ordinarily no real problem to the large employers, and the intention is not so much to encourage industry to choose an abnormal location as to induce it to draw on a different sector of the population for its labor force. Let us take a brief look at an approach to the problem in Great Britain that focuses on subsidizing wages.

In 1967 the Department of Economic Affairs in Great Britain introduced a proposal for a regional employment premium. The essence of the proposal was "that the existing grants and other assistance for capital investment should be supplemented for a period of years by payments towards the labour cost of manufacturing industry in the Development Areas."[18] The department directly addressed the need to subsidize labor if capital subsidy is not to further aggravate the structural unemployment caused by increases in labor productivity:

The proposed assistance towards labour costs would act in conjunction with the existing incentives to capital investment. It would help to meet the criticism which is sometimes levelled against special regional investment incentives that, in the absence of assistance towards labour costs, they tend to tip the balance in favour of locating capital-intensive projects in areas of labour

17. McShane interview with Ken Mueller of the OEDF, April 16, 1970.
18. Great Britain, Department of Economic Affairs, H.M. Treasury, *The Development Areas: A Proposal for a Regional Employment Premium* (London, 1967), para. 18.

surplus rather than in areas of labour shortage. The investment grants by themselves could not be further raised to produce an additional stimulus comparable with the effect of the proposed employment premium—if only because the total of capital expenditure capable of attracting grant is much smaller than the labour costs which would attract employment premium. In manufacturing industry the annual wage and salary bill is about five times the total annual investment and about seven times the annual investment in machinery.[19]

The employment premium is "across the board"—that is, any manufacturing employer in a development area receives the subsidy on all wages paid. Opinion in the United States would probably reject such a "loose" program that gives payments irrespective of the target population. An employment premium in the United States, therefore, would have to be paid only to those employers who have employed statistically defined hard-core unemployed.

John Kain outlined such a tight wage subsidy program in his presentation to the congressional Joint Economic Committee. The essentials of his scheme were that the employment service would simply certify workers who have been unemployed beyond a certain period of time (the long-term unemployed) for participation in the program. Any employer hiring one of these certified workers would receive an hourly cash subsidy. "There should be an increasing scale depending on the worker's duration of unemployment, so that firms would have a stronger incentive (larger cash subsidy) for hiring the really hard-core unemployed. . . . There should be a declining subsidy for weeks worked on the presumption that the productivity of workers increases with training and experience on the job."[20] Experimenting with these rates over a period of time should allow the most effective scales to be established.

In accord with his conviction that programs should be designed to reduce the social and economic isolation of the ghetto, Kain "would prefer a wage subsidy that would apply only to the hiring of the long-term unemployed by suburban employers—more specifically those

19. *Ibid.,* para. 28.
20. U.S. Congress, *Employment and Manpower Problems in the Cities: Implications of the Report of the National Advisory Commission on Civil Disorders,* Hearings before the Joint Economic Committee, Congress of the United States, 90th Congress, 2nd Session, May-June 1968, Statement by John F. Kain, Dept. of Economics, Harvard University and the MIT-Harvard Joint Center for Urban Studies, p. 66.

located further than a certain minimum distance from the ghetto." However, he admits "to the logic, on narrow cost effectiveness grounds, of a flexible wage subsidy available to firms . . . anywhere in the metropolis."[21]

In his journal and in interviews, Amory Bradford expressed the wish to see large corporations such as General Motors take an interest in the EDA. One reason that such corporations show little interest is that the agency offers the wrong incentives. The Survey of Current Business observed that "three-fifths of all capital funds used by corporate business in the postwar period has been derived from internal sources, i.e., retained earnings and depreciation allowances. An additional one-fifth has been raised in long-term markets, . . . while the remainder has involved increases in short-term debt, principally accounts payable and bank debt."[22] It would be difficult to argue that, given these conditions, a large corporation would be unable to find financing through regular channels, and this presumably explains why Bradford was unable to interest large employers. A subsidy on wages, however, may well be an incentive to them precisely because they do employ so many men and in jobs that typically require short training periods.

One of the most attractive aspects of any labor subsidy or employment premium is that it is paid out only on performance. Capital subsidy plans are, however, always paid out on a promise. The applicant says, "If you give me a low cost loan of $100,000, then I shall employ twenty hard-core unemployed." What happens is all too likely to follow the pattern described by a black woman to whom Bradford talked about the employment plan machinery:

Let me get this straight. You have some employer, who files a Plan saying he will employ twenty of our people. We approve his plan, and he starts up with your money. But then he chisels a little bit, and only employs eighteen, and takes two others from outside, maybe his cousins or something. Does this committee then say, "You fire those two, and take on two of ours"? And if he won't, then you call his loan, and put him out of business, and the other eighteen lose their jobs? I don't like the sound of that.[23]

21. *Ibid.*
22. U.S. Department of Commerce, *Survey of Current Business,* September 1957, p. 8.
23. Bradford, p. 165.

The employer was, in fact, more likely to employ only five rather than twenty new men because he substituted new capital for labor. He could claim good faith but add that "things hadn't quite worked out as expected." Bearing in mind Almon's anticipated increase in labor productivity with any rapid increase in investment, it would prove difficult to demonstrate bad faith. The dilemma of performance *versus* promise was to plague the EDA throughout its operation in Oakland. A labor subsidy, which pays on performance, avoids these problems altogether and has the attractive characteristic that failure of the program costs no money.

"Payment on performance" is a useful premise on which to base employment policy in distressed areas. One of the advantages of an employment subsidy is that money is paid out only on performance, that is, the hiring of a worker and if no workers are hired, then no money is spent—an appealing attribute for the taxpayer. If policy analysts carry bumper stickers, they should read, "Be Simple! Be Direct!" or "PAYMENT ON PERFORMANCE."

Our preferred economic theory has been proposed with the invaluable benefit of hindsight. Had we been around at the time, we might not have thought of it. Had we been subjected to the same extreme time pressure as the actual participants in the public works and business loans programs, all thought of alternatives might have been driven from our minds. The fact that the legislation establishing the EDA lacked specific reference to (though it did not prohibit) wage subsidies might have contributed to the lack of innovation. It may also be that a program to subsidize labor precisely because it was innovative might have run up against as many or even more obstacles than the other programs. Indeed, it might not have been able to get off the ground at all.

We would like to believe that legislators and administrators fully cognizant of the difficulties of implementation would have cast about for simpler and more direct methods of accomplishing the desired result. Under the self-imposed necessity of undertaking immediate action, they might not have considered the differences between a depressed neighborhood and a depressed region. But they would have searched first and foremost for a program that would connect their activities with the production of jobs, avoiding intermediary steps like the plague. This is a suggestion for the future. Our purpose, in any event, is not to lay blame for perfectly understandable error but to suggest how policy might have been improved by making implementation a part of its essential conception.

A WORD OF CAUTION

On the side of substantive policy recommendations, we may have overestimated the likely effectiveness of a labor subsidy. It would not be difficult to find plausible arguments against our suggestions. Consider, for instance, applying the literature on the so-called dual labor market to the problem at hand.[24] The central idea is that poor people with little skill (often black males) are confined to a set of jobs characterized by low wages and status and lack of opportunity. There is no normal path of advancement for these workers within the firm's employment structure. Their turnover is high. This turnover is part of a mutually reinforcing process. Employers count on an unstable work force for the jobs, so they are designed in such a way that there are frequent hirings through "shape-ups," where the men must appear in person on the spot. Not much time is lost, therefore, when one man quits and another man is hired. Under these circumstances, a firm is not likely to invest much in training or anything else affecting the employee. At the same time, the bad qualities of the jobs and the ease with which men go from one to another—nothing is lost in the transition since the jobs have no seniority attached—means that the workers themselves develop capricious behavior, quitting frequently, working irregularly, and thereby completing the self-fulfilling prophecy of both employer and employee. The latter expects to be laid off and treated badly, so he leaves; and the former, expecting his workers to be unreliable, gives them scant consideration and is not surprised to discover that they live up to his predictions.

How would a policy of subsidizing wages fit into such a differential market? To subsidize everyone would be inefficient because there would undoubtedly be money spent on people whom the firm would have hired anyway. A more selective plan might still run into similar difficulties. A firm might merely substitute "certified hard-core unemployed" for people of equal skills whom they otherwise would

24. See, in this connection, Michael Piore and Peter Doeringer, *Internal Labor Markets and Manpower Analysis* (Lexington, Mass.: D.C. Heath, 1971).

have hired. Making certain that the increment of employment generated by the subsidy is real and goes to the people intended is no simple matter. Moreover, since turnover is a big problem in the market, the idea of diminishing the subsidy over time might prove counterproductive. It might make more sense to give a larger subsidy the longer a man stays on the job, thus rewarding the firm for reducing turnover. Naturally, this approach would prove expensive. Without carrying the discussion further, enough has been said to suggest that there is no easy road to creating long-term jobs for the hard-core unemployed.

On the political side, the American federal system will continue to pose severe problems for policies initiated by the national government. After studying the pitfalls encountered in implementing Title I (compensatory education) of the Elementary and Secondary Education Act, Jerome T. Murphy arrives at judgments similar to our own:

To blame the problems on timidity, incompetence, or "selling out" is to beg the question. I have identified a number of contributing causes: the reformers were not the implementers; inadequate staff; a disinclination to monitor; a law and tradition favoring local control; and absence of pressure from the poor. The primary cause, however, is political. The federal system—with its dispersion of power and control—not only permits but encourages the evasion and dilution of federal reform, making it nearly impossible for the federal administrator to impose program priorities; those not diluted by Congressional intervention can be ignored during state and local implementation.[25]

No one supposes that the federal system is going to disappear. If the federal principle maintains its vitality, then it means precisely that state and local organizations must be able to oppose, delay, and reject federal initiatives. When these kinds of actions can no longer be undertaken, there is no state or local independence and hence no operative federalism. The form might still be visible but the substance will have disappeared. American cities may become more internally cohesive, but they probably will not. They may all be alike, so that knowledge of one can be extended to the others, but it would be hard to find anyone who would bet on it. Consequently, formula-

25. Jerome T. Murphy, "Title I of ESEA: The Politics of Implementing Federal Education Reform," *Harvard Educational Review* 41 (1971): 60.

tors of federal programs will be faced with cities of uncertain unity and will find it difficult to gather accurate and up-to-date political intelligence about them. No matter how the federal government is organized and reorganized, virtually all social programs will cut across the jurisdictions of different bureaus, departments, and overhead agencies. While the number of clearances could be cut down by organizing with a single set of programs in mind, there is no organizational arrangement that will minimize clearances for all programs, past and future. New entrants are likely to find, as did the EDA in Oakland, that they must fit into arrangements that have been made with other purposes in mind. The requirement that the Economic Development Administration and the Small Business Administration collaborate in the administration of loans programs, for instance, added new clearance points and an inherently antagonistic relationship to an already difficult program. Getting one agency to assist another in this way met the value of reducing overlap and duplication of personnel, but it was not helpful for immediate programmatic purposes.

Moreover, the EDA itself could not have acted unilaterally to reduce the number of clearance points. Other federal actors, whose consent was uncertain and whose attention to the problem at hand was minimal—Congress and the Budget Bureau—were required to act before certain previously necessary steps could be omitted. Finally, there may be people who think that someone can issue a ukase forbidding undue haste in the design of federal programs, but we think that the tendency will be extremely difficult to resist. We still believe that difficulties of implementation can be mitigated, but we urge continued skepticism when anyone suggests that inherent features of political life can be summarily abolished.

8

Implementation as Evolution (1979)

GIANDOMENICO MAJONE
and
AARON WILDAVSKY

The study of implementation is becoming a growth industry; tens, perhaps hundreds, of studies are underway now. Yet researchers are visibly uneasy. It is not so much that they expect to discover all the right answers; they are not even sure they are asking the right questions. Amidst the flurry of activity is an underlying suspicion that the phenomenon to be studied—implementation—eludes understanding. But this uneasiness is not surprising, for the attempt to study implementation raises the most basic question about the relation between thought and action: How can ideas manifest themselves in a world of behavior?

"WHO'S ON FIRST?"

Let us begin with the initial source of enlightenment (or, if you prefer, confusion) in defining the domain of implementation, the effort in the first edition of *Implementation* to distinguish a stage of implementation from a stage of policy when these are intertwined. Is it appropriate to separate objectives and actions when, analytically, language and behavior have joined them together? Having said that there must be a goal against which to judge implementation, Pressman and Wildavsky went on to say that the goal and the implementing actions are part of a process of interaction. What comes first, then, the chicken of the goal or the egg of implementation? The authors answer that "each element is dependent on the other," so that "program implementation thus becomes a seamless web." Now you see it (implementation of course); now you don't. Having just indicated that implementation involves forging a causal chain from objectives to results, the authors immediately reverse the direction of causality. "We oversimplify . . . once a program is underway implementers become responsible both for the initial conditions and for the objectives toward which they are supposed to lead."[1]

If implementation is everywhere, as one of the authors suggested in another connection,[2] is it *ipso facto* nowhere? Indeed, the authors warn that "the separation of policy design from implementation is fatal." Yet if they cannot be separated, what place is there for policy analysis or, indeed, for anything but action? "Though we can't isolate policy and implementation for separate discussion," the authors of *Implementation* continue, "the purpose of our analysis is to bring them into closer correspondence with one another." It just possibly may be reasonable to separate in the mind subjects that must be joined in action. To what purpose? To improve policy design. But aren't policies always being redesigned? Yes, there's the rub. No doubt this is why students of implementation complain that the subject is so slippery; it does depend on what one is trying to explain, from what point of view, at what point in its history.

IMPLEMENTATION AS CONTROL

One way to conceptualize the split between policy and implementation is to merge them into each other. One may absorb implementation into planning and design; what is supposed to be, will be, when the grand design unfolds; some may deny the existence of anything preceding implementation so that implementation is absorbed into interaction. Which position one takes depends on how one answers the question: What sort of entity is a "policy" before it is implemented? Is policy a fully articulated plan, needing only enforcement,

1. See Preface to First Edition.
2. Aaron Wildavsky, "If Planning Is Everything, Maybe It's Nothing," in *Policy Sciences*, vol. 4, no. 2 (Amsterdam: Elsevier Scientific Publishing Co., June 1973).

or is policy the necessary premise for everything that follows? Or is the preimplementation stage a limbo where policy ghosts await the arrival of a merciful implementer? In the following pages we shall argue that both positions—reification and nullification—discount important features of policy development.

In the planning-and-control model of implementation, the initial plan, call it P_0, and its realization, call it P_1, are on the same logical level. The implementation problem, as the users of the model see it, is to transform one into the other by a suitable theory or "production function." Barring design errors P_1 is logically implied by P_0 and good implementation is the irresistible unfolding of a tautology. The model prescribes clearly stated goals, detailed plans, tight controls and—to take care of the human side of the equation—incentives and indoctrination.

This view of implementation—which we have caricatured just enough to make its main features stand out—has the intuitive appeal of all teleological or means-end theories, which seem to embody the very essence of rational action. As description, it leaves out the detours, the blind alleys, the discarded hypotheses, the constraints tightened and loosened, the lumpy stuff of life in favor of a predigested formula consisting of a ranking of objectives, a considering of alternatives, and a criterion that chooses among them. Presentation of the end of inquiry provides prescription for its beginning and its middle. No one does (or should) think like that if only because divorcing available resources from desirable objectives stultifies policy analysis. As prescription, this prevailing paradigm of rationality encourages consistency in ranking objectives at the expense of effectiveness in making policy preferences live in the world. But, at least in the area of public policy, it is neither descriptively nor prescriptively adequate. In this view, for instance, implementers must know what they are supposed to do in order to be effective. Yet, "street-level" bureaucrats are notorious for being too busy coping with their day-to-day problems to recite to themselves the policies they are supposed to apply. Even high-level officials do not seem to be particularly committed to the idea of making correct deductions from firmly established principles. Writing about the administrative process in the regulatory commissions of the New Deal era, James Landis recalls how "one of the ablest administrators that it was my good fortune to know, I believe, never read, at least more than casu-

ally, the statutes that he translated into reality. He assumed that they
gave him power to deal with the broad problems of an industry and,
upon that understanding, he sought his own solutions."[3]

The planning model recognizes that implementation may fail because the original plan was infeasible. But it does not recognize the
important point that many, perhaps most, constraints remain hidden
in the planning stage, and are only discovered in the implementation
process. Moreover, feasibility conditions keep changing over time:
old constraints disappear or are overcome (e.g., through learning),
while new ones emerge. The solution space undergoes continuous
transformations, shrinking in one direction, expanding in another.
Consequently, the implementer's left hand must be probing constantly the feasibility boundary, while his right hand tries to assemble
the various program components.

This sort of ad hoc, trial-and-error searching for a feasible solution is a far cry from the deliberate procedures suggested by the
planning model. The complicated flowcharts purporting to "structure" the implementation process only show how close implementation analysts of this stripe can come to the same infinite regress that
has plagued all other planners: since there is good and bad implementation (as there is good and bad planning), it is not enough
simply to "implement"; one must choose the *right* implementation
plan. But then, by the same logic, one must know the *right* way to
implement the implementation plan, so that there is no way to tell
where the implied regress ends. In practice, implementing a policy
is a unitary process or procedure, not a tandem operation of setting
a goal and then enforcing the plan that embodies it.

IMPLEMENTATION AS INTERACTION

The second major model in implementation analysis minimizes the
importance of goals and plans. An authoritatively adopted policy is
"only a collection of words" prior to implementation.[4] At most it is
a point of departure for bargaining among implementers. Policy
standards—establishing requirements for how policy goals shall be

3. James M. Landis, *The Administrative Process* (New Haven: Yale University Press, 1966 [1938]), p. 75.
4. Eugene Bardach, "On Designing Implementable Programs," to appear
in *Pitfalls of Analysis*, ed. G. Majone and E. Quade (London and New York:
John Wiley and Sons, 1979).

implemented—"represent no more than exhortations: they are inanimate messages that must be communicated to those in charge of
executing the policy."[5] The more consistent analysts of this school
actually deny any meaning to expressions such as: "the implementation process translates a policy mandate into action"; "implementation realizes policy goals"; or "implementation transforms prescriptions into results." For, as Bardach carefully points out, such
locutions suggest that words can somehow become deeds (he con-
cedes, however, that these "words" can create expectations and
thereby influence behavior).[6]

These analysts correctly sense that a yet-to-be implemented policy
and an implemented one do not belong to the same logical category,
but their words/deeds dichotomy is too crude, in our opinion, to be
useful analytically. This dichotomy implies, among other things, that
in success or failure, implementation is completely divorced from
policy success or failure. The process is the purpose. The next logical
step, which in fact has been taken by some writers, is to assert that
the central problem of implementation is not whether implementers
conform to prescribed policy, but whether the implementation process results in consensus on goals, individual autonomy, and commitment to policy on the part of those who must carry it out. But
these problems are pervasive; they are not the product of functional
distinctions among different groups of actors in a policy problem.

At a deeper level, we disagree with the idea that the function of
the implementation process is to satisfy the psychological and social
needs of the participants, regardless of the actual policy results. This
view is strangely reminiscent of old syndicalist doctrines summarized
in once-popular slogans like "The Railroads to the Railroadmen,"
and "The Mines to the Miners." The syndicalists' demand for "industrial democracy" actually concealed a view of production as an
end in itself rather than as a means of satisfying consumers' wants.
We feel the emphasis on consensus, bargaining, and political maneu-
vering can easily lead (and has, in fact, led) to the conception that
implementation is its own reward.

The interaction model of implementation carries interesting evo-

5. Carl E. Van Horn and Donald S. Van Meter, "The Implementation of
Intergovernmental Policy," now in *Policy Studies Review Annual*, vol. 1, ed.
Stuart S. Nagel (Beverly Hills and London: Sage Publications, 1977), p. 108.
6. Bardach, "On Designing Implementable Programs."

lutionary overtones. The results are not predictable, an element of surprise is maintained, and the outcomes are likely to be different from those sought by any single participant. Does an evolutionary conception of implementation imply that any path, any product of a number of active forces, is appropriate so that, as Hegel said, the real is right? Certainly not, but that is the impression one often gets from the writings of advocates of the interaction model. The model is inadequate for assessing the intrinsic worth of policy ideas and their significance for policy evolution. Hence, interpretations based on it are, at best, partial. Consider, for example, the "capture theory" of governmental regulation in the United States. The theory holds that regulatory commissions inevitably become captured by the interests—truckers, airlines, drug companies—they are supposed to regulate because these are the forces that care most about what the commissions do. With the understanding that this capture may ebb and flow according to the political seasons, this scenario appears to be a reasonable description of reality. However, the economic critique of regulation is more parsimonious and, at the same time, more fundamental. For the economist argues that the policy idea is defective at its roots: compared to market adjustments, government regulations are inevitably ill-informed, slow to respond, and detrimental to consumers because they reduce competition. Explaining policy failure in terms of the quality of the policy idea seems to work at least as well as explaining it in terms of social forces capturing and corrupting the implementation process.

POLICIES AS DISPOSITIONS

Having rejected the idea of reifying goals and programs (policies do not grow from small but true replicas of their mature form) as well as the idea of reducing them to mere "words" (evolution presupposes a genetic basis), it is appropriate for us to propose an alternative viewpoint.

We begin by observing that the essential constituents of any policy are objectives and resources. In most policies of interest, objectives are characteristically multiple (because we want many things, not just one), conflicting (because we want different things), and vague (because that is how we can agree to proceed without having to agree also on exactly what to do). So if the objectives are not uniquely determined, neither are the modes of implementation for them.

Because of cognitive limitations and the dynamic quality of our environment, moreover, there is no way for us to understand at first all the relevant constraints on resources. We can discover and then incorporate them into our plans only as the implementation process unfolds. As long as we cannot determine what is feasible, we cannot carry out any well-defined policy univocally; all we can do is carry along a cluster of potential policies. Implementation begins neither with words nor deeds, but with multiple dispositions to act or to treat certain situations in certain ways.

Plans, programs, judicial decisions, and administrative regulations may be evaluated as specific occurrences or results by the legislative draftsman, the lawyer, the administrative expert, or the historian. As far as the implementation analyst is concerned, these exist only as potentialities, and their realization depends both on intrinsic qualities and on external circumstances. If we want to think of a plan as a tool in the hands of the implementer, we must bear in mind that even a tool is only a cluster of dispositions. To say that something is a tool is to say that it can produce certain results under appropriate circumstances; it is not to say that it is drilling, sawing, or welding at any particular moment.

Now Webster's definition of disposition ("the tendency of something to act in a certain manner under given circumstances") obscures the important point that many dispositions—and certainly those relevant to the present discussion—are generic rather than specific. They do not find expression in a unique function or activity, and it may even be impossible to determine, a priori, the specific forms in which they will be realized. Even a highly specialized tool can be employed for uses other than the normal ones: *faute de mieux*, one can hit a nail with a shoe or with a fat dictionary. Dispositional terms like "skillful," "intelligent," "fair," "knowledgeable" (and their opposites) imply wide ranges of possible actions and types of behavior rather than tendencies toward, or capabilities of, specific achievements.

Policies grow out of ideas, and ideas are inexhaustible. What can be done with them depends as much on their intrinsic richness as on the quality of the minds and the nature of their environment. As problems are truly understood only after they have been solved, so the full implications of an idea can often be seen only from hindsight, only after the idea has been used and adapted to a variety of circumstances. Hence the beginnings of an idea are, generally speaking, an insufficient measure of its capabilities or its scope. Any new idea, Cardinal Newman once observed, has unknown amplitude:

It will, in proportion of its native vigour and subtlety, introduce itself into the framework and details of social life, changing public opinion and supporting or undermining the foundations of established order. Thus in time it has grown into an ethical code, or into a system of government, or into a theology, or into a ritual, according to its capabilities; and this system, or body of thought, theoretical and practical . . . will after all be only the adequate representation of the original idea, *being nothing else than what that very idea meant from the first—its exact image as seen in a combination of the most diversified aspects, with the suggestions and corrections of many minds, and the illustration of many trials.*[7]

Is the policy idea, then, what it was or what it became or what it might have been? And how do we credit the contributions of those "many minds" and "many trials?"

IMPLEMENTATION SHAPES POLICY

Policies are continuously transformed by implementing actions that simultaneously alter resources and objectives. Varying the amount of resources need not require doing more or less of the same thing: one might do quite different things with $1 million than if one had $10 million. Altering objectives may change the significance of behaviors that are seemingly the same. Suppose the actual purpose of a system of effluent charges gradually shifts from pollution control to raising general revenue. The fiscal and administrative mechanisms may remain the same, but the policy would change significantly. When social security changes from insurance to income redistribution, the same name covers very different realities.

Which objectives are to be implemented, in what order, with what proportion of available resources? Constraints are also objectives. There is no such thing as "the objective"—reducing poverty or improving health. There are always constraints as to time allowed,

7. John Henry Newman, *An Essay on the Development of Christian Doctrine* (Harmondsworth, Middlesex, England: Penguin Books Ltd., 1974 [1845]), pp. 98–99; our italics.

money permitted, procedures allowable, liberties held inviolable, and so on. That we focus our attention on a particular one, singling it out as our objective, does not mean there are not others within which we must also operate or, at least, find ways to relax or overcome. Knowing only the avowed programmatic objective without being aware of other constraints is insufficient for predicting or controlling outcomes. When we are able to confront the multiplicity of objectives and constraints—so little inflation versus so much unemployment—or to observe the juggling acts of ill-fated commissions on national goals, in which the early objectives are likely to catch the worm of scarce resources, then the necessity to continuously readjust the means and ends becomes evident.

The goal of the British National Health Service Act of 1946 was the "improvement in the physical and mental health of the people of England and Wales, and the prevention, diagnosis, and treatment of illness." "The services so provided," the Act continues, "shall be free of charge, except where provision of this act expressly provides for the making and recovery of charges." But how is the government to provide, at no cost to users, services whose demand elasticity is on the average quite high, and whose costs keep rapidly rising? No independent economist or government adviser seems to have raised this question at the time the National Health Service was created. Instead, the advocates of the new system relied on three implicit assumptions: (1) that health needs could be determined on the basis of purely medical criteria; (2) that it was possible to meet those needs without placing too heavy a burden on the national resources; and (3) that by reducing ill health, the Service would contribute to increased production, and would in fact become "a wealth-producing as well as health-producing Service."

Experience has shown that the first two assumptions were incorrect, and the third one is still highly doubtful.[8] The costs of the Service soon proved much higher than initial estimates. It became necessary to introduce charges for drug prescriptions, dentures, spectacles, replacement of surgical appliances and equipment, and for hospital treatment following road accidents. Because the prevailing ideology has prevented the development of a coherent system for rationing medical services, unplanned rationing took place, resulting

8. Walter Hagenbuch, *Social Economics* (Cambridge: Cambridge University Press, 1958), pp. 282–283.

in congestion, and, in the opinion of many observers, a decrease in quality of services. Since available resources were not even sufficient to meet current demands, very little investment in new facilities was possible, and the goal of prevention kept receding into the distant future. In sum, the goals of the National Health Service had to be adjusted and readjusted as the impossibility of efficiently providing "free" services with high elasticity of demand became increasingly clear.

Conversely, the discovery that some constraints are no longer binding can suggest to implementers possibilities that the original planners did not envisage or desire. Significant developments in social security in the United States since 1935 (in particular, the repeated extensions of coverage to new groups) appear to be due not only to political pressures, but even more to organizational breakthroughs in data collection and information handling.[9]

How well policies respond to opportunities, how well they facilitate adaptation and error correction, are qualities insufficiently discussed. For our purposes, however, it is more important to observe that keeping things going rather than getting things started is the ordinary condition of administration. It is not policy design but redesign that occurs most of the time. Who is to say, then, whether implementation consists of altering objectives to correspond with available resources (as social welfare spending decreases, inflation increases), or of mobilizing new resources to accomplish old objectives (as the United States buys foreign currencies to defend the dollar)? Indeed, old patterns of behavior are often retrospectively rationalized to fit new notions about appropriate objectives. We do not always decide what to do and succeed or fail at it; rather, we observe what we have done and try to make it consistent in retrospect.[10] If Head Start finds it difficult to demonstrate lasting improvement in children's reading abilities, it may stress its clear capacity for increasing parents' involvement, which in turn may lead to educational improvement in their children. We choose after the act as well as before. For example, policymakers often come to certain conclusions under the pressure

9. Eveline Burns, *Social Security and Public Policy* (New York: McGraw-Hill, 1956).

10. Karl Weick, *The Social Psychology of Organizing* (Reading, Mass.: Addison-Wesley Publishing Co., 1969); and Aaron Wildavsky, *Speaking Truth to Power: The Art and Craft of Policy Analysis* (Boston: Little, Brown, 1979).

of events, or previous commitments, or the force of their own convictions. A policy may come into being still lacking a doctrine capable of explaining it, and yet gaining support and finding an ecological niche in a crowded policy space. Though they have seldom been discussed, such late doctrinal developments are part of the implementation process and exert a considerable influence on policy evolution.

BUT DOES POLICY SHAPE IMPLEMENTATION?

Biologists tell us that embryonic tissue of the fruitfly *Drosophila* is capable of developing into a wing, a leg, or an antenna, according to the influences brought to bear on it. Also, the tissues of the flank of a newt are capable of developing into a leg, but it would be impossible to induce a fish to develop a leg, or a horse to develop a wing. Whereas policies can assume marvelous new forms during implementation, in order to understand policy evolution (or indeed any type of evolution), it is as important to understand what cannot happen as what can.

Although the literature is rich in examples of implementation failures (or, at least, of outcomes that do not meet certain standards, though they may be considered functional on other grounds), implementation monsters—policy outcomes bearing no recognizable relationship to the original idea—seem to be rare. As Bardach writes, most participants in the implementation process "act within a context of expectations that *something will happen* that bears at least a passing resemblance to whatever was mandated by the initial policy decision."[11] This expectation, it seems to us, is precisely what needs to be explained. Why is it reasonable to assume that the final results will be genetically related, however indirectly, to the original policy idea? And why does implementing policy decisions appear to be so much more problematic in some areas than in others?

In discussing the "capture theory" of governmental regulation we have already pointed out that some implementation failures can be explained satisfactorily by inadequacies in the theory. This suggests that such objective properties of a policy as its substantive content and its theory ought to be included among the variables used to ex-

11. Eugene Bardach, *The Implementation Game* (Cambridge: MIT Press, 1977), p. 50.

plain implementation results. We would argue, for example, that the difficulties of implementing federal pollution control programs cannot be ascribed only to the destabilizing effects of the federal intrusion into a delicately balanced political situation,[12] but must also be related to the technical and scientific inadequacies of current environmental policies. Enforcement would be easier if more were known about the health and other effects of pollution and about methods of controlling particular types of pollutants. Environmental standards, for instance, could be based on generally accepted scientific evidence. In a situation in which controversy over questions of fact was greatly reduced, conflicting interests would probably prefer to fight their battles during the policy adoption stage rather than during implementation. Similarly, the implementation of innovative educational policies is much more difficult because of a widespread lack of confidence in the underlying cognitive theories.

Some of the ways in which policy affects implementation are fairly obvious. Policy content shapes implementation by defining the arena in which the process takes place, the identity and role of the principal actors, the range of permissible tools for action, and of course by supplying resources. The underlying theory provides not only the data, information, and hypotheses on which subsequent debate and action will rely, but also, and most importantly, a conceptualization of the policy problem. For instance, the mode of implementing a large-scale program of multiphasic health screening (MHS) would depend significantly on which of two alternative philosophies of MHS were adopted: MHS can be seen merely as a multiple screening program, or as the basis of an alternative method of delivering primary care, one in which prevention is considered an important factor.

Is the empirical evidence supplied by the growing number of case studies sufficient to indicate systematic relationships between different policy characteristics and classes of implementation problems? Although we can do little more than open up the question at present, this seems to be one of the most promising approaches to the study of implementation. Armed with such knowledge, the analyst would be able to work out the set, large but not unbounded, of possible policy developments.

12. J. Clarence Davies, 3rd and Barbara S. Davies, *The Politics of Pollution*, 2nd ed. (Indianapolis: Pegasus, 1975).

EVOLUTIONARY IMPLEMENTATION

In the interaction model, implementation is the continuation of politics by other means. According to the planning model, implementation is an extension of organizational design. To say that implementation should be part of design is to suggest that policy theory be formulated with a view toward its execution. This may mean at least two things: policy relevance—the variables in the theory should be manipulable by those with authority; and the specification of a variety of conditions that might occur, with instructions as to what to do under different circumstances. In view of our limited knowledge, this list would be relatively short and inevitably insufficient. Although it is usual to speak of making authority commensurate with responsibility, it is rare for an official to coerce all others, both because the political system divides authority and because it is costly to use up persuasiveness for this purpose. Additional authority therefore must be acquired along the way without necessarily being able to anticipate objections from all interested actors.

Since administrative discretion can be used as a cover for arbitrary behavior that is unrelated to policy intentions, some authors feel that the problem of administration is, purely and simply, one of controlling discretion. Controlling it how? Unless one is willing to assume that policies spring fully armed from the forehead of an omniscient policymaker, discretion is both inevitable and necessary. Unless administration is programmed—a robot comes to mind—discretion can be controlled only by indirect means. Again, we must rely on learning and invention rather than on instruction and command. In punishing his generals for failing to execute his orders faithfully even when their disobedience brought him victory, Frederick the Great of Prussia was at least consistent. We require the impossible when we expect our bureaucrats to be at the same time literal executors and successful implementers of policy mandates. Something has to be left to chance. In a world of uncertainty, success is only loosely correlated with effort, and chance can never be ruled out as the main cause of either success or failure. To the extent that success *is* related to effort, it depends more on "knowing how" than on "knowing that," on the ability to select appropriate types of behavior and rules of conduct, more than on abstract knowledge of decision rules or on blind obedience to directives.

When problems are puzzles for which unique solutions exist, technicians can take over. But when problems are defined through the process of attempting to draft acceptable solutions, then analysts become creators as well as implementers of policy. "This particular problem may not be solvable," they tell their clients, "but how about substituting one that can be solved?" In other words, if problems are best understood through solutions, then implementation includes not only finding answers, but also framing questions. Reformulating problems means changing solutions. Policy ideas in the abstract (assuming only minimal logical coherence) are subject to an infinite variety of contingencies, and they contain worlds of possible practical applications. What is in them depends on what is in us, and vice versa. They have no resting point, no final realization; they are endlessly evolving. How then, and why then, separate analytically what life refuses to tear apart?

Reducing, bounding, limiting contingencies is the analytic function. Discovering the constraints under which policy ideas may be expected to operate—applying negative knowledge, if you will—is the main task of analysis. Fixed prescriptions—"knowing that"—give way to "knowing how"—adopting the right rule at the right moment as events unfold, in order to bring out one potential result over many others. Knowing how is a craft, not a science.

How effectively can implementation bring out one rather than another range of results? The more general an idea and the more adaptable it is to a range of circumstances, the more likely it is to be realized in some form, but the less likely it is to emerge as intended in practice. The more restricted the idea, and the more it is constrained, the more likely it is to emerge as predicted, but the less likely it is to have a significant impact. At one extreme we have the ideal type of the perfectly preformed policy idea; it only requires execution, and the only problems it raises are those of control. At the other extreme, the policy idea is only an expression of basic principles and aspirations, a matter for philosophical reflection and political debate. In between, where we live, is a set of more or less developed potentialities embedded in pieces of legislation, court decisions, and bureaucratic plans. This land of potentiality we claim as the territory of implementation analysis.

Implementation is evolution. Since it takes place in a world we never made, we are usually right in the middle of the process, with events having occurred before and (we hope) continuing afterward. At each point we must cope with new circumstances that allow us to actualize different potentials in whatever policy ideas we are implementing. When we act to implement a policy, we change it. When we vary the amount or type of resource inputs, we also intend to alter outputs, even if only to put them back on the track where they were once supposed to be. In this way, the policy theory is transformed to produce different results. As we learn from experience what is feasible or preferable, we correct errors. To the degree that these corrections make a difference at all, they change our policy ideas as well as the policy outcomes, because the idea is embodied in the action.

EVALUATING IMPLEMENTATION

In the world of what Herbert Simon calls programmed decisions—a world in which objectives are known, agreed upon, and singular, so that all that remains is to make the required calculations—people supposedly know how to distinguish the quality of an implementation from the quality of a decision. The four possibilities can be represented in tabular form:

Implementation in a Preprogrammed World

	Decision	
	Good	Bad
Execution — Good	1. No problem (too good to be true)	3. The policy problem
Execution — Bad	2. The control problem	4. No problem (or: how two bads = one good)

If both the decision and the execution are good (#1), then evidently there is no problem; if both are bad (#4), then we can only be grateful that poor decisions are made ineffective by worse actions. If the decision is good but the execution is bad (#2), then the problem can only be one of control (ineptitude, laziness, or whatever) in connecting premises to conclusions. Here the implementation problem is indistinguishable from the control problem. If implementation is good but the decision is bad (because the result is suboptimal or even infeasible) (#3), then there is, in this preprogrammed world, nothing the implementer can do about it. Since decision is the only active element, the only place to go is back to the drawing board.

Outside the static world of programmed decisions, "good" and "bad" take on multiple meanings. In an evolutionary context "good" means "faithful," but interestingly enough, it might also mean "faithless." A faithful translation of an ill-formed policy idea or theory would bring into being all the inconsistencies, inadequacies, and/or unfortunate consequences inherent in the pristine conception. A faithless interpretation would straighten out logical defects and/or alter elements so that the consequences were more desirable than those in the original plan. But immediately an objection springs to mind: this is not the original policy idea at all, but a new one transformed into something quite different. Quite right! If the implementation were faithful, then an imperfect idea would have been nursed along only to produce unsatisfactory effects. Evidently then, if imperfect policy ideas can be compatible with good implementation, it must be possible for implementation to alter policy. Indeed, if all activity is composed entirely of behaviors that incorporate inseparable ideas and actions, then any change in implementation must bring about a change in policy.

Consider government subsidies for medical care, such as Medicaid for the poor. The policy is designed to increase access to medical services for the poor by reducing the cost to them, but it is also designed to raise the quality of service without raising the cost of care for others. In practice, however, since the medical system absorbs all monies, the entry of additional funds paid essentially on a cost plus basis has raised the price of medical care for everyone. Equal access, higher quality, and lower cost seem to be incompatible. What are we to do? The conflict between cost and quality is most acute in the hospital sector, where prices have been rising at a phenomenal rate. Government could try to specify allowable treatment for all ailments, ruling out more expensive methods and monitoring each individual transaction. Access to care would still be independent from the patient's ability to pay, but the problem of administrative calculation would be virtually insuperable. Or government could work out a formula to give each hospital a lump sum which it could allocate among services and patients. Calculations might become manageable, costs might be contained, but quality and equality would probably suffer because it would be no longer possible to mandate the precise services that had to be performed for each potential patient. Or government might give poor people a direct subsidy, a medical voucher, allowing them to buy services up to a specified level. Cost containment would be more certain but the chances for equal access and high quality would fall.

Clearly, none of the available alternatives meets all the criteria for the original policy. Any change in implementation—lump sums to hospitals or vouchers to patients—changes what the policy does, alters the mix of values, and shifts the relationships among quality, cost, and access. How then should we evaluate the implementation of this policy?

Or how should we evaluate the implementation of the British National Health Service Act? Is this a case of implementation failure (because no efficient system of rationing was used), of policy failure (because the theory proved inadequate), or no failure at all (since, as a British economist puts it, "there is now a consensus among all segments of British society and among all shades of political opinion that health should be distributed in accordance with need rather than ability-to-pay, in other words 'Communism in health' ").[13]

Is what has been said of successful scientific theories also true of policies, that they never prove to be "right," but only gain increasing acceptance? One cannot discount the possibility that successful implementation may be made possible only by a lowering of standards, a reformulation of evaluative criteria, or a shift in viewpoints (from the goals of the U.S. Office of Education or of federal granting agencies to those of local school districts and states receiving grants-in-aid).

Faithful implementation is not a vacuous notion: it may be tested in several different ways. But there is no need to feel guilty about failing to carry out a mandate inherent in a policy in a literal way, because literal implementation is literally impossible. Unless a policy matter is narrow and uninteresting (i.e., preprogrammed), the policy will never be able to contain its own consequences. Implementation

13. Mark Blaugh, *Economics of Education* (Harmondsworth, Middlesex, England: Penguin Books Ltd., 1972), p. 324.

will always be evolutionary; it will inevitably reformulate as well as carry out policy. Perhaps implementation angers as well as intrigues us because, after the deeds have been done, we wish that implementation had been cowardly or courageous, killing off the idea or making it successful, so that either way, without specifying which way in advance, the blame would not be ours.

Implementation is worth studying precisely because it is a struggle over the realization of ideas. It is the analytical equivalent of original sin; there is no escape from implementation and its attendant responsibilities. What has policy wrought? Having tasted of the fruit of the tree of knowledge, the implementer can only answer, and with conviction, it depends. . . .

9

What Should Evaluation
Mean to Implementation? *(1983)*

ANGELA BROWNE AND AARON WILDAVSKY

Evaluation research is a robust area of activity devoted to collecting, analyzing, and interpreting information on the need for, implementation of, and impact of intervention efforts to better the lot of humankind by improving social conditions and community life.[1]

Most everyone who writes on the subject of evaluation is tempted to invent their own labels and to offer a personal conceptualization of this activity. This intellectual ferment may be attributed to the fact that evaluation is a rapidly growing branch of social research. This growth began in the mid-sixties, fed by the vast infusion of federal funds for evaluating social programs of the Great Society. Disappointment with the results of these programs has led evaluators to extend their reach to cover the various theoretical perspectives and the sources of error in practice they soon discover.

But in order for evaluation to be effective in its expanding domain—to be of use during implementation—it must be aimed at generating data that can be used to improve the implementation

---

1. Peter Rossi and Howard Freeman, quoted in Dennis J. Palumbo and David Nachmias, "The Pre-Conditions for Successful Evaluation: Is There an Ideal-Type?," paper prepared for presentation at the International Political Science Association Meetings, Rio de Janeiro, Brazil, August 9–14, 1982, p. 5; subsequently published in *Policy Sciences* 16 (1983):67–79.

process. Evaluation must also allow future implementation processes (and their designers, organizations, operators, and critics) to learn from errors. Because implementation is always occurring, evaluators, having extended their reach to this arena, can contribute to a continuing refinement in comprehension of why programs and policies do or do not work. Implementers can help them do so by understanding the differences between the various forms that evaluation takes.

In asking "What should evaluation mean to implementation," this chapter looks both at the separation of implementation and evaluation and at the connections that do exist between them. Having infringed on the tasks of implementers, evaluators also take over their problems—which involves reconciling knowledge with power.

EVALUATION AS IMPLEMENTATION

According to Dennis J. Palumbo and David Nachmias:

> The field of evaluation is undergoing an identity crisis. From its initial surge in the 1960s when evaluation research clearly was dominated by a single methodology and evaluation researchers believed that its potential was unlimited, it has undergone a metamorphosis. Rather than a single orientation, a number of alternative approaches to evaluation have sprung up and a nagging doubt about its future has crept into a number of recent publications.[2]

Ernest House writes that "the current evaluation scene is marked by vitality and disorder. The scale, ubiquity, and diversity of evaluation activities make comprehension difficult, even for those operating within the field."[3] Yet,

> it has not always been this way. During the 1960s and early 1970s the ideal type of evaluation research that was conducted then . . . was aimed at determining whether goals were being achieved; it was not much concerned with the relationship between the evaluator and program manager; and it optimistically believed that evaluations would automatically be used to improve the socio-political processes. Today there is considerable doubt about all of these things.[4]

It is the plunge into the cold bath of implementation that has given evaluation the chills.

2. Ibid., p. 1.
3. Quoted in ibid., p. 1.
4. Ibid.

The main trend in evaluation research, Howard E. Freeman and Marian A. Solomon say, is its emphasis on relevance. This trend manifests itself by an interest in utilization of evaluation. Programs should be designed "to build a shared understanding and, if possible, to achieve consensus on evaluation requirements and strategies to maximize the applicability of results and increase the likelihood of program improvement."[5] This trend toward utilization (read implementation) is the same one that Daniel Mazmanian and Paul Sabatier posit as their preferred direction for implementation studies.[6] Yet the closer evaluators come to program managers, the greater the temptation of evaluators to fudge the results.[7] Indeed, the disappointment with lack of utilization has led some analysts to argue in favor of a political model in which evaluators take a partisan stance, marshaling evidence in favor of the policies they are asked to evaluate. Since evaluation inevitably turns up negative aspects of programs, Palumbo and Nachmias believe its results will be rejected. "Thus," they conclude, "it is not possible for the evaluator to be independent or engage in scientific 'objectivity.' " Needless to say, such severe criticism from within the evaluation community is bound to be contested.

The failure to implement evaluation, that is, to utilize its results, has led to challenges to prevailing assumptions. This line of thought and action is made brutally clear by Palumbo and Nachmias:

> Most evaluations that are done today assume that decision makers analyze the situation first, then act; the assumption is that decision makers, *before they act*, identify goals, specify alternative ways of getting there, assess the alternatives against a standard such as costs and benefits, and then select the best alternative (the rational model). But if organizations in fact do the opposite—if they act first and then analyze what they did—then evaluations based on the rational paradigm will be out of resonance. . . . Rationalistic evaluations are likely to miss the mark because organizations (decision makers, individuals in organizations) are not looking for the one best way or most efficient alternative for solving a problem. They are instead searching for sup-

5. Howard E. Freeman and Marian A. Solomon, "Evaluation and the Uncertain '80s," *Evaluation Studies Review Annual* 6 (1981):1–23.

6. See chapter 10, "Implementation as Mutual Adaptation," of this volume. See also Daniel Mazmanian and Paul A. Sabatier, *Implementation and Public Policy* (Palo Alto, Calif.: Scott, Foresman, 1983).

7. Aaron Wildavsky, "The Self-Evaluating Organization," *Public Administration Review* 32 (September/October 1972):509–20.

port for action already taken, and for support that serves the interest of various components of the policy shaping community (Walker, 1981). Evaluations, therefore, should *not* seek 'objective truth,' but attempt to discover what societal needs have been met by the action that has been taken. They should *not* attempt to see if policy goals have been achieved because . . . they cannot do this; instead, they should determine which stakeholders' interests are served by organizational action.[8]

The substitution of partisan analysis for enlightenment as the primary function of evaluation is bound to be controversial.

Contact with implementation has spread the utilization virus. Are evaluators to become poor politicians, then, abandoning the concern for error that made them methodologically rigorous and politically neutral,[9] or can they make use of their newly found organizational sophistication to improve their work without sacrificing its quality?

AN IMPLEMENTER'S GUIDE TO THE CHARACTERISTICS OF EVALUATION

Concern over the dollar volume of expenditures on evaluation and related services has been intensified by suspicion that evaluation research has a low level of utility. Three common criticisms of evaluation are:

(1) Weak methodology.—Validity and credibility are endangered by problems of proper procedure.

(2) Irrelevance.—Research findings either lack timeliness or would not, in any event, make a difference to decision making.

(3) Underutilization.—The resulting information is not disseminated or, if received, is not used.[10]

---

8. Palumbo and Nachmias, "Pre-Conditions for Successful Evaluation," pp. 9–11.

9. And, can they do this without impeding implementation? Negative evaluations that are incorrect can cause good programs to be terminated, or they can create unfavorable public opinion. Slow evaluations can impede implementation of decisions based on awaited findings. Thomas Cook, "Book Reviews," *Knowledge* 4 (March 1983): 463–65.

10. Freeman and Solomon, "Evaluation and the Uncertain '80s," p. 16. On dissemination, see Jack Knott and Aaron Wildavsky, "If Dissemination Is the Solution, What Is the Problem?," *Knowledge* (June 1980):537–78. See also Carol H. Weiss and Michael J. Bucuvalas, "Truth Tests and Utility Tests: Decision-Makers' Frames of Reference for Social Science Research," *American Sociological Review* 45 (April 1980):302–13.

Though evaluation is undoubtedly, as Carol Weiss terms it, a "growth enterprise," it is growing not only in size but in scope, threatening to become coterminous with policy analysis itself.[11] This conceptual imperialism, we believe, is grounded in the desire to produce perfect policy. As soon as a major category of policy defects is uncovered, recommendations are made to improve the evaluation process. Soon enough the purview of the evaluator becomes so broad (does the expert's desire for power and professionalization lurk here?) that it is difficult to say what evaluation is not.[12]

Let us begin by trying to say what evaluation *is*. Peter Rossi and Richard Berk provide a broad description, which includes evaluation as policy analysis during implementation:

> Evaluation research may be conducted to answer questions that arise during the formulation of policy, in the design of programs, in the improvement of programs, and in testing the efficiency and effectiveness of programs that are in place or being considered. Specific policy questions may be concerned with how widespread a social problem may be, whether any program can be enacted that will ameliorate a problem, whether programs are effective, whether a program is producing enough benefits to justify its cost, and so on.[13]

As evaluative activity increases, it strives to develop a clear identity separate from that of merely a stage in policy formulation. This distinct identity may be enhanced by considering evaluators' answers to five basic questions about their craft, with an emphasis on the last two questions:

(1) When?

(2) Where?

(3) For whom?

(4) What?

(5) Why?

11. Carol Weiss, *Evaluation Research* (Englewood Cliffs, N.J.: Prentice Hall, 1972), p. 34.

12. William Meyers refers to the "entrepreneurial willingness" to accept evaluation contracts "bearing little relationship to . . . previous competence" of social research firms. William R. Meyers, *The Evaluation Enterprise* (San Francisco: Jossey-Bass, 1981), pp. 43–44.

13. Peter H. Rossi and Richard A. Berk, "An Overview of Evaluation Strategies and Procedures," *Human Organizations* 40 (1981):287.

WHEN?

Evaluation can occur at any time. It may be "retrospective," a characterization that many definitions of evaluation prefer,[14] inquiring into how well a program has done in the past, or "prospective," considering how a program is likely to do in the future. If it continues during a program, it is "formative." If it is both formative and retrospective, then it is "ongoing." When it occurs before and after a treatment is administered, it is "integrative."[15]

The evaluative questions asked will vary according to time phase. The emphasis on outcome measures, selection of investigative methods, and even the purpose of an evaluation will be affected by its timing.

Retrospective and prospective evaluation.—Retrospective evaluation, depending as it does on history, cannot be accomplished without efforts to implement the program in question. So we can say that without implementation there can be no retrospective evaluation. Only prospective evaluation can conceivably occur without a prior record of implementation. We doubt whether it is helpful to designate as evaluation the analysis of a program without a past, that is, without consequences to evaluate.

Continuous evaluation.—Evaluation can occur once or continuously, by a single study or by many. A "continuous evaluation" is performed "proactively to help improve a program as well as retroactively to judge its worth."[16] At its best evaluation is "a social procedure that is the cumulative result of many efforts rather than just one."[17] The effects of purposive evaluative behavior can be additive, resulting in continuing advances in the perceptual capacities

14. In 1976, the Symposium on the Use of Evaluation by Federal Agencies reached a consensus on the definition of evaluation that included the stipulation that evaluation be retrospective. Eleanor Chelimsky, *An Analysis of the Proceedings of a Symposium on the Use of Evaluation by Federal Agencies*, vol. 2, November 17–19, 1976 (MacLean, Va.: Metrek, 1977), p. 5.

15. William N. Dunn, *Public Policy Analysis: An Introduction* (Englewood Cliffs, N.J.: Prentice-Hall, 1981), pp. 51–61, 358.

16. Daniel L. Stufflebeam and William J. Webster, "An Analysis of Alternative Approaches to Evaluation," *Evaluation Studies Review Annual* 6 (1981):70–85.

17. Aaron Wildavsky, *Speaking Truth to Power: The Art and Craft of Policy Analysis* (Boston: Little, Brown, 1979), p. 7.

of actors in the policy process. Perhaps this was an underlying intention of the recently proposed "Master Plan for Services to California's Children and Youth," which noted that program objectives "often are not clearly stated, measurable, or agreed upon, which makes it difficult to accurately evaluate their degree of accomplishment," and that "these programs do not operate in isolation of other children services and social and economic events." This predicament generates "a need to develop mechanisms to accurately and continuously measure and evaluate the quality of children services. Evaluation is necessary to determining the redirection of funds and for decision making regarding future program development."[18] Thus evaluation becomes a generic activity aiming at enlightenment.

Continuous evaluation is an attempt to generate perpetual feedback. "Responsive evaluation" is one through which evaluators learn about their clients' perceived needs for information.[19] Since client behavior is part of the process of implementation, information about the perceptions in terms of which they act is essential.

WHERE?

As evaluators descend from the general, formal, and national locus to the specific, less formal, and local setting, they intervene in the system of information generation at increasingly lower levels, which affects the nature of their evaluations. Structure and formality increase at higher levels of bureaucracy and organization. Rules are written, studies are planned, meetings are held. At local levels, evaluation may be managed by "peak associations," such as leagues of cities, or not done at all, except informally.

There are organizations especially devoted to evaluation. These range from units within government, such as the General Accounting Office, to not-for-profits, like the Council on Municipal Performance, to private-for-profits, like the big management consultants or the famous "beltway bandits" that ring the nation's capital. Independence, objectivity, and capability vary across and within all

18. Office of Statewide Health Planning, State of California, "Proposed Master Plan for Children and Youth: Executive Summary," Public Hearing Draft (Sacramento, 1980), p. 14.

19. Robert A. Stake, *Evaluating the Arts in Education: A Responsive Approach* (Columbus, Ohio: Charles E. Merrill, 1975).

these categories. The perspectives from which they do their work vary with their clientele, as we can see by looking at exactly for whom the evaluation is being performed.

FOR WHOM?

Evaluators are naturally obligated to their sources of funding; they must address their employer's or sponsor's evaluative concerns. However pressing and clearly defined these concerns, evaluators may perceive the existence of other interested parties. There are numerous stakeholders in the delivery of a publicly funded social service. Among them may be the recipients of the service, the sociopolitical groups within the community in which the service is delivered, the congressmen who voted to fund this service, the political party with which the related policy is identified. Additional stakeholders who are responsible for the implementation of this service delivery program include overseeing agencies of government, administrators, managers at the local level, and first-line service workers. If the service is contracted, the provider may have an added interest in the findings of an evaluation about its activities.

Multiple perspective evaluation.—The recognition of multiple stakeholders may have a liberating effect on the otherwise constrained evaluative focus. Perceptions of program goals and underlying values may expand. "The focus, use and power of evaluation will vary, then," Michael Patton concludes, "depending on who is identified as the relevant decisionmaker(s) and information user(s)."[20] The sponsoring client's need for information is frequently distorted by the push and pull of the multiple stakeholders' interests in the outcome. And whether there are multiple and conflicting stakeholders or a single unified stakeholder in the evaluative process, there always remains the possible discrepancy between the values of the employer and those of the evaluator.

WHAT?

When evaluative energy is expended without a primary motivation to analyze, the scope of the study is narrowed by omitting policy implications from among the research questions. The research ques-

20. Michael Quinn Patton, *Utilization-Focused Evaluation* (Beverly Hills, Calif.: Sage Publications, 1978), p. 145.

tions address the efficiency of selected processes,[21] but generally they do not focus on the relationship between these processes of implementation and their implications for future policy change.[22]

Pseudo-evaluation.—Certain forms of evaluation purport to study both process and outcome but do not actually do so. William N. Dunn labels studies that employ evaluative techniques but do not evaluate outcomes as "pseudo-evaluations."[23] In their delineation of thirteen forms of evaluation in education, Daniel L. Stufflebeam and William J. Webster describe two forms of pseudo-evaluation, both "politically oriented." A "politically controlled study" is initiated by a client who must defend or maintain his "sphere of influence." A second form of pseudo-evaluation, consisting of a "public relations inspired study," is based on a "propagandist's information needs" for data that construes a positive image of a policy or program.[24] Other pseudo-evaluations are merely innocuous assessments that do not ask questions relevant to policy.

Quasi-evaluation.—In between process and outcome lies what is called "quasi-evaluation." This "question-oriented" evaluation begins with a query, such as, "How many people does this program serve?" or "How can we be certain it is serving them?" Techniques are employed to answer these questions. Questions designed to generate information about outcomes (i.e., how did these outcomes occur, and what is the distribution of valued outcomes among the population?) are not given priority. The quasi-evaluative "focus . . . is too narrow or is only tangential to the questions of worth."[25] Variables that might affect implementation are ignored.

Accountability studies and standardized testing programs are common quasi-evaluations. Standardized tests have been widely used since the 1930s to evaluate the quality of education. Performance

21. See Howard E. Freeman, "Boundaries of the Evaluation Research Field," *Evaluation Studies Review Annual* 2 (1977): 25; and Harry P. Matry, Richard E. Winnie, and David M. Fisk, *Practical Program Evaluation for State and Local Governments* (Washington, D.C.: Urban Institute, 1981), p. 4.

22. For analysis of the differences between outputs, outcomes, and inputs, see Frank Levy, Arnold Meltsner, and Aaron Wildavsky, *Urban Outcomes* (Berkeley and Los Angeles: University of California Press, 1973).

23. Dunn, *Public Policy Analysis*, p. 343.

24. Stufflebeam and Webster, "An Analysis of Alternative Approaches to Evaluation," p. 71.

25. Ibid., p. 73.

of individual students is monitored and summed; the teacher's time is accounted for. Now the desire for accountability has spread beyond education. Clients, advocates, taxpayers groups, and opponents of many social programs have created a demand for competing measures of accountability such as process equity and process effectiveness in service delivery.[26] The implementers of social programs are held accountable for their actions, as if their actions guaranteed the desired outcomes. The program is not questioned; its operators must fulfill its specifications, even when these specifications are irrelevant, vague, even counterproductive.[27]

"Objectives-based" quasi-evaluations intend to discover whether or not specific goals are being achieved. Without questioning the desirability of the objectives themselves, the use of experimental designs allows investigators a limited focus on suspected causal relationships.

Goal-fixed evaluation.—As Huey-Tsych Chen and Peter H. Rossi designate it,[28] "Goal-fixed evaluation" is a quasi-evaluation that focuses on expected outcomes. Evaluation is conducted on the basis of "policy-program objectives that have been formally announced."[29] A good example was the Office of Economic Opportunity's use of project evaluation at the local level of federally funded programs: "Very often," R. O. Washington concludes, "this form of evaluation simply compares project results with performance objectives on baseline conditions."[30]

Restriction to formal objectives narrows the focus of evaluation.

26. Sumner J. Hoisington, "Accountability in Social Welfare," *Encyclopedia of Social Work* (National Association of Social Workers, 1977), p. 207.

27. The concept of "accountability" in clinical social work practice (as well as in other fields) is related to several unresolved issues, one of which is whether accountability has increased at all. Some say that a "pseudo-accountability" has developed in response to public and administrative pressures. They allege that quantities of insignificant data are collected in time-consuming and costly ways, with little bearing on the substance of clinical social work. Florence Haselkorn, "Accountability in Clinical Practice," *Social Casework* 59 (June 1978):330–36.

28. Huey-Tsych Chen and Peter Rossi, "Multi-Goal, Theory-Driven Approach to Evaluation: A Model Linking Basic and Applied Social Science," *Evaluation Studies Review Annual* 6 (1981):40–41.

29. Dunn, *Public Policy Analysis*, p. 345.

30. R. O. Washington, *Program Evaluation in the Human Services* (Milwaukee, Wisc.: University of Wisconsin, n.d.), p. 2.

Accreditation-certification studies, for example, specify guidelines for professionals, lay persons, or self-reporting institutions to determine whether an institution is "fit to serve [the] designated functions." Guidelines such as these restrict the outlook of evaluators in any field of study.[31] Consider the evaluator of a suicide prevention hotline. The pre-specified goal of the project may be to prevent anonymous callers from committing suicide. If so, an output measure, such as the number of calls per month, reveals very little about implementation—about potential suicide victims' use of the hotline, the needs of callers, or the hotline's success in meeting these needs.

Fixed-objective evaluations are confined to description—what has or has not happened. Pseudo- or quasi-evaluations either ignore or obscure causality: "What," not "why," is their question. Each of these forms of evaluation serves a purpose, but each is inherently limited in its capacities to produce knowledge relevant to policy implementation: the evaluator may suspect something is wrong but, without knowing why, cannot, on that basis, devise better policies. By contrast, comprehensive evaluations strive to clarify causality by connecting inputs and processes to outcomes.

Comprehensive evaluation.—"Comprehensive evaluation" is the ideal form, Howard Freeman argues, combining analysis of process and of program impacts as they relate to previously specified goals.[32] The synergism of process and impact data in comprehensive evaluation has the potential for an increased understanding of what is happening and why. There are many fields, however, in which it is difficult to identify significant process variables and their relationships to outcomes because the multitude of factors influencing implementation have yet to be delineated. One of these fields is family services. The interactions between a counselor and a client family during a given number of sessions can be represented in terms of total hours, number of times voices were raised, or other quantitative depictions of activity. Yet even when the pre-specified goal seems clear enough—removal of the family's need for family service—the process of achieving this outcome may be obscure. Some of the crucial causal variables may actually exist outside the treatment program (i.e., income level, public health, maturation of family

31. Stufflebeam and Webster, "Analysis of Alternative Approaches to Evaluation," p. 76.
32. Freeman, "Boundaries of the Evaluation Research Field," pp. 26–27.

members, etc.).[33] Comprehensive evaluation is only as comprehensive as the understanding of the process.

Inferential evaluation.—Barclay Hudson tells us that "inferential evaluation" "goes beyond facts to attempt a clarification of cause and affect relationship," asking "was Y caused by X?"[34] Value is not emphasized, but causality is. A program given credit for positive outcomes (families improve their quality of life due to counseling, for example) or receiving criticism for failure (e.g., a crime has not been prevented due to poor policing) may be the benefactor or the victim of poor causal reasoning.

The problem of identifying causality is prominent in the evaluation of group home-treatment programs. To date, Michael Jang and Herbert Hatanaka report, there is only "fragmentary evidence" that "demonstrates the efficacy of programs for particular adolescent problems." Lacking a sound information base, "most group home studies deal with the issue of effectiveness in a roundabout way by first examining salient attributes of these programs and only later inferring their effectiveness in helping the adolescent residents."[35] In an effort to avoid such fallacious inferences, research is designed to "help make explicit the overlay of concepts and judgment that is needed to extract causal inference from inert facts."[36] This identification and separation of causal factors is desirable, if, in fact, it can be accomplished. In inferential evaluation, alternative causes and objectives can be considered. Insight into causality is freed from the confines of a single model. But pre-fixed goals continue to limit the study of outcomes in that the questions remain fixed. "Did X cause Y?" is a good question; even better would be "If not Y, then what did X cause?" or, "If not X, then what caused Y?" The discovery and evaluation of these connections have political overtones.

The objectives of public policy are likely to be multiple, con-

33. John R. Schuerman, "Do Family Services Help?", *Social Services Review* 49 (September 1975):367.

34. Barclay Hudson, "Domains of Evaluation," *Social Policy* 6 (September/October 1975):79–81.

35. Michael Jang and Herbert Hatanaka, "Group Homes for Adolescents: A History, Ideology, and Organizational Analysis," Office of Human Development Services, Grant no. 18–P–0017–9–01 (San Francisco: Institute for Scientific Analysis, 1980), pp. 58–59.

36. Hudson, "Domains of Evaluation," p. 81.

flicting, and vague.[37] The price of agreement among stakeholders is likely to be vagueness, allowing them to fight their battles another day. Policy and program objectives are multiple so as to create a sufficiently broad coalition of support. Contradiction comes in because objectives held by different interest groups (for example, lowest cost per person placed versus finding jobs for the hard-core unemployed; quality versus cost of medical care) may well be opposed. It follows that evaluators may be hard put to discover single, specific, compatible objectives to use as criteria for judging policy. As programs to carry out policy evolve, moreover, the objectives of the stakeholders may change. New information about the workability of programs is gained during their implementation. Unforeseen consequences occur that may accomplish objectives that, while generally considered desirable (say, preschool education helps mobilize parents for community action), were on no one's explicit agenda. Yet the new objectives, new workability issues, and new unanticipated consequences are unlikely to be examined if the evaluation criteria are restricted to formally predetermined goals.

Goal-free evaluation.—The escape from this myopic goal-oriented research design into "goal-free" evaluation is proposed by Michael Scriven, who claims that "consideration and evaluation of goals" is "unnecessary" and that it may "contaminate" the findings. An evaluator should seek out "actual" rather than "alleged effects." The evaluator, in knowing as little as possible about goals and "program rhetoric," will be free of a condition in which the researcher sees exactly that which is being sought.[38]

Whether or not goals are realized, there may be outcomes of a program or policy that do not relate to the original goals. This is a natural result of the "complex web of exchanges" required to formulate and implement a policy "that changes the rules of the game, but not necessarily the interests of the consumers."[39] Students of health and medical policy are particularly aware of perverse consequences.

37. See Wildavsky, *Speaking Truth to Power*, pp. 10–11, 21–25.

38. Michael Scriven, "Prose and Cons About Goal-Free Evaluation," *Evaluation Comment: The Journal of Education Evaluation* 3 (December 1972):1–7.

39. Philip Jacobs, *The Economics of Health and Medical Care* (Baltimore: University Park Press, 1980), p. 250.

Each of the public and private "players" involved in the distribution and consumption of health care have different goals. Public funders may have partisan motives. Private-sector providers are generally profit-oriented. The consumer of a medical service is presumably health-oriented. But the distribution of "health" is not necessarily the actual objective of the funders and suppliers. And the acquisition of "health" by service recipients is not always the outcome of a health-care program. Among the actual effects of the Medicare program, for example, is the growth in health-care expenditures. Whether this results in improved health among the recipients of the service is difficult to say. Suppliers may be responsible for inducing unessential demand, while overlooking cases of actual need. Or medical care may, in large measure, be irrelevant to most health problems.[40] A goal-fixed approach to the evaluation of health programs and policies may overlook competing goals, undesigned consequences, and conflicts in the underlying definitions of health. A goal-free evaluation may escape these confines.

Goal-free evaluation has its share of shortcomings. This creative approach to program evaluation necessarily involves the covert imposition of the evaluator's perspectives and preferences as distinguished from the overt kind involved in acceptance of fixed goals. And it is not geared to unearthing alternative theoretical explanations for outcomes. An evaluator must have some means of selecting from among the infinite range of potential perceptions and effects those which are to be studied. Goal-free evaluation does not specify criteria for such a decision. Evaluators are in a peculiar predicament: "There is no theoretical limit to how they must define the problem to which they apply their skills. The limits are political."[41]

When expected benefits do not occur, programs are considered to be less than effective. In these instances, which are common, it appears that programs cannot bear evaluative scrutiny. Yet closer inspection may reveal weaknesses in the evaluation itself.

Both programs and evaluations of them may be ineffective, Chen and Rossi write, but the actual

---

40. See Aaron Wildavsky, "Doing Better and Feeling Worse: The Political Pathology of Health Policy," *Daedalus* 106 (Winter 1977):105–23.
41. Robert Nakamura, in a letter to Aaron Wildavsky, May 16, 1983.

problem lies in the articulation of research design and program design. Evaluation researchers have not adequately mapped social programs onto the research designs that are used. . . . There is nothing wrong with the formal structure of conventional research paradigms, nor are there necessarily serious defects in the programs. Rather the problem lies in the extent to which programs have been properly interpreted by evaluation researchers.[42]

Implementation may have been successful but ability to evaluate program effectiveness may be lacking. Here we have the evaluator's dilemma: is it the implementation or the evaluation that has failed?

Multi-goal evaluation.—A variety of potential outcomes are identified in multi-goal evaluation. Recognition of possibilities is greatly expanded, but in a more structured way than in a goal-free evaluative free-for-all. The evaluator looks at program goals and beyond them to treatment effects. In so doing, the "conventional official-goal-fixed approach" (i.e., passive evaluative behavior) is abandoned. Instead, evaluators actively develop theoretical models to lead to discovery of a wider range of potential impacts.

Chen and Rossi describe the role of social science evaluation as one that reviews "all of the outcomes deemed possible by social science theory" from "the pool out of which outcomes are to be selected for evaluation testing."[43] This theory-driven method would contribute to the body of social science research. But it may have little effect on the implementation of policy unless it can provide program operators with more substantial information on modes of improvement.

True evaluation.—A "true evaluation," Stufflebeam and Webster say, "sets out to identify and assess, for society or some segment of society, the merits of competing policies."[44] "True" is not opposed to "false" evaluation but merely a designation for a more comprehensive approach to the subject. It differs from inferential evaluation (which reviews multiple sources of causality) and from multiple-goal evaluation (which considers a variety of impacts) in that a wider range of values are involved. In their eyes, a "policy study"

42. Chen and Rossi, "Multi-Goal, Theory-Driven Approach . . . ," p. 39.
43. Ibid., p. 46.
44. Stufflebeam and Webster, "Analysis of Alternative Approaches to Evaluation," p. 71.

is an example of true evaluation. Costs and benefits of alternatives
are evaluated to determine "which of two or more competing policies
will maximize the achievement of valued outcomes at a reasonable
cost."[45]

Difficulties with certain studies arise when stakeholders propose
competing policies while they value similar outcomes or when conflicting stakeholders propose similar policies while valuing contrasting outcomes. Politicians often seek agreement on a general policy,
postponing what the parties to the bargain think they are going to
get out of it or how.[46] Either way, the difficulty encountered in inferential evaluation remains: causality cannot be guaranteed. Competing stakeholders not only propose alternative policies and value
contrasting results, but their underlying assumptions of causality
may be radically different without any certain method of deciding
between them.

Decision-theoretic evaluation.—Dunn's "decision-theoretic evaluation" also addresses outcomes, but these are "explicitly valued by
multiple stakeholders."[47] By combining sponsor-initiated studies
with client and consumer-oriented studies, a more global picture of
the values at stake may be produced. Stakeholders may have intended
or even hidden goals. Decision-theoretic evaluators strive to unearth
these goals and weigh them against and along with the publicly
stated ones.

A version of this form of evaluation may be especially useful in
the evaluation of programs aimed at "prevention" of a known evil.
A social investment in prevention is often viewed as an expenditure
for an evil that does not yet exist. The economic value of a prevention program (such as immunization drives, anti-smoking and pro-
seatbelt campaigns, water fluoridation, and prenatal screening for
birth defects) consists of the avoidance of future costs. Yet imagining these costs may involve considerable conjecture on the part of
all of the competing stakeholders.[48] These preventative programs
appear prima facie to be desirable, but interspersed among them
may be not a few nostrums, and deciding which ones ought to be

45. Ibid., pp. 76–77.
46. A seminal study of the dynamics of agreement is E. Pendelton Herring,
The Politics of Democracy (New York: Rinehart, 1940).
47. Dunn, *Public Policy Analysis*, p. 348.
48. Richard M. Scheffler and Lynn Paringer, "A Review of the Economic
Evidence on Prevention," *Medical Care* 18 (May 1980):473–84.

implemented may take more knowledge than anyone can command.

Meta-evaluation.—An "evaluation of evaluation" is advocated to ensure its continued refinement.[49] These "meta-evaluations" may be conducted either during or after the primary evaluation. They may examine the research design, evaluative techniques, and the conclusions. A review of the literature can be included. Evaluations of similar programs may be compared. Reevaluation and even replication of the original study can verify or question its results.

An independent, simultaneous, heterogeneous evaluation of evaluation is the ultimate meta-evaluation. It is conducted by persons who are not connected with the primary evaluators. It is concurrent and thus able to avoid maturation and various other time-related threats to its own validity.[50] And this meta-evaluation applies different evaluative techniques, in order to better test the primary findings.[51]

Validity, credibility, and relevance are increased with such a meta-evaluation. But, is it feasible? Will the expense be prohibitive? Not necessarily. The simultaneous secondary evaluation need not be large and costly. Several small meta-evaluations, coupled with a small primary evaluation, may each be a fraction of the size of one larger primary evaluation. Thomas D. Cook and Charles Gruder argue that

> in some circumstances several independent evaluations might require a total number of respondents and sites that is not larger than a single evaluation would require. But even when it is advisable to have one large evaluation, it may still be useful . . . to yoke this to a smaller evaluation that is more explicitly focused.[52]

Restricting the number of respondents, focusing on target groups, limiting the research questions, and sharing responsibility for the product of an evaluation are all part of the simultaneous evaluative activity. In a sense, otherwise overabundant and superfluous evalua-

49. Thomas D. Cook and Charles Gruder, "Metaevaluation Research," *Evaluation Studies Review Annual* 4 (1979):469–513.

50. "Maturation" is a process in which the subjects under study change due to the passage of time, such as "growing older, growing hungrier, growing more tired." See Donald T. Campbell and Julian C. Stanley on "Factors Jeopardizing Internal and External Validity," in *Experimental and Quasi-Experimental Designs for Research* (Chicago: Rand McNally, 1966), p. 5.

51. Cook and Gruder, "Metaevaluation Research," pp. 480–84.

52. Ibid., p. 507.

tive behavior is streamlined by such meta-evaluative behavior. A potentially beneficial aspect of meta-evaluation is the pressure co-evaluators may exert on themselves to examine carefully the construct validity of their models. A potentially destructive aspect may be the encouragement of feelings that, since the evaluations differ, anything goes; in the end, superfluous evaluation may be encouraged or at least permitted. Every Eden, even the enlightenment of evaluation, has its serpent.

WHY?

Swimming in a sea of complexity, evaluators begin to wonder if it is all worthwhile: why should they struggle so hard to produce information about programs and policy if no one is going to use it? Recall two of the common criticisms of evaluation: irrelevance and underutilization. By introducing themselves into the maelstrom of policy making, evaluators hope to make their profession meaningful. If the evaluative information is actually absorbed by a policy implementing organization, it should affect policy outcomes.

It follows that information users (often these are implementers) should work with evaluators to analyze and interpret the data. The dissemination of information is a cooperative effort. Hence evaluators have to involve decision makers and information users who work at all levels of implementation in all stages of the evaluation.

Yet even the continuous and responsive production of feedback does not guarantee that the information will be recognized and absorbed. When the information is absorbed, it may not be utilized. Implementation is, after all, the acid test of evaluation.

Utilization-focused evaluation.—If the wrong questions are asked by evaluators, Michael Patton contends, they are wrong because they are not going to generate information that will be utilized. In his utilization-focused evaluation, evaluation designs should have a "built-in utilization component appropriate to the unique circumstances they encounter."[53] This form of evaluation requires the identification of decision makers and information users. Relevant questions are listed and focused. User need and not just program relevance is emphasized. According to Patton, the fundamental question should always be: "What difference would it make to have this information?

53. Patton, *Utilization-Focused Evaluation,* p. 20.

How would the information be used and how would it be useful?"[54] In this model of evaluation for implementation—the active imposition of a framework by the evaluator on clients in order to elicit their reactions—the evaluator is "active-reactive-adaptive."[55] Clients will react by contributing their own goals, perceptions, and questions. This dialogue is supposed to lead to the adaptation of the research design, via clarification of the issues. Whose objectives should be implemented, those of the adaptor or the adapted, is presumably up for grabs.

Utilization-focused evaluation involves the people who intend to implement the evaluation research. These participants are asked to define the questions to be asked by evaluators.[56]

Interactive evaluation.—"Interactive evaluation" brings implementers right into the very act of evaluation. Evaluation, Jolie Bain Pillsbury and Kathy Newton Nance explain, should become "the shared responsibility of evaluators and direct delivery staff." "Direct delivery," of course, is another term for "implementation." Together, evaluators and staff define questions and construct a process of analysis. A "continuous feedback loop becomes an integral part of service delivery."[57] Presumably, mutual agreement and commitment to evaluation is generated when this happy circumstance occurs so that staff no longer view outside evaluators as threatening. Pillsbury and Nance extend interactive evaluation from the programmatic levels to the decision-making levels of organization and policy. Thus the organization becomes self-evaluating.

Though responsive evaluators attempt to adapt their behavior to the demands of each new task, this may not be enough to guarantee the utility of an evaluation. Utilization-focused research is only as effective as a program or policy is evaluable. Continuous evaluation of something that has not been constructed to be evaluable is wasted work.

Evaluability assessment.—During the latter half of the 1970s, the United States and Canadian governments became concerned about the inevaluability of programs. "Evaluability assessment" (also

54. Ibid., p. 286.
55. Ibid., p. 289.
56. Ibid., p. 20.
57. Jolie Bain Pillsbury and Kathy Newton Nance, "An Evaluation Framework for Public Welfare Agencies," *Public Welfare* 36 (Winter 1976), pp. 47–51.

known as "exploratory evaluation" and "accountability assessment")
was developed in response. According to Joseph Wholey, it is "being
used to stimulate agreement on realistic, measurable program objectives, appropriate program performance indicators, and intended
uses of program performance information. . . ."[58] Program objectives
are analyzed for their consistency with program design, for the likelihood that they can be realized, and for their measurability. Proposed
information utilization procedures are scrutinized. An evaluability
assessment can provide advance warning when a proposed treatment process will be impossible to evaluate.

In evaluability assessment, evaluation has come a long way from
an activity to determine whether a policy is working, to an integral
part of policy design so one can tell whether it works. Error detection is no longer incidental; it becomes integral to evaluation.

Learning evaluation.—Is it possible that a hybrid of all of the
evaluations—a continuous, responsive, utilization-focused, interactive evaluation, accompanied by evaluability and meta-evaluations—
would contribute to "gradual, cumulative improvement" in processes, programs, and policies?[59] Would it overcome the common criticism of irrelevance and underutilization in evaluation?

How would such an evaluation become relevant to policy? Must
the evaluation findings be fed back to the locus of initial policy decisions? Or are evaluations conducted during policy and program
implementation relevant to policy as soon as they affect implementation itself?

In that the attempted fulfillment of policy objectives is a test of
the workability of a program, any policy implementation is already
based on a tacit policy evaluation. How far beyond the informal
connections between implementation and evaluation, the question
is, should formal studies go? Should they, for instance, go to the very
objectives that are supposed to be evaluated? An explicit evaluation
that promotes the amending of objectives is self-forming. This morphogenetic or self-organizing evaluation might ask, "What are the
emerging issues?" rather than, "Is this program reaching predetermined policy goals?"

58. Joseph S. Wholey, "Using Evaluation to Improve Program Performance," *Evaluation Studies Review Annual* 6 (1981): pp. 59–60.
59. Erwin C. Hargrove, *The Missing Link: The Study of the Implementation of Social Policy* (Washington, D.C.: Urban Institute, 1975), p. 55.

Either the old objectives may be inappropriate to new circumstances, or they may be vague or contradictory. Thus a new program may be forced to develop its objectives during implementation rather than prior to it. In the emerging field of mental health care for the victims of violent crime, for instance, Susan Salasian proposes an ongoing evaluation of services on a case-by-case basis. As a victim's course of psychological recovery is unpredictable, the successful program must be continuously responsive around a flow of information regarding the client's mental health.[60]

Existing programs are forever confronted with new programmatic issues. At this level of operation, evaluation is a necessary component of program development and implementation. A morphogenetic evaluation could be part of a "continual in-house trial policy," such as that maintained by the California Youth Authority. The CYA contends that it has learned from its trial programs (e.g., community parole centers and within-institution counseling), which are conducted at only one or two facilities at a time. CYA claims to have a better record than "other organizations with different approaches to correctional change." Although many of its findings are negative, the information generated allows CYA to refrain from further investment in "fruitless" programs, and to seek out and develop the best methods of lowering recidivism rates.[61] Going along with the fad for naming new types, we can call the CYA approach Hippocratic evaluation—doing no harm when you cannot do good.

SEPARATING IMPLEMENTATION FROM EVALUATION

In the world of action, implementation and evaluation are often carried on by the same people—public officials. They act and ob-

60. Susan Salasian, "Evaluation as a Tool for Restoring the Mental Health of Victims," *Evaluation and Change*, Special Issue (1980):25.

61. Daniel Glaser, *Routinizing Evaluation: Getting Feedback on the Effectivenesss of Crime and Delinquency Programs*, National Institute for Mental Health, Department of Health, Education, and Welfare, publication no. ADM 76–369 (Rockville, Md., 1976), pp. 158–59. Many issues covered in the literature on ethics in social experimentation are pertinent to the evaluation of social experiments and programs. "Large scale experimentation is so new that the moral and ethical dilemmas it raises have not yet been addressed systematically." Alice M. Rivlin and P. Michael Timpane, eds., *Ethical and Legal Issues of Social Experimentation* (Washington, D.C.: Brookings Institute, 1975), pp. 2, 115–18.

serve, observe and act, combining program execution with intelligence about consequences, so as to reinforce or alter behavior. Doing well or doing badly, hardly conscious of the analytic distinctions involved, participants in the policy process act simultaneously as evaluators of the programs they implement and implementers of the programs they evaluate.

It has to be so. Even where there is a formal attempt to separate policy from administration, whether this is between the legislative and executive branches or between policy analysis units and program administration, the vast bulk of activity is carried on in the field. Outside forces are overwhelmed in numbers and expertise by men and women inside the organization. Given the size and scope of contemporary government, most intelligence about events and their consequences has to come from close to the ground.

It is well to understand that formal evaluators, being once (if they work in agencies) or twice (if they are part of overhead units, like the Office of Management and Budget or the General Accounting Office) or three times (if they are outside government) removed from the scene of action, cannot substitute for or replace public officials themselves.[62] This would be undemocratic; it would also be cognitively unfeasible. If mankind sees "through a glass darkly," what shall we say of those who see almost entirely through other people's prisms?

Because implementation and evaluation take place together in organizations, the character of these organizations matters more than one can say for the quality of the endeavor. Yet the world continues to be one that evaluators never made. No skill can replace the organizational context or make up merely out of the mind for the anti-evaluative proclivities of some kinds of organizations. Failure is inherent in an enterprise that runs counter to deep-seated tendencies in the organizations through which the work has to be done. No one gets it all, as President Kennedy said, and no evaluator should expect to be successful most of the time.

In the world of theory, distinctions may be made that are, of necessity, blurred in practice. There, if we have the wit, we can control

62. Of course, public officials' "very proposal to evaluate has political impact." This singles out a program for evaluation, signaling its vulnerability. See Lee J. Cronbach, *Toward Reform of Program Evaluation* (San Francisco: Jossey-Bass, 1980), pp. 163–64.

concepts instead of being dominated by them. In that world of abstractions, evaluation may be distinguished from implementation. The question is whether it is intellectually satisfying and practically useful to do so.

By blurring the distinction, evaluation becoming preoccupied with utilization and implementation taking up monitoring, the two subfields merge into a single-seamed concern with policy analysis. Designing policies to be evaluable and implementable, discovering new alternatives, bringing in new values and constituencies, recommending choices among possible programs, establishing coalitions to support preferred programs, and more, much more, from political feasibility to organizational incentives, become part of the task of evaluators-cum-implementers. A sense of power and responsibility is gained. A sense of differentiation, appropriateness, and hence professionalization is lost.

Evaluators are able to tell us a lot about what happened—which objectives, whose objectives, were achieved—and a little about why—the causal connections. Cumulating evaluations should add to the store of information relevant to policy. The broader the viewpoints from which evaluation is done, the more valuable the information generated. Were they particularly fortunate or perspicacious, evaluators might just barely know a little about which instruments of policy are likely to be efficacious in securing desired results, without necessarily recommending particular policies.

Selling evaluation goes with the job. Making it more attractive to different constituencies or organization units is part of being persuasive. So is writing well. Why shouldn't evaluators go "whole hog" by superintending the actual implementation of programs themselves?

Evaluators have tried to become implementers. This is both good and bad—good because evaluation becomes more relevant, bad because it becomes less knowledgeable. Being useful is one thing; acting as if one were responsible for implementation is another. Monitoring the consequences of programs, which up until now has been the central core of evaluation, requires a certain openness to go where the evidence leads. The evaluator must always be prepared to discover that the consequences (or objectives) hitherto considered are not the only ones. That breadth of vision is sacrificed when evaluation becomes indistinguishable from implementation. Where an absence of interest in utilization is stultifying, an exclusive concern with immediate use results in subordination of intelligence to action. In the end, if this path is taken, only self-serving evaluations will be made. Why care, then, whether evaluations whose conclusions are prejudged are utilized or not? If we care, it is only to see that there is as little of this sort of "evaluation" as possible. Demarcating the domain of implementation helps maintain the distinctiveness and integrity of evaluation.

Implementation might be conceived, following Jan-Erik Lane, as joining the traditional public administration concern with the executive to the newer interest in evaluation.[63] The evaluator collects and analyzes data to provide information about program results. The implementer consumes this information, using it to check on past decisions and to guide future actions. Implementation is, as we said, about learning from evaluation. It is in their production and consumption of information (that is, learning) that implementers and evaluators engage in complementary relationships.

These two generic aspects of policy analysis share an interest in the clarification of objectives. There must be prior objectives against which to measure subsequent achievement. But objectives need not, indeed should not, "be forever." Both implementation and evaluation are concerned with the relationship between resources and objectives, though in different directions. Evaluation is concerned with the causes of outcomes and implementation with utilizing causal knowledge to alter outcomes. If, as we claim, however, implementation takes place within an evolutionary framework, it becomes difficult to assume the prior existence of objectives against which to assess accomplishment. Objectives cannot be held constant while they are changing. Neither can the policy preferences of different people. It is intelligent to alter objectives to fit resources,[64] to adjust programs to face facts, as well as to fit resources to objectives.

In his perceptive paper, Lane asks, "Is implementation analysis the same as evaluation analysis? The concept of implementation as evolution amounts to a strong denial of any identity between the two, because if objectives and outcomes continuously interact, how could

63. Jan-Erik Lane, "The Concept of Implementation," *Statsventenskaplig Tidskrift* 86 (1983):17–40.

64. See the extensive discussion in Wildavsky, *Speaking Truth to Power*, pp. 21–141.

the outcomes be evaluated in terms of a fixed set of objectives?"
Evaluators need not stand still when they need to keep moving. They
are wise, then, not to fix prematurely on immediate utilization amidst
the flux of life, wise also to infuse their own evaluations with multiple
possibilities, some of which may be more important in the future
than they are now. The conceptual distinction between evaluation
and implementation is important to maintain, however much the two
overlap in practice, because they protect against the absorption of
analysis into action to the detriment of both.

10

Implementation as Mutual Adaptation (1983)

ANGELA BROWNE AND AARON WILDAVSKY

What is it that distinguishes implementation analysis from the general body of evaluation study? There are few methodological differences. In fact, many of the conceptual issues in the study of evaluation are becoming apparent in research on implementation.[1]

That there is a conjoining of these fields is not surprising; by a sort of evaluative imperative, eager evaluators have felt compelled to expand their domain: when the program under review fails in some respect, the evaluator can fix it as if he or she were also the implementer. If everything that might be controlled to transform policy into action must be controlled, it follows that even the mysteries of implementation can be unraveled through a comprehensive evaluation of its defects.

The basic questions that evaluators ask about their task—When? Where? For whom? What? Why?—are shared by implementation analysts. Choices as whether to undertake a retrospective, concurrent, or prospective study (the When?); decisions as to the scope of activity and selection of sites to be studied (the Where?); responsi-

---

1. The term "mutual adaptation" was introduced (to the fields of policy and implementation analysis) by Paul Berman and Milbrey W. McLaughlin, in *Federal Programs Supporting Educational Change*, vol. 1, *A Model of Educational Change*, Grant no. R–1589/1–HEW (Santa Monica, Calif.: Rand Corporation, 1974).

bilities toward an employer, a profession, or an interest group (the For whom?); factors to be measured (the What?); and motivations for the study (the Why?) are also significant concerns of implementation analysts.

IMPLEMENTATION AS POLICY EVALUATION

WHEN?

Of the basic five questions, that of "When?" is probably the most crucial in an evaluation of the implementation process. The prospective approach of including considerations crucial to implementation in policy design has been criticized because present knowledge is often insufficient to predict the future—the actual implementation. Similarly, a prospective implementation analysis, or a "forward mapping" of an anticipated implementation, is a weak analytic strategy.[2] Preanalysis is inherently limited: in preanalysis, the hypothetical relation of policy to program remains as yet untested by attempts at implementation.

Richard Elmore suggests that prospective implementation, or "forward mapping," "begin with a statement of congressional intent."[3] Regulations and administrative behavior are mapped out in anticipation of compliance with this original mandate. Responsibility is divided among agencies. In accordance with the expressed congressional intent, the desired outcome is stated. If the map is a detailed one, it outlines (or "codes," as the term is sometimes used) strategies for compliance, the means of encouraging political support, and the methods for the transfer of technology. The basic premise of forward mapping holds that the more explicit the policy, the more of its implementation can be controlled by those who mandated it, the elected or appointed officials at the top. This "top-down" perspective leads those who would analyze an implementation process to undertake their evaluation from the standpoint of a forward map. Here the question of "When?" is not when to evaluate but where in time to locate the original causes of the failure or success

2. Richard F. Elmore, "Backward Mapping: Implementation Research and Policy Decisions," in Walter Williams, et al., eds., *Studying Implementation: Methodological and Administrative Issues* (Chatham, N.J.: Chatham House, 1982), p. 19.

3. Ibid., p. 19.

of implementation. The attention of the forward-mapping implementation analyst is drawn to the beginning; in policy time, this is usually the moment of the enactment of a law or the rendering of a court decision. This moment is, as might have been said in an earlier age, the original (policy) sin.

Adaptation (an evolutionary characteristic of implementation) occurs when a policy or program evolves in response to its environment as each alters the other. Mutual adaptation, the product of environmental response to policy intent, is unavoidable. Undesigned consequences must be expected in any process of adaptation during implementation. Top-down forward mapping in policy development —which always predicts the future inaccurately or incompletely— does not prevent the evolutionary processes of implementation from manifesting themselves, yet top-down mapping in implementation analysis tends to ignore these processes.

Elmore's antithesis to forward mapping, which he so aptly terms "backward mapping," is an analytic approach compatible with our view of implementation as an evolutionary process. The assumptions maintained by backward mappers are that "the closer one is to the source of the problem, the greater is one's ability to influence it; and the problem-solving ability of complex systems depends not on hierarchical control but on maximizing discretion at the point where the problem is most immediate."[4]

During adaptation, decision-making authority is dispersed. The outcome of the resulting chain of implementation decisions cannot be predicted or measured according to indicators of formal, top-down hierarchies of control. The analytic onus is better placed on the decentralized, sometimes informal, and often unanticipated points of decision. Community politics, the behaviors of individuals outside the implementing domains, and the behaviors of individuals and groups within implementing organizations are recognized as determinants of policy outcome in backward mapping.

What would it take to map implementation accurately? Concurrent evaluations can provide information about the behavioral mechanisms working at each of the points of adaptation or decision in the implementation chain. These are process evaluations: if conducted continuously, they provide feedback that can be applied to each of

4. Ibid., p. 21.

the decisions to be made. Hence, the importance of goal-fixed evaluations is diminished, as even the goals of implementers are subject to change each time a program is adapted to its environment. Because the program is most intimate with its environment at the point of service delivery, much of the evaluation should occur there. In policies directed toward local service delivery and community development, a useful backward map is especially detailed in its rendering of the work at the bottom of the formal hierarchy.

The "When?" of implementation analysis in backward mapping is therefore better answered by a "rather later than sooner" perspective. Only after the fact can the course of evolution be ascertained. The difficulty is that this may be too late. It is important to gauge the timing of analysis against the utility of the findings: is something learned that can be transferred to other implementation processes? Or, better yet, is something learned that can influence the very process being studied? If so, implementation and the analysis of it merge in a process resembling the previous chapter's concept of continuous evaluation.

WHERE?

Next to timing, focus is a basic consideration in the design of an implementation study. Implementation analysts have indicated at least an intuitive awareness of the significance of the particular (local delivery site) over the universal (federal policy directive) in their propensity for the case study—so much so that, according to Paul Berman, as of 1978 the literature consisted "mainly of atheoretical case studies of varying quality . . . whose claims to generality are questionable because they cannot be easily compared."[5] He argues that implementation analysts' selection of subject matter is problematic, and he questions whether there is any transferrable knowledge to be gained. (Can the implementation problems of education policy, for instance, be compared to those of transportation policy?) Even if the scope is narrowed and restricted to the implementation analysis of a single policy, there are research design dilemmas: should the student of implementation study single sites or multiple sites, via longitudinal or cross-sectional designs or by a combination of them?

5. Paul Berman, "The Study of Macro- and Micro-Implementation," *Public Policy* 26 (Spring 1978):158.

Sophisticated field-network evaluations, involving nationwide cross-sectional and longitudinal studies concerned with large-scale federal programs, usually conducted by big research organizations, are costly and time-consuming.[6] In these studies, large numbers of field sites are analyzed by researchers, under the direction of a central research unit, for several years. Such a project may be more apt to emphasize the complexities of research methods than those of actual implementation. This shift in emphasis is due to the difficulties inherent in most research, such as competition among researchers, the effects of personal biases on findings, and the resistance of local officials to intrusive studies.[7] Beyond human factors, practical issues such as those of data collection, data analysis, and research design demand so much attention that the ultimate purpose of the study—to analyze the problems of the implementers—may take a back seat.

FOR WHOM?

The objectivity of implementation analysts is threatened by more than the "Where?" (focus and scope) of the research design. Whenever analysts decide to scrutinize an implementation process, they must answer to their employers and sponsors and identify other parties as being concerned stakeholders. This is a conflict shared by all evaluators involved in the analysis of public policies. Researchers conducting organizational analyses are subject to personal involvements with staff or management or client objectives. The dividing line between analysis and advocacy may fade when an insider's knowledge is necessary for in-depth research. Some degree of personal involvement with critical issues affecting clients, staff, and organizational processes may be unavoidable. Yet this close involvement clouds the "For whom?" question in implementation analysis.

Some of this confusion surfaces in the conflicts between the roles of neutral researcher, organizational consultant, advocate, and outright activist.[8] Analysts must clarify their purposes. Are they to

6. John Stuart Hall and Susan A. MacManus, "Tracking Decisions and Consequences: The Field Network Evaluation Approach," in Williams, et al., eds., *Studying Implementation*, pp. 100–118.

7. Ibid., pp. 106–11.

8. For a discussion of the researcher-consultant model, see Betty Jane Narver and Walter Williams, "The Consultant/Researcher Role: Implications for Studying Public Management Problems," in Williams, et al., eds., *Studying Implementation*, pp. 149–79.

remain neutral, unbiased reporters or should they constructively try to affect the implementation process and thus its outcome? Whose perspectives should they employ in their evaluations of implementation processes? Often, too, after properly preselecting one evaluative perspective only to arrive at another during their research, researchers become divided in their allegiances.

In deciding for whom they are evaluating, analysts must consider measures of constituency satisfaction. Rather than focus only on outcome measures, it is the "modification and compromise of goals in an effort to reconcile conflicts and accommodate the concerns of those constituency groups, whose goals may shift over time," that Robert Nakamura and Frank Smallwood identify as important in the analysis of implementation.[9]

Support of policies and those who make them is essential for implementation, but the specific clients or consumers of the policy outcome may represent only a fraction of the interested or affected public. That is why Nakamura and Smallwood include "clientele responsiveness" in their list of criteria for the evaluation of implementation. They indicate that an emphasis on "consumer and clientele satisfaction" necessitates an "experimental approach to policy implementation, which places a high premium on program adaptability, flexibility, and accommodation in its attempts to meet consumer and clientele needs and demands."[10] Again, implementation becomes evolutionary.

The gravity of the question "For whom?" in implementation research is especially apparent to researchers who identify themselves with the recipients or would-be recipients of programs. (The very purpose of the study of implementation is called into question when these clients are neglected.) Implementation failures, in which actual policy results fall short of expected outcomes, are especially painful for target populations, who were supposed to have benefited. At the end of the implementation chain, they are often left with unrealized promises, promises that perhaps should never have been made if they could not have been kept.

The guarantee of equal opportunity in education is an example of the easy-to-make, hard-to-keep type of promise. "The great hopes

9. Robert T. Nakamura and Frank Smallwood, *The Politics of Policy Implementation* (New York: St. Martin's Press, 1980), pp. 149–50.

10. Ibid., pp. 150–51.

raised by P. L. 94–142," John Gliedman and William Roth write, "may be cruelly disappointed regardless of how well or how poorly the schools translate the law's provisions into practice."[11] Public Law 94–142 ensures, without exception, all handicapped children a free public education.[12] In so doing, it has met with the standard obstacles to implementation, such as a shortage of resources, a lack of co-ordination, and poor planning. But a more subtle problem for implementation analysts can be discerned in the P. L. 94–142 predicament. For all its impressive procedural innovations, each one of these is "ultimately no better than the vision of the handicapped child that informs its implementation."[13] Researchers who seek to identify underlying resistance to implementation may discover the persistence of old ways of thinking. The long-standing view of physical handicap as a deviant characteristic was not ended with the enactment of a law. Analysts of its implementation must, with the would-be beneficiaries of this policy in mind, consider the qualitative and very human obstacles to implementation success. The question of "For whom?" is therefore more variegated than the identification of sponsors and stakeholders.

WHAT?

Quantitative measures of goal attainment (i.e., number of people served, miles of roads built) and efficiency (i.e., people served well or roads built adequately at a reasonable cost in a reasonable amount of time) are perhaps the most obvious criteria of successful implementation.[14] But these measures are only a beginning. The ability of a policy to effect change in behavioral, organizational, or environmental conditions is dependent on the technology required to effect that change, which itself may be unsatisfactory, and the size of the problem, including the extent of the population and the degree of change required. A formal policy can be viewed in terms of whether

11. John Gliedman and William Roth, *The Unexpected Minority: Handicapped Children in America* (New York: Harcourt Brace Jovanovich, 1980), p. 197.

12. Garry D. Brewer and James S. Kakalik, *Handicapped Children: Strategies for Improving Services* (New York: McGraw-Hill, 1979), p. 343.

13. Gliedman and Roth, *The Unexpected Minority*, p. 197.

14. Policy goal attainment and efficiency criteria are two of the ways to evaluate implementation listed by Nakamura and Smallwood, *Politics of Policy Implementation*, pp. 146–48.

it possesses the ability to structure the implementation process by means of clear objectives and priorities, a valid theory of causality connecting instruments of policy to desired objectives, adequate financial resources at the start, and sufficient power—cooperation among implementing organizations and the ability to get the clientele involved to do as desired. Policy makers tend to neglect these important variables of control, leaving the administrative domain to struggle with the production of an expected outcome.

A policy, Daniel Mazmanian and Paul Sabatier add, can do more than affect the design of implementing agencies; it can encourage or discourage the participation of outside actors, such as program beneficiaries and private and other governmental bodies.[15] Given Eugene Bardach's interpretation of the implementation process as a system of games,[16] in a pluralist polity this political aspect of policy design must be a major determinant of implementation success or failure. Not everyone agrees to cooperate or can be coerced, persuaded, or induced to do so. After all, we have seen that the problematic interactions of various "players" can cause delay, low performance, unwieldy costs, noncompliance, and undesigned consequences.

Many nonstatutory variables have these effects on the implementation process. Those identified by Mazmanian and Sabatier include "socioeconomic conditions," "public support," "attitudes and resources of constituency groups," and the "commitment and leadership skill of implementing officials." Listing these variables, however, is not the same as estimating or controlling them.

Whether it be the limiting of the discretion of implementers or the incorporating of outside players (stakeholders) into the implementation framework, a policy potentially exerts greater control when it addresses these issues at the start. Because there will always be unknowns, however, policy makers can only expect to make a few of the variables that matter part of statute.

Anticipation of the stages of implementation may be useful in controlling the other contingencies during policy formulation, as well as during implementation. Regarding the revision phase, Mazmanian and Sabatier state, "Just as the passage of a statute (or other basic

15. Daniel A. Mazmanian and Paul A. Sabatier, *Implementation and Public Policy* (Palo Alto, Calif.: Scott, Foresman, 1983), p. 28.

16. Eugene Bardach, *The Implementation Game: What Happens After a Bill Becomes a Law* (Cambridge, Mass.: MIT Press, 1980), pp. 55–58.

policy decision) should be viewed as the starting point for an analysis of implementation, so the revision/reformulation of that statute should be viewed as the culminating stage of the process (although the process may be repeated several times)."[17] For analytic convenience, implementation processes may be regarded as distinct replays, but for the players it is one continuous repeat performance.

Between the starting and ending points, the opportunity for on-the-spot learning from evaluation presents itself. This is an active version of implementation analysis. As an aid to management, program evaluation can directly influence implementation. In this spirit, the Canadian Departmental Program Evaluation Plan serves as "a source of information for resource allocation, program improvement and accountability in government."[18] Just as attempted implementation constitutes the raw material of evaluation, so evaluation modifies implementation.[19] Without the one—the errors of implementation—there cannot be the other—the learning from evaluation.

WHY?

Once we determine the "What?" of implementation analysis, we must still ask why such studies are undertaken. The answer, presumably, is that analysis of implementation is supposed to influence what happens. Can an implementation analysis directly influence an implementation process? A recent study of local health departments' preventative health services in California identified factors that influence negotiations between state and local offices, including the effects of state requirements on local performance. The authors of the study (Philip Weiler et al.) have developed a model for program modification through state-local negotiation. During a test negotiation, local and state agencies were asked to list process and outcome objectives in several program areas, as well as to describe the current status of each of these objectives. This joint effort entailed the development of new indicators quantifying specific health objectives. Each local agency was required to set out an increase in the delivery of

17. Mazmanian and Sabatier, *Implementation and Public Policy*, p. 38.

18. Treasury Board of Canada, Comptroller General, Program Evaluation Branch, *Guide on the Program Evaluation Function* (Ottawa, 1981), p. 4.

19. See Canada, Office of the Auditor General, *Audit Guide: Auditing of Proceedings for Effectiveness, Subject Matter Series* (Ottawa, 1981), pp. 17–19 and appendix A, pp. 45–52.

services within its jurisdiction to be achieved within one year and also to include a means of measuring this achievement.[20] The major difficulties inherent in the implementation of these performance standards became apparent during the preliminary negotiations. There was disagreement between state and local officials regarding jurisdiction and objectives as well as inadequate or inappropriate data. Overall, the effects of negotiations and self-assessment were viewed as positive. Although the primary determinant in the realization of one-year objectives proved to be the availability of resources, the negotiations served to increase communication between state and local health agencies and to improve the implementability of performance standards. Sufficient resources and realistic objectives, somewhat more money and somewhat lesser standards, came together. Implementers were participants in the negotiations. In a world of flux, it is only through continuous negotiation between administrators, implementers, and decision makers that any "congruence between program design and program implementation" (mentioned as essential in the literature) can ever be achieved.[21]

Acting as if everything was up for grabs—as if the policy itself can be modified, perhaps even reversed, during negotiations between the immediately interested parties—raises serious questions about democracy as well as about implementation. What happens to public authority when change is delegated to private organizational interests? What happens to implementation when it is deemed desirable to disregard guidelines that some would say should have been considered authoritative? What is it about the very analysis of implementation that invites the undermining of the original and democratically defined objectives of a policy?

The "Why?" of implementation analysis involves striking a balance between national and local interests. We have learned a great deal about the convolution of objectives during the local level implementation of federally funded social welfare programs. First, "local influentials" oppose the taxation of their communities for federal programs, and then they vie for the allocation of a "fair share" of

---

20. Philip Weiler, et al., "The Implementation of Model Standards in Local Health Departments," *American Journal of Public Health* 72 (1982):1230–37.

21. Peter H. Rossi, Howard E. Freeman, and Sonia R. Wright, "Monitoring Implementation," in Rossi, Freeman, and Wright, *Evaluation: A Systematic Approach* (Beverly Hills, Calif.: Sage Publications, 1979), p. 157.

these program dollars. Most of these social welfare programs, R. Allen Hays asserts, would never have been mandated by local officials, most of whom are "philosophically opposed to government expenditures for the disadvantaged . . . [and to] the use of local taxes for such purposes."[22] But when it is time for implementation, this philosophical opposition to redistributive policy is overwhelmed by hunger for a piece of the redistributive pie. Suddenly the agency that administers a social welfare program becomes a strong advocate, not necessarily of its disadvantaged clients, but of the program itself.[23] And it mediates between its favorite local elites and outspoken client groups all during program implementation, so much so that mediation and implementation are indistinguishable processes.

Whether it be the combat over perceived priorities in the cutback or termination of public programs,[24] the power struggle between agencies implementing Oakland's EDA or the fiery participation of interest groups in the decision to bring seismically hazardous buildings up to code, the politics of implementation is the ultimate determinant of outcome. The latter instance, the implementation of hazard controls, is an example of the sort of good ideas that are difficult to make operational. Who would ever think that a decision to bring 8,000 pre-1933 structures (built of unreinforced, earthquake-vulnerable masonry) up to code would be an issue of high conflict potential? But in Los Angeles this meant that multi-million-dollar decisions affecting affluent property owners, "displaced businessmen, threatened tenants, low-income neighborhood organizations, civil rights groups, contractors," and many others were held up.[25] Why would anyone object to the avoidance of calamity? Because knowledge is limited, no one knows for sure when and if calamity will strike. Thus there is disagreement over who should pay the costs of anticipation. The "Why?" of implementation analysis must always

22. R. Allen Hays, "Social Welfare Programs and Political Conflict in Local Communities: The Mediating Function of the Implementing Agency," *Policy Studies Journal* 11 (December 1982):235.

23. Ibid., p. 236.

24. Peter de Leon, "Policy Evaluation and Program Termination," The Rand Paper Series, P–6807 (Santa Monica, Calif:. Rand Corporation, 1982), pp. 17–23.

25. Richard Stuart Olson and Douglas C. Nilson, "Public Policy Analysis and Hazards Research: Natural Complements," *The Social Science Journal* 19 (January 1982):95.

seek to identify the reasons for the obstruction of implementation and the means for their alleviation. It is only in implementation analysis that a kaleidoscopic understanding of the relationship between policy intent and policy outcome can be achieved.

DUAL IMPLEMENTATION

There are, then, two implementation processes. One is the initially perceived, formally defined, prospectively expected set of causal links required to result in a desired outcome; the other is the unexpected nexus of causality that actually evolves during implementation.

The formal source of the expectation is in the policy decision; at this point a policy and its programmatic flesh is imbued with its coding. What constitutes coding? Any prescribed action, such as a regulation or standard operating procedures, incorporated into the original policy mandate is a form of coding. This notion of prescribed action is illustrated in the literature on "mandating." Max Neiman and Catherine Lovell state that "a mandate is any responsibility, action, procedure or limitation that is imposed by one sphere of government on another by superior constitutional, legislative, executive or judicial authority as a direct order or as a condition of aid." In their typology, Neiman and Lovell include "requirement mandates" that "indicate what it is that must be done" by specifying goals, programmatic actions, responsibilities, and amounts of service to be provided, and that require procedures for putting into production some service outcome, such as reporting, fiscal monitoring, personnel recruitment, evaluation, and performance levels. There are also "constraint mandates" that "limit the amount and type of *locally* derived resources that can be extracted and/or employed to support services." There is a "continuum of compulsion" from the most to the least compelling requirements.[26] Policy directives of any sort provide varying degrees of compulsion in diverse degrees of detail. There is a continuum of direction with low and high degrees of implementation detail. Toward the higher end of this continuum are intricately specified rules, regulations, and statutes. Toward the lower end of this spectrum, courts are often instructed to reconsider their

26. Max Neiman and Catherine Lovell, "Mandating as a Policy Issue—The Definitional Problem," *Policy Studies Review Annual* 9 (Spring 1981): 667–71; see also Neal Gross, et al., eds., *Implementing Organizational Innovations* (New York: Basic Books, 1971), pp. 19–40.

decision without direction. Legislators may attempt to rewrite statutes in accord with Supreme Court decisions, only to have state courts rule them unconstitutional. Implementers may hinge their activities on vaguely worded directives such as "equal opportunity" and "current service budgets." Policy makers who incorporate little implementation coding in original mandates reveal their inability to legislate unknown processes; instead, they attempt to compel outcomes—leaving the unknown "hows" to the implementers.

Policy formulators, including legislators, judges, and executives, do not and cannot foresee all of the difficulties of implementation. They are confronted with a coding dilemma: should they prospectively employ prespecified, explicit, controlled implementation directions or use unspecified, implicit, discretionary implementation coding? How much adaptation should they want or expect?

A special example of this predicament is found in the field of "intelligence" (including counterintelligence and covert action). Federal funds are appropriated with the knowledge that it is difficult to "hold secret intelligence agencies accountable for their actions," whether retrospectively (via evaluation) or prospectively (via prespecified implementation).[27] Consequently, there is considerable reliance on unspecified and unreported implementation activities.

Even in nonsecretive activities, there are obscure and unplanned processes. The troubled implementation of the 1965 Elementary and Secondary Education Act evidenced the presence of unknowns in the implementation of "social innovations."[28] According to Louise Comfort, the "full implications of the ESEA were scarcely envisioned, let alone anticipated or included in the planning for the implementation of the policy." This is not surprising, as it is impossible to design a policy that "can be implemented with a modicum of effectiveness

27. "Intelligence Failures, CIA Misdeeds Studied," *Foreign Policy/ National Security* (September 20, 1975), pp. 20–25.

28. The Berman-McLaughlin model of "social innovation" is a three-stage process: (1) initiation, (2) implementation, and (3) incorporation. Paul Berman and Milbrey McLaughlin, "Implementation of Educational Innovation," *Educational Forum* 40 (March 1967):347–70. At the heart of the obscure social innovation process directed toward social change are the issues of organizational willingness to implement the results of evaluation (see the prior chapter). Even when evaluation during implementation produces new information that may enhance the implementation process, an organization may resist changing its objectives accordingly.

and fidelity throughout the multiple units of the multilevel educational bureaucracy," especially an innovative (i.e., untested) policy.[29] But we need not belabor the subject of educational policy. Policies that induce tax cuts may not result in desired investment, and those that provide for accelerated depreciation may simply support projects that would have been undertaken anyway. We would not like to be on the receiving end of an evaluation of monetary policy.

Because the implementability of a policy decision cannot be comprehensively considered during policy formulation, there will always be uncharted territory in the implementation process. Implementers forge new links in unpredicted environments. They are pioneers.

This picture of dual (anticipatory and resilient) implementation is further complicated by the descending shifts in levels of government and social organization during policy implementation. Walter Williams divides the "long federal governance process from Congress to local service project operators" into three domains:

(1) The 'decision domain,' where 'big decisions' are made,
(2) The 'administrative and support domain,' which ranges from middle-federal to local administrative levels, and,
(3) The 'operators' domain,' in which 'social service delivery organizations (are) dealing directly with project participants.'[30]

Thus, in the effort to distinguish policy from its implementation, the (in)famous "policy-administration" dichotomy rises again.

The EDA employment project was implemented across these three domains. Using a public works program, federal policy makers intended to give impetus to community-level changes. The administration of this thrust could not be handled at a distance. In Seattle, the regional office vied for the expansion of its administrative domain, while the necessary local-level orchestration of administrators and operators was obstructed. The actual operations, such as filling the bay in the construction of a marine terminal and designing an aircraft maintenance terminal and employing laborers to build it, were comprised of many parts. The decision domain had not anticipated

29. Louise K. Comfort, *Educational Policy and Evaluation: A Context for Change* (New York: Pergamon Press, 1982), pp. 2, 37.
30. Walter Williams, "The Study of Implementation," in Williams, et al., eds., *Studying Implementation*, pp. 6–9.

the complexities (fire regulation, contract negotiation, project costs, etc.); the administrative domain was unable to simplify them; the operators' domain failed to implement the program within the time specified.

In order to integrate the notion of domains into a model of implementation based on mutual adaptation, each domain can be conceived of as a realm of duty for the forging of a particular series of causal links. The least compact, most extended species of implementation is one in which a lengthy process with many actors working at several levels of government requires an elaborate distribution of responsibility. The decision domain sets the process in motion. The administrative domain expands in response to the dispersion of duty. Renate Mayntz, in an analysis of environmental policy in Germany, finds the policy structure of environmental protection characterized by a "high degree of horizontal differentiation" that "causes problems of co-ordination." The number of decision points is increased, the possibilities for consensus are diminished, and unexpected shortcomings in environmental protection ensue.[31] The operators' domain encounters many of the environmental obstacles to implementation. The greater the distance from the top of the decision domain to the bottom of the operators' domain, the greater the number of opportunities for undesigned consequences to occur.

One of the lessons of the EDA project is that we should expect new programs to experience difficulties. Given that the span of influences on implementation can never be entirely preconceived, the actual implementation process will always be less structured than the expected process. The lack of concern for the side effects of a policy may be attributed to a common human characteristic, the limited "capacity for attention" beyond initial purposes.[32]

The effects of many policies are not foreseen. The purpose of court-ordered school desegregation, for instance, was to remedy marked racial imbalances in school districts. It appears instead to have resulted in "court-induced white flight": white families moved away

31. See Renate Mayntz, "External Pressures and Conflicts in the Formation and Implementation of Environmental Policy" (Berlin: International Institute of Management, 1975), pp. 3–4.

32. Lewis A. Dexter, "Undesigned Consequences of Purposive Legislative Action," *Journal of Public Policy* 1 (October 1981):415–17.

from the desegregating districts. The side effect of desegregation was resegregation.[33]

Some of the unplanned effects of policies are difficult to avoid. The Federal Reserve has the capacity to break an interest rate spiral by means of credit controls. In recent years, tightening of credit in order to slow money expansion has had an undesigned side effect: a public sensitivity to this process has developed. Financial markets act in *anticipation* of credit controls by rushing to increase borrowing before their imposition. This, in turn, aggravates the need for credit control. And, the financial markets' "hair-trigger reaction to each blip in money growth" profoundly complicates the job of Federal Reserve policy.[34] "Supply-side" tax cuts, under the Reagan Administration during a period of monetary contraction, widen rather than narrow budget deficits.

The problem of illegal immigration generates a compounding of conditions, each of which, when addressed, aggravates the other. Estimates are that 2.5 million people enter the United States illegally each year, and at least one-half million stay, creating a sizeable population of four to six million who live and work in the U.S. unprotected by our laws. The situation is complicated by economic instability and population pressure beyond our borders that interact with America's global role and its internal economic conditions to underscore the absence of a policy response to the problem of illegal immigration. A policy response to only one factor within this constellation of factors risks aggravating other difficulties. To close the borders is costly. It may be detrimental to international relations and deny Mexico its safety valve. To require a counterfeit-proof worker's identification card in lieu of closing the borders and then to impose

33. Social scientists have debated the cause of white flight. Declining white birth rates, residential out-migration related to employment, and other factors have been suggested as alternatives to the white flight explanation for desegregation. David J. Armor, "White Flight and the Future of School Desegregation" (Santa Monica, Calif.: Rand Corporation, 1978), pp. 187–225. See also Armor, "The Evidence on Busing," *The Public Interest*, no. 28 (Summer 1972), pp. 90–126; and Armor, Thomas F. Pettigrew, and James Q. Wilson, "On Busing: An Exchange," *The Public Interest*, no. 30 (Winter 1973), pp. 88–134.

34. Harold van B. Cleveland and Ramachandra Bhagavatula, "The Continuing World Economic Crisis," *America and the World: 1980 Foreign Affairs* 59 (1981):595–97.

sanctions against employers of illegals may drive illegals even further underground than they already are.[35]

Instead of mandating certain outcomes, public policy may leave it to be determined by bargaining among the immediately affected parties. The troubled implementations of air and water pollution and other environmental control laws are cases in point. In this realm of policy, voluntary compliance is the emphasized method of enforcement. Laissez-faire compliance helps secure consent by business, but it also contributes to delay and resistance in meeting mandated standards. States do not enforce federally-defined emission requirements in a systematic way, and temporary exceptions are granted, sometimes repeatedly. Levels and time controls are chiseled away through continued negotiation.[36] Where formal notice of violations is actually issued, administrative enforcement is often slow and weak, reluctant and confused. On the local level, city halls end up with the job of resolving goal conflicts, as in Renate Mayntz's example of the local implementation of waste disposal requirements.

> While the cost/benefit relationship of an orderly *removal* of garbage and sewage may favor the rendering of these services which are visibly in the interest of the local population, this is different where the orderly *disposal* and waste water purification required by law are concerned. No visible benefits accrue to the local population in recompense for the sizable funds the local government has to expend in building and maintaining a high quality incinerator or purification plant.[37]

And even if all were in agreement, "implementation incentive systems" (monitoring, sampling, inspection, reporting) would still be handicapped by the elusive nature of air and water "quality." The inadequate technology to measure and provide continuous compliance limits the power of environmental policy to control its outcome.[38]

Fortunately, some undesigned consequences are positive even when prespecified goals have not been achieved. Project Head Start,

35. Sylvia Ann Hewlett, "Coping with Illegal Immigrants," *Foreign Affairs* 60 (Winter 1981/82):358–78.

36. Paul B. Downing and James N. Kimball, "Enforcing Pollution Control Laws in the U.S.," *Policy Studies Journal* 11 (September 1982):56–57.

37. Mayntz, "External Pressures and Conflicts . . . ," pp. 10–11.

38. See Gordon L. Brady and Blair T. Bower, "Effectiveness of the U.S. Regulatory Approach to Air Quality Management: Stationary Sources," *Policy Studies Journal* 11 (September 1982):66–67, 73–76.

which may or may not have achieved its goal (the controversy continues) of promoting long-range academic performance, has at least sensitized parents and communities to other local issues.[39] Whether effective or not, the implementation of a social program tends to make target populations a general subject of social concern.[40]

Policies with unforeseen consequences are being implemented daily. The responsibility for generating expected results is in the hands of implementers, yet the very act of implementing a policy may result in its undesigned consequences. Are these consequences good or bad? That depends on how much we value spontaneity.

It may be that the purpose of a particular policy analysis is to achieve a fixed objective. The purpose of the policy-analytic process, however, given a great many analyses, is to help us decide what we ought to prefer. Otherwise, we would remain mired forever in early (and possibly infantile) longings. Even this is too straightforward. What we want depends on what we can get. Resources affect objectives. What we ought to prefer depends both on what is desirable and what is feasible. Negotiating between the two is what being grown up is about—neither unlimited resources nor insatiable desires.[41] Learning is not only a matter of means—how to achieve pre-fixed objectives—but also of ends, i.e., learning to educate our preferences.

Learning to perfect preferences imposes broader obligations on policy analysis (and thus, also, its component parts, such as implementation and evaluation). A wider array of values should be considered in case these might be preferable. A broader range of groups, who generate these values, should also be taken into account because they may matter more in the future or because their perspectives may illuminate obscure aspects of current programs. By broadening the spectrum of stakeholders, the range of causal connections—the "Why?" of policy analysis—is enlarged.

39. Richard B. Darlington, et al., "Preschool Programs and Later School Competence of Children from Low-Income Families," *Science* 208 (April 1980):202; and Jeanne Nienaber and Aaron Wildavsky, *The Budgeting and Evaluating of Federal Recreation Programs* (New York: Basic Books, 1973), p. 14.

40. Richard Weatherly and Michael Lipsky, "Street-Level Bureaucrats and Institutional Innovation: Implementing Special Education Reform," *Harvard Educational Review* 47 (May 1977):194.

41. This is a major theme of Aaron Wildavsky's *Speaking Truth to Power* (Boston: Little, Brown, 1979).

Supporters of smaller government are likely to argue that unless a program is proved efficacious, it should be diminished or eliminated. Adherents of larger government would rather continue an unsatisfactory program than risk losing an effective one. People's political perspectives guide them toward the kind of error they would rather make—and, consequently, the kind of learning they would rather attempt. Those who see government as a source of coercion may take limited knowledge of social causation to imply that the spontaneous action of individuals, as in private markets, will evolve solutions better than can be designed. Believers in bigger government take mankind's lack of knowledge in connecting policies to consequences as a challenge to learn by doing.

The importance of a philosophy of error (what kind of mistake would we like to make?) is underscored in Charles M. Judd and David A. Kenny's book on quantitative methods for *Estimating the Effects of Social Interventions*, in which they say that applied researchers should prefer type two errors (rejecting the right hypothesis) to those of type one (accepting the wrong one). They write that

> all too often in the last 20 years, evaluations of education, rehabilitation, and social welfare programs conclude that these programs have little effect. In part this may be due to failures to detect effects when in fact they exist. Given the expense of putting together and administering these social welfare programs, it is crucial that any effects that they engender be detected.[42]

On an a priori basis, one might well say that accepting the wrong hypothesis is just as bad as failing to accept the right one. Indeed, the belief in some quarters that evaluations done under academic auspices are higher in quality than those done by entrepreneurial private research entities may be due to the prospect that an even-handed approach (that is, a more unbiased one) is less likely to find effects when they are not there. Henry Aaron's *Politics and the Professors* argues that since it is inordinately difficult to ascertain causal relations, analyses are biased against finding positive effects.[43] Unless values are to drive out facts altogether, thus denying any recourse

42. Charles M. Judd and David A. Kenny, *Estimating the Effects of Social Interventions* (Cambridge: Cambridge University Press, 1981), p. 29.
43. Henry J. Aaron, *Politics and the Professors: The Great Society in Perspective* (Washington, D.C.: Brookings Institution, 1978).

to experience, some findings must still be accepted. How much credence to place in them depends on the values of the evaluator, as well as on the merits of what is being evaluated.

THE EVOLUTIONARY PERSPECTIVE

Consider the interaction between a project and its local organizational setting. Paul Berman stresses the role of "mutual adaptation" in effective "micro" (local-level) implementation. He offers the example of the federal Right-to-Read Program, in which a "step-by-step management plan" for the improvement of students' reading scores was provided to schools. In most cases, teacher strikes and parental resistance or superficial adoption of the plan without any actual classroom changes resulted in "ineffective implementation." Students' scores appeared to improve only in a few instances where the plans were adapted to particular characteristics of specific classroom settings and where this was paralleled by adaptation on the part of teachers and administrators. Berman perceives the crucial adaptive processes in effective micro-implementation to "consist of many decisions made over time by many local actors."[44]

Such a series of decisions made over time eventually delayed and confounded the outcome of the EDA's minority employment project in Oakland. In the study of the project presented earlier, it was observed that "programs can be delayed, modified, scaled down, and otherwise adapted or distorted to fit their environment."[45] In its effort to meet its dual objectives, the construction of public works and the creation of jobs for the hardcore unemployed, two corresponding strings of actions were initiated by the EDA. However simple the original goals, the eventual series of adaptive decisions by federal and local actors resulted in the delay of the never more than partially completed project. Implementation of the job training program was encumbered by disparate organizational objectives. At the federal level EDA and HEW disagreed on the very development of the training program. Implementation within the Oakland community involved negotiation between constituency groups and the syn-

44. Paul Berman, "The Study of Macro- and Micro-Implementation," *Public Policy* 26 (Spring 1978):172–74.
45. This book, p. 110.

chronization of the public's expectations of the EDA and "the feds' " expectations of "the locals."[46] A policy alters its form as it evolves into a program confronted with myriad organizational and community (environmental) pressures.

Both beneficial and detrimental adaptation can be expected during the progressive dispersion of responsibility from one central site to many local sites during the implementation of an original mandate. As a federal policy mandate is expressed downward toward local delivery in the implementing hierarchy, its local programs, with the same directives, are translated differently in dissimilar environments. This tendency toward divergence during adaptation was made evident when organizational units within the EDA itself drew different conclusions about the program's authority structure. The Western Area Office expressed its demand for greater authority in the process that was formally, if feebly, controlled by Washington.[47]

EDA's Oakland employment project was the site of but one local implementation. Imagine the multiplication of this series of adaptations from the federal level to each of the local delivery sites in any community-oriented federal program. The possibility of divergence in perspectives is bound to rise as the number of local implementation areas increases. Do we give up on implementation as overwhelmed by complexity or do we reconceptualize our understanding?

An evolutionary perspective may serve to ease the unsettling sense of discontinuity experienced by students of implementation. The implementation process may be seen as part of a larger process, the policy process, its activities corresponding to those of other organizing forces in the world, for all living things implement, evaluate, learn to adapt and evolve.[48]

In primitive life forms, data collection is accomplished through

46. Ibid., p. 47.
47. Ibid., p. 51.
48. James W. Valentine, "The Evolution of Multicellular Plants and Animals," *Evolution: Readings from "Scientific American"* (San Francisco: W. H. Freeman and Company, 1978), p. 68; and Edward D. Wilson, "Animal Communication," *Animal Societies and Evolution: Readings from "Scientific American"* (San Francisco: W. H. Freeman and Company, 1981), pp. 10–17. Two excellent accounts of evolution are Ernst Mayr, *The Growth of Biological Thought* (Cambridge, Mass.: Harvard University Press, 1982); and Theodosius Dobzhansky, Francisco J. Ayala, G. Ledyard Stebbins, and James W. Valentine, *Evolution* (San Francisco, Calif.: W. H. Freeman and Co., 1977).

osmosis. The single-cell animal evaluates information from its surroundings. Its behavior is always reflective of an ever-changing environment. In other animals, the need for feedback is met in more sophisticated ways. A bat finds its bearings by means of echolocation. It emits sound waves and monitors their rates and angles of return. It adjusts its flight according to the feedback it generates and receives from its environment.

Humans are not born with policy-evaluative abilities. As a society, we are learning them. There is no specific genetic program behind our plans for social action. We have no formally planned policy echolocation process that would enable us to make our policies "fly right." If implementation is flight, in this sense, then evaluation should serve as a kind of policy-program echolocation during implementation.

Policy implementation requires a greater degree of discretion than does the flight of a bat. More than chemical osmosis or sonar echolocation, policy evaluation is a conscious attempt to generate and learn from policy-relevant feedback. At this we are novices. Our ideal is that of increasing the effective utilization of information; evaluation during implementation should engender not a summary but a continuous learning process.[49]

Social policies and analyses of them are intertwined; they evolve together. If policy analysis is intended to improve policy making, implementation analysis must aim to improve program execution as it takes place. This adaptive analytical function should serve as a feedback mechanism. Policy objectives need not be blindly pursued but may be reconsidered as they are pursued. Several characteristics of implementation lend themselves to this evolutionary perspective.

Our view is based on the premise that a policy evolves during its implementation by adaptation. Words on paper, mandated by an executive or administrative order, a statute, or a court ruling are translated into actual operations in a real environment. The process of adaptive translation subjects a policy to the most fundamental evolutionary test, that of its viability within the environment.

Most genetic alterations occur over thousands and even millions of years. By contrast, some of the most critical transformations of policy take place during its comparatively short-term implementation

49. See chapter 11 to the third edition of this book for a discussion of single-loop and double-loop learning.

phase. The original genetic coding sets a range within which the organism can develop; the original policy mandate delineates the range of program development. But that is all it can do. The characteristics of the program are determined by the interaction of its inherited structure with its social environment. A necessary corollary to this statement is that the environment must, in turn, be malleable in order to coexist and evolve along with intervening policies and programs.

IMPLEMENTATION AS MUTUAL ADAPTATION

During the 1970s and early 1980s, implementation studies have proliferated.[50] Yet the effects of all this implementation research have not registered themselves in more predictable relationships between policy objectives and program outcomes. And the myriad of variables that generate these outcomes have yet to be discovered and agreed on by analysts.[51] In reaction to what is widely perceived as a dismal record, students of implementation, like the evaluators before them, have sought to guard themselves against failure. Instead of learning from error as it is occurring, they hope to prevent failure before it takes place. Since there can be little learning without mistakes to learn from, however, the field of implementation is caught in a double bind: too much error suggests incompetence and too little inhibits learning.[52]

Some of the recent literature has taken a theoretical approach to the analysis of implementation. Five stages in the implementation of regulatory policy are specified by Paul Sabatier and Daniel Mazmanian: (1) "policy outputs (decisions)" require (2) "compliance . . . with those decisions" in the next stage. Compliance leads to (3) "actual impacts," which result in (4) "perceived impacts." Eventually, the original policy output is affected through (5) evaluation by the political system "in terms of major revisions (or attempted

50. Robert K. Yin, "Studying the Implementation of Public Programs," in Williams, et al., eds., *Studying Implementation*.

51. Neal Gross, Joseph B. Giacquinta, and Marilyn Bernstein, *Implementing Organizational Innovation* (New York: Basic Books, 1971), pp. 39–40.

52. Gregory Bateson developed the "double bind" concept of schizophrenia: the double bind is viewed as a trap or a closed system; escape from it requires learning, that is, moving to a higher level of understanding.

revisions)" in the content of the policy.[53] This cyclical process results in a continuous modification of policy decisions.

Sabatier and Mazmanian separate the variables affecting the realization of policy objectives into three categories. The first division consists of variables that denote the "tractability" or manageability of the problem. Many social problems are grandiose and/or amorphous. Their measurement is difficult and their resolution is dependent on numerous interrelated adjustments. Few problems can be precisely defined, and of those that seem to be definable, few are wholly solvable. The second set of variables describes the ability of the policy (and the statute embodying it) and its operational programs to control, structure, and guide implementation. Sanctions and inducements, resource adequacy, and "specificity of policy directives" are among the components of this set. The third set of factors reflect the effect of political variables, such as existing support for statutory objectives, on the implementation of a law.

We have no quarrel with this sophisticated model of implementation. There is none better in the literature. All we wish to do is observe that it, like similar statements, turns the subject matter around. In the beginning, the purpose of implementation studies was to help make policies workable. It was the workability problem that required study. If a policy was already implementable, its objectives politically palatable and attainable by available instruments and theories of policy, then there would be no need for further implementation analysis. Were there in existence a proven formula for implementation and for the modes of its control (i.e., resources, sanctions and inducements), all that would remain would be to press the administrative button: a desired policy outcome would simply emerge.

What has happened to the literature on implementation is that its objectives have become its preconditions. Instead of ending up with more effective implementation, it is apparently deemed neces-

53. Paul Sabatier and Daniel Mazmanian, "Toward a More Adequate Conceptualization of the Implementation Process—With Special Reference to Regulatory Policy," (University of California, Davis, 1978), p. 26. Report is based on research supported by National Science Foundation grant no. ENV77–20077. See also, by the same authors, *Effective Policy Implementation* (Lexington, Mass.: Lexington Books, D. Heath and Co., 1981), pp. 3–35.

sary to begin with it. Implementation analysts, therefore, work toward influencing policy design instead of policy implementation, establishing a prospective approach (a "forward map") to implementation analysis. What is worse is that we all do this. After all, no one wants to be a perpetual loser. Analysts of implementation would rather operate in a world where preconditions appear to facilitate desired outcomes than have to scrounge around for workable objectives along the way. By anticipating future difficulties, analysts hope to avoid or meliorate them. Unfortunately, wishing away the difficulties does not avoid them. To cope with new difficulties, we need resilience, the capacity to bounce back and do better under existing circumstances.[54] We need the capacity to learn during implementation. Implementation, rather than being a static subject, its ends safely tucked within the prescribed means, needs to become dynamic, with implementers learning how to overcome unforeseen obstacles. These obstacles (lack of knowledge, power, etc.) cannot be entirely avoided by prospective, anticipatory policy design: they cannot be assumed away. A prospective, anticipatory view of implementation concentrates on designing policies in advance so they are less likely to fail. Its opposite, a retrospective view, emphasizes the ability to cope after things break down. In our evolutionary (or learning) view of implementation—implementation as mutual adaptation—a little anticipation and a lot of resilience go a long way. Combining the two so that there is continuous mutual adaptation between program and experience, implementation then being both prospective and retrospective, is admittedly a compromise. It is neither insistent on existing programs or on systemic change but on the gradualism implied in the evolutionary metaphor. Error remains, but, we think, it is not as great as if either approach were followed alone.

This book on implementation is written from a reformist perspective. We speak of it as "dual" because we do not wish to give up our connection to the past or our desire for change in the future. Dual

54. C. S. Holling, "Resilience and Stability of Ecological Systems," *Annual Review of Ecology and Systematics* 4 (1979):1–23. See also, Aaron Wildavsky, "Trial Without Error: Anticipation Versus Resilience as Strategies for Reducing Risk," paper presented at the 1983 Faculty Seminar on "Private Enterprise, Regulatory Reform, and Risk Assessment: The Role of the University," sponsored by the Chair of Free Enterprise, College of Engineering, University of Texas at Austin, April 15–17, 1983, and to be published in the proceedings of the seminar.

implementation, partially retrospective, partially prospective, both backward and forward mapping, in Elmore's evocative phrase, is a compromise. Why? Because we are compromisers. Were we to desire keeping existing policies intact, we would choose prospective implementation. Should we desire to change them, we could choose retrospective implementation. Since we desire a little of both, i.e., to pursue "the middle way," we embrace our contradictions, ending up as unabashed supporters of implementation as mutual adaptation.

11

Implementation as Exploration (1983)

ANGELA BROWNE AND AARON WILDAVSKY

> We shall not cease from exploration
> And the end of all our exploring
> Will be to arrive where we started
> And know the place for the first time.
>
> T. S. ELIOT

Looking back, retrospectively rationalizing their behavior, implementers may say that what they did is what they always meant to do, especially if they wish to justify such behavior in the future. Perhaps this desire to reinterpret the past to serve future policy is an important reason why each generation rewrites history in its own terms. Looking forward, however, the question of causality continues to trouble the study of implementation. Changes in the desired direction may occur (for example, a decline in the crime rate due to a decrease in the teenage population) despite the fact that the program in question is irrelevant or actually moves in the opposite direction. On the other hand, failure to secure change may be attributable to forces entirely outside the program's control (say, budget cuts due to inflation). Given that there are a multitude of forces at work on any particular program or agency, the same difficulties that bedevil evaluation may frustrate the attempt to locate the responsibility for implementation.

The trade-offs policy analysts are used to considering in policy design, between development and distribution or between efficiency and equity, also have to be made in implementation.[1] Rufus Brown-

---

1. For further discussion see Frank S. Levy, Arnold J. Meltsner, and Aaron Wildavsky, *Urban Outcomes: Schools, Streets and Libraries* (Berkeley and Los Angeles: University of California Press, 1974).

ing, Dale Rogers Marshall, and David H. Tabb make this point particularly well:

> Efforts to benefit minorities, like efforts to improve the environment or achieve any other desirable end, must balance the benefits of high federal control to achieve that end against the disadvantages. The traditional opposition of local units to federal control and the appeal to the norm of local home rule are important political realities and accurate reflections of the inherent technical or logistical limitations of central control in large complex political systems. Grants with high federal control are often rejected by or not given to jurisdictions most in need of change but resistant to federally imposed changes. An argument can be made that with a given amount of federal funds programs with less national control . . . actually bring about more change than more coercive programs, like Model Cities, because more local jurisdictions participate. Even though the level of change benefitting minorities in each jurisdiction may be less, the total change is greater.[2]

Browning, Marshall, and Tabb end their paper with a provocative statement: "Implementation research has contributed to the growing awareness of the complexity of translating public policy into practice and to increasingly sophisticated analyses of the multi-causal interactive patterns. At some point this kind of applied research merges with more basic research into the processes of change in political systems and the optimistic view of policy as an easily manipulable leverage point begins to fade. We think the study of implementation is reaching that point." Should this be so, should it prove difficult to disentangle changes desired in implementation of a particular program from all the changes going on elsewhere, the difficulties experienced in trying to carve out a well-defined domain for implementation would become more understandable. Since some changes cannot easily be separated from others, judging implementation by the degree to which original intentions have been met is not always (or often) possible. As Alex Radian wrote to Aaron Wildavsky in a letter:

> Suppose we (implementation theorists) were present at the creation (of policy), what could we say that would be at the same time useful, possible and desirable? I argue that the study of implementation is

2. Rufus Browning, Dale Rogers Marshall, and David H. Tabb, "Implementation and Political Change: Sources of Local Variation in Federal Social Programs," in *Effective Policy Implementation*, edited by Daniel Mazmanian and Paul Sabatier (Lexington, Mass.: D. C. Heath, 1981).

self-centered and therefore has not produced policy relevant knowledge. By self-centered I mean that the question asked is always why has implementation failed and how can policies be made so that they will be more implementable. The inherent assumption is that what is good for implementation is necessarily good for policy and politics and that if we would only find the key to effective implementation we would be able to incorporate it into policy. It is much like the error that public finance theorists have been making for years, if we could only find optimal tax structures policy makers will adopt them. Your notion of simplicity suffers from this weakness. In the tax field policy makers are forced to make increasingly complex policies because that helps to make the tax burden vague and because every pressure group demands its own special benefit. True it is more difficult to implement complex policies, but unless the rules of politics are changed it is not possible to make simple policies.[3]

If change—altered relationships among participants leading to different outcomes—is the idea behind implementation, the continuous adjustment of objectives is called for just as much as modification of instruments for attaining them. Implementation ceases being static; it becomes dynamic by virtue of incorporating learning of what to prefer as well as how to achieve it. Implementation is no longer solely about getting what you once wanted but, instead, it is about what you have since learned to prefer until, of course, you change your mind again. As implementation becomes a moving target, the vocabulary of creation and completion becomes less appropriate than the language of evolution.

EVOLUTION SANS LEARNING

That learning occurs does not mean it will prove effective. Because change takes place at different levels of organization, the entire entity may not learn a single lesson but different lessons located on different levels. Since the preferences of participants are also changing and the time for learning is short, elements of the organization may discover that they are marching for the right reasons in the wrong directions. As James March and Zur Shapira observe:

> In the typical case, it is possible to show how a simple set of adaptive rules will permit the organization to find optimal, or near optimal, choices if experience is prolonged enough, the environment and organizational tastes are stable enough, and the search terrain is orderly

3. Alex Radian to Aaron Wildavsky, February 2, 1979.

enough. In such situations, learning and selection become comparatively powerful tools of the intendedly rational organization or individual. The interest for students of behavioral decision theory in this perspective might lie both in the linkage it makes between the intelligence of calculation and the intelligence of adaptation, and in the opportunities for exploring the results of adaptive processes where experience is relatively brief, the environment and tastes are changing, and the search terrain is filled with local optima. Individuals, like organizations, might be seen as learning in a changing, ambiguous environment that can make the lessons they learn misleading.[4]

Not all evolution is desirable. Nor is all implementation. There are many ways in which immediate feedback may prove misleading over the long term. As Stephen Jay Gould tells it:

> All evolutionary textbooks grant a paragraph or two to a phenomenon called 'overspecialization,' usually dismissing it as a peculiar and peripheral phenomenon. It records the irony that many creatures, by evolving highly complex and ecologically constraining features for the immediate Darwinian advantage, virtually guarantee the short duration of their species by restricting its capacity for subsequent adaptation. Will a peacock or an Irish elk survive when the environment alters radically? Yet fancy tails and big antlers do lead to more copulations in the short run of a lifetime. Overspecialization is, I believe, a central evolutionary phenomenon that has failed to gain the attention it deserves because we have lacked a vocabulary to express what is really happening: the negative interaction of species-level disadvantage and individual-level advantage. . . . The general phenomenon must also regulate much of human society, with many higher-level institutions compromised or destroyed by the legitimate demands of individuals.[5]

Overspecialization, an individual-level advantage, turns out to be an overall disadvantage for the species. Another form of overspecialization is found in organizations' and individuals' overemphases on the prospective approach to policy design long after implementers have deviated from the design.

If immediate feedback can be misleading, delayed feedback can be dangerous. Policies that treat problems may appear to be successful, although, in fact, they overlook the less visible but more over-

4. James G. March and Zur Shapira, "Behavioral Decision Theory and Organizational Decision Theory," in G. Ungson and D. Braunstein, eds., *Decision Making: An Interdisciplinary Inquiry* (Boston: Kent Publishing Co., 1982), p. 112.

5. Stephen Jay Gould, "Darwinism and the Expansion of Evolutionary Theory," *Science* 216 (April 1982):380–86.

whelming growth of the actual cause(s) of the problem. A wall designed to prevent a mud flow in one place may have little effect on the cause of the flow or on the other directions the flow will take if it is blocked in only one spot. Critics of poverty programs argue that programs that "throw money at the poor" may appear to work, while the cause of poverty—something about which these programs generate little information—persists unabated.

Even when individuals believe their deeds are efficacious, they may be wrong or they may be thinking in terms of self-interest, not of social service. This dissociation of original intent and outcome may take place because the behavior of an organization is wrongly considered to be adaptive when it is in reality only geared toward achieving formal goals in predetermined ways. Individuals and their organizations may surrender increased adaptation to enhanced internal stability. According to Donald Campbell:

> A process of habit meshing takes place within any organization, in that each person's habits are a part of the environment of others. Encounters which are punishing tend to extinguish [the habit]. . . . Rewarding encounters increase the strength of behavioral tendencies on the part of both parties. Thus any social organization tends to move in the direction of internal compatibility, independently of increased adaptiveness.[6]

The members of the organization become more compatible but the organization itself becomes less adaptable.

Karl Wieck goes on to explain how selection may be adverse:

> Whenever the different members of a group contribute portions of a finished product, and the group is given feedback about performance only in terms of the group product (e.g., it is acceptable, it is unacceptable), individual members have no way of knowing how adequate their *individual* contributions were. If the outcome is judged acceptable, this could mean that individual members will repeat their actions even if they were actually irrelevant or detrimental to the outcome. Thus we would have yet another instance in which certain behavior was selected (reinforced due to the success of the group) without any relation to adaptation.[7]

6. Donald T. Campbell, "Variation and Selective Retention in Socio-Cultural Evolution," in H. R. Barringer, G. I. Blanksten, and R. Mack, eds., *Social Change in Developing Areas* (Cambridge, Mass.: Scheukman, 1965), pp. 19–49.

7. Karl E. Weick, *The Social Psychology of Organizing* (Menlo Park, Calif.: Addison-Wesley, 1969), p. 63.

Habit meshing, when combined with adverse selection, helps explain how individuals and units in an organization can believe they are doing well, for others as well as for themselves, when their clienteles or other people outside their purview see it quite differently.[8]

Overspecialization and habit meshing are forces that countervail the mutual adaptation between program and environment required during implementation. They evolve but they do not learn.

We have come to the recalcitrance of human endeavor. Policy design may well be inappropriate and, if not, will almost certainly have to be adapted to its milieu. Yet these very adaptations may lead us astray. If policy planning is precarious and program evaluation may be perverse, what hope is there for implementation?

More monitoring evidently is in order to check on whether and to what degree current objectives are being met. And if these objectives are not being met, which ones are? Since selection may be adverse, and outcomes unanticipated, it is important to understand which objectives are actually being implemented. Causal analysis grows in significance as people ask, "What effects does this program cause and why?" Answers to such questions are sought in the field of evaluation research. When evaluation is seen as an aid to implementation, knowing that things are wrong, and perhaps why they went wrong, may help put things right. Maybe, but not necessarily.

Organizations may not wish to detect or correct errors. There may be no need for them to do so, because resources are abundant, or no way for them to act because resources, including past experience and present knowledge of what to do, are insufficient. Most organizations reject the evaluations they sponsor because the results are antithetical to established forces or unfeasible in view of limited resources. Success in implementing and evaluating can hardly be guaranteed. What to do?

Just as public policy evolves, so, too, does policy analysis. Just as policy in a democracy seeks popularity, so do evaluation and implementation. In the political process, however, politicians know that sometimes they will lose. Parties and politicians are sometimes voted out of office. Avoiding loss forever would transform the political system in an undemocratic direction. Evaluators and implementers are under no such imperative. They can respond to repeated reports of

8. This paragraph is taken from Aaron Wildavsky, *Speaking Truth to Power* (Boston: Little, Brown, 1979), pp. 75–76.

failure by trying to overcome each and every difficulty. Thus the
evolution of implementation analysis is met not by selection out but
by inclusion in. It is not only government that grows larger but also
the scope of implementation and evaluation. In part this growth by
accretion is desirable; without all this thrashing about there would
be far fewer new perspectives from which to advance our understanding, even if many are discarded along the way. Insofar as this growth
represents overreaching for an unobtainable conclusiveness, as if
adding yet another set of considerations would end error, it must be
rejected as utopian. Like the process of perfecting our preferences,
merging intent entirely into outcome remains valuable as an ideal
only so long as it is recognized that perfect implementation is perfectly unobtainable. It is the process of falling short and yet trying again
that is most worthy.

LEARNING TO LEARN

In elucidating his classification of learning, Gregory Bateson began
with the notion that learning is change.[9] When an organism changes
its response to a signal or stimulus, it has learned. Bateson developed
a theoretical ladder of learning based on the idea that a change takes
place each time something is learned. In this ladder, the lowest rung
of learning is the mere "receipt of a signal" (or "learning zero").
Learning-zero is, in essence, "non-learning." It does not involve
evaluation of experience. The same error is indefinitely repeated;
there is no change in response to a continuing stimulus.

The next order of learning, "learning one" or simple learning,
incorporates feedback from the original event into the organism's
memory. When a child touches a hot iron, his reflex is to remove his
finger away from the hot metal. If he touches the hot iron again, no
learning or learning-zero has occurred. When presented with the hot
iron a third time, the child may know better than to touch it. If he
does not touch the iron, he probably has learned from the previous
experience.

A higher order of learning is "learning-to-learn" or "deutero-
learning." This "learning-to-learn" is described as "learning to learn
to receive signals." In this "double-loop" process, the one-to-one

9. Gregory Bateson, "The Logical Categories of Learning and Communication," *Steps to an Ecology of Mind* (New York: Ballantine, 1972), pp. 279–
308.

correlation between a stimulus and a change in behavior is super-seded. Information that speeds the process of change is recognized and then purposively selected from the environment.[10]

Students of organizational learning, especially Chris Argyris and Donald Schon, have applied Bateson's concepts.[11] Based on their application, we can say that in "single-loop" organizational learning, error is detected, its sources are discovered, and strategies for its correction are devised. A non-learning organization, by contrast, repeats the same error infinitely. In single-loop processes, each simple learning experience constitutes an increment of change in an organism or organization.

In double-loop or "deutero" learning, the processes are more profound. Evaluative learning generates a context for organizational change—expected and continuous change through learning. A climate of evolution through continuous self-analysis is born. "Morphogenesis" (i.e., ongoing self-evaluation and self-development) becomes the goal. In "learning to learn to receive signals," an organization may even refine its evaluative behavior (the behavior evaluating all its other behavior). The intake of policy-relevant knowledge should increase as the organization learns to learn to interpret and evaluate new signals. Its ever-improving learning and evaluative processes are deposited into an accessible organizational memory, and they are reactivated in each appropriate circumstance, facilitating organizational learning and change.

What types of organizations, programs, and policies are prepared to redesign themselves? Bo Hedberg, Paul Nystrom, and William Starbuck contend that a "self-designing organization functions most smoothly if its ideology cherishes impermanence." And, members of the self-designing organization not only "define problems for themselves and generate their own solutions, [they] . . . also evaluate and revise their solution-generating processes."[12] If this "self-designing

10. On learning and incorporating concepts, see Donald Campbell, "Reforms as Experiments," *American Psychologist* 24 (1969):409–29; and Donald Campbell, "Methods for the Experimenting Society," paper delivered to the Eastern Psychological Association, April 17, 1971.

11. Chris Argyris and Donald A. Schon, *Organization Learning: A Theory of Action Perspective* (Menlo Park, Calif.: Addison-Wesley, 1978), pp. 7–29.

12. Bo T. Hedberg, Paul C. Nystrom, and William H. Starbuck, "Camping on Seesaws: Prescriptions for a Self-Designing Organization," *Administrative Science Quarterly* 21 (March 1976):43.

organization" is the ideal, however, what happens to the original objectives that were supposed to be implemented? If both objectives and the programs designed to implement them are changing, implementation would be determined not only by looking back, so as to assess the fit between objectives and accomplishment, but also by looking forward to new, more informed relationships between ends and means.

The role of evaluation during implementation is one essential to the learning process, especially learning to redesign. Current demands for retrenchment and termination suggest that certain programs must be willing to redesign themselves, lest others do it for them. But should they redesign without learning or without evaluating? As Peter de Leon states, "The policy terminator must rely heavily on the evaluation community." Because most public programs in most public sectors in most industrialized countries are confronted with the demand to reduce expenditures, gaining understanding of how to do so is an important activity. De Leon suggests that the policy evaluation community, in conducting "careful program analysis could compensate for political inadequacies of the system."[13] It could systematize this particular redesign process and facilitate the transfer of learning from one redesigning organization to another. Without political support from external constituencies and internal organizational actors, however, the institutional reinforcement of learning is problematical.

In a report on "governmental learning," Lloyd Etheredge terms action effective when it generates information that will contribute to constructive change.[14] These changes should be evidenced by "increased differentiation of thinking about a problem (recognizing and articulating its elements) and by increasingly coherent integration and perspective on the problem and how one is thinking about it."[15] Observe a subtle switch: good decisions are those based on learning; better decisions are those that bring forth new learning. The latter are self-directing decisions in the sense that they demand

13. Peter de Leon, "Policy Evaluation and Program Termination," The Rand Paper Series, P–6807 (Santa Monica, Calif.: Rand Corporation, 1982), pp. 4, 22.

14. Lloyd Etheredge, *Government Learning: An Overview*, report sponsored by the National Science Foundation (Cambridge, Mass.: MIT Center for International Studies, 1979), p. 6.

15. Ibid., "Executive Summary," p. 2.

evaluation and redesign rather than an a priori defense of the status quo. Obviously, learning includes learning about how to realize objectives as well as about whether and to what extent they are worth achieving.

Etheredge is concerned with the development of "organizational memories that can codify experience and learning." He views improvement of evaluation and implementation of "high policy decisions to solve major problems with multi-billion dollar programs" as crucial. So he asks:

> Fifteen years after the Great Society, have Executive Branch agencies codified their organizational memories to learn how to implement programs—and how to design programs that can be implemented? And why not? In thirty years of foreign aid, what have they learned? In eighty years of hemispheric (and then global) intervention?[16]

Like many other observers, Etheredge is not impressed.

A recent General Accounting Office (GAO) report speaks eloquently to Etheredge's concerns about institutionalizing learning and memory.

GENERAL ACCOUNTING OFFICE REPORT TO THE ADMINISTRATOR, AGENCY FOR INTERNATIONAL DEVELOPMENT   EXPERIENCE—A POTENTIAL TOOL FOR IMPROVING U.S. ASSISTANCE ABROAD

DIGEST

The Agency for International Development committed, but unspent, project assistance funds increased by 325 percent—from around $1.6 billion in 1975 to nearly $5.3 billion as of Semptember 30, 1981.

Many causal factors both within and outside Agency influence have contributed to the recent slow project completion record. Prior GAO and AID reports have shown that problems hindering the success of development projects are not unique and continue to exist. The Congress has expressed concern that AID should improve development projects on the basis of lessons learned and that AID must ensure replication of successful projects elsewhere in the world. Accordingly, GAO reviewed how AID identifies, records, and uses the knowledge and experience gained from development projects.

APPLYING LESSONS LEARNED

GAO found that the Agency staff does apply lessons learned in developing new projects. The application of this information, however, is

16. Ibid., p. 20.

restricted primarily to the personal initiative and experience of individuals involved in a particular project. This personal experience network for finding and using lessons learned is weakened due to staff turnover.

RECORDING LESSONS LEARNED

GAO also found that lessons learned are neither systematically nor comprehensively identified and recorded during the life of a project by those directly involved with the project. Little encouragement or incentive is provided to AID staff members to routinely identify and record the lessons they learn.

GAO believes that the AID "institutional memory" system for projects—the Development Information System—is a potentially valuable and useful tool that can complement personal experience and other sources which AID staff members currently use. However, the use and the value of this system are limited due to

—lack of staff knowledge about the system,
—lack of user feedback,
—the necessary documents not being forwarded . . . and subsequently entered into the system, and
—lack of a[n] information analysis service for AID staff.

The AID information system has become virtually inoperative in providing information to project designers.[17]

This report sees evaluation and implementation as interconnected processes of learning. The quality of evaluation can improve over time, taking implementation with it.[18] Congress is concerned that AID has not improved its development projects, that it does not transfer knowledge from one site to the next. Opportunities for learning during implementation are overlooked, as are opportunities to learn from previous implementations. This is because organizations, programs, and policies are not designed with learning in mind: the general organizational resistance to change supplants the organizational tendency to learn.

It may be that the inability to learn (or, more accurately, for elements of AID to learn from each other) is a purely administrative defect. Perhaps better record-keeping and enhanced attention to disseminating the results are all that is necessary to improve learn-

17. General Accounting Office, ID–82–36, June 15, 1982.
18. Eleanor Chelimsky, "The Nature, Definition, and Measurement of Quality in Program Evaluation," *GAO Review* 17 (Fall 1982):46.

ing.[19] Yet efficient administration cannot counterbalance vacillation in policy goals. It is well known that the objectives of foreign aid have undergone considerable change and, indeed, that from the very beginning they have been in turmoil. If the purpose of aid is merely to support the group that governs (think, say, of Zaire), it might not make much difference how the money is spent or that anything is learned while spending it. Should AID officials discover that efforts to improve projects based on other experiences bring down complaints that they are destabilizing friendly governments, their interest in learning may be diminished. Their attention may be diverted toward the preferences of an existing government in a specific nation, away from the people who are supposed to be benefited by the project and away from any form of large-scale organizational learning. What is worth learning, apparently, depends on what is worth implementing. Were this supposition to have a certain merit, the implementers (in this case, AID agents in the field) would not shoulder all the blame. Instead, the difficulties in learning attributed to implementers in the field might better belong to policy makers at home, who cannot quite make up their minds whether their programs should serve the populace or the government of the host country, and whose goals are often vague and vacillating.

Come to think of it, policy making, whether foreign or domestic, is often inconsistent. When the emphasis is on controlling the cost of medical care, for instance, programs become restrictive; when the emphasis is on access, programs become more open; and when quality of care is at the forefront, both cost-control and coverage may suffer. For the realization of which of these objectives, concurrent and conflicting as they are, should implementers be held responsible?[20]

LEARNING TO IMPLEMENT FOR WHAT?

In pluralist polities, the visible play of organized interests results either in objectives that change, because different forces vie for control of the area of policy in question; or objectives that are vague,

19. Robert B. Garey and John F. Sacco, "Everyday Bureaucratic Realities and Program Evaluation," *GAO Review* 17 (Fall 1982):30.

20. Theodore Marmor, "Can the U.S. Learn from Canada?," in S. Andreopoulos, ed., *National Health Insurance: Can We Learn from Canada?* (New York: Wiley, 1975).

because the conflicts are compromised; or objectives that are contradictory, because first one side and then another receives priority
treatment. Always, the implementers are faced with the consequences: they cannot win because even a coherent policy is bound to
disaffect someone. Working with conflicting expectations, the implementer plays a no-win game. So some students of public policy blame
the political system that leads them to behave as they do.

   This attribution of "system blame" seeks to show that the existing
polity is flawed. In *The Fiscal Crisis of Capitalism*, for example,
James O'Connor argues that the capitalist political system is inherently contradictory. It must provide ever-increasing amounts of
welfare payments to "buy off" the discontent of the populace, but
then it discovers that taking these funds out of the productive process
leaves it too poor to continue paying off.[21] More modest flaws are
alleged in the literature on the capture of regulatory commissions by
the industries they are supposed to regulate. Because the private
interests involved have a more palpable stake in the decisions these
commissions make, they end up exerting the most influence.[22]

   Pluralism itself may be deemed the villain. Instead of celebrating
the virtues of political competition, for example, Theodore J. Lowi,
in *The End of Liberalism*, castigates the government for failing to use
its formal authority to propound and enforce norms of policy embodying the public interest. This reformist criticism is most relevant
for students of implementation because it makes the gap between
government objectives and poor performance the central feature of
its analysis, blaming not the administrators but the politicians for
failing to enunciate and stick to clear and consistent policies.[23] Who
is to be blamed has an effect on what is to be implemented. People
who wish to blame the capitalist system and people who wish to

21. James O'Connor, *The Fiscal Crisis of the State* (New York: St. Martin's
Press, 1975).
   22. Marver Bernstein, *Regulating Business by Independent Commission*
(Princeton: Princeton University Press, 1955). Of course, advocates of leaving
decisions to private markets take the opposite position: it is governmental
interference that creates the monopolies that favor the regulated. See any
issue of *Regulation* magazine.
   23. Theodore J. Lowi, *The End of Liberalism: The Second Republic of the
United States*, 2nd ed. (New York: W. W. Norton, 1979). See, for example,
pp. 272–94.

blame the bureaucracy have to learn quite different modes of implementing their paradigms.

Learning is a golden concept. Everyone is for it. That alone should give us pause. Different parts of organizations may learn different and perhaps opposed lessons. Lessons are often learned by subparts of the whole political system, while resisted by other subparts. Is learning to implement public programs learning how to achieve pre-existing goals, learning how to alter the mix of objectives and the resources employed to achieve them, or learning how to change the political system that produces the policies that deserve to be carried out? Is learning confined to discovering better means to old ends or ought it also to be concerned with learning what to prefer? If studies of implementation look more and more like "the house that Jack built," each step depending on others that have come before and go on afterward, that is not because anyone is opposed to learning but, on the contrary, because there are deep philosophical differences over what sort of learning there ought to be—programmatic, policy-oriented, or systemic. Reactionaries (those who favor past programs) want to learn how to get rid of present-day programs and reinstitute those of another era. Conservatives (who favor the status quo) want to learn how to better implement existing programs. Reformers want to learn how to implement policies with somewhat different objectives, and radicals want systemic change. Radicals favor prospective, future-oriented implementation so they can work with a clean slate, unencumbered by the past; reactionaries favor retrospective implementation, looking back to the original program; and reformers, keeping, as always, to the middle, want it both ways—retrospective for the parts of the past they wish to preserve and prospective for the future they wish to change. The field of implementation, dealing as it must with the relationships between what is desired, done, and achieved, is bound to reflect these differing views regarding the good (or, at least, better) government that brought this field into being.

RECONCEPTUALIZING IMPLEMENTATION

Why is it so difficult to rethink the role of the implementer? Is it because the implementer is, by definition, implementing a policy or plan of action that has been designed by others located at a higher point in the hierarchy? Mandates are sent downward—resources enabling their implementation to trickle down—and, finally, information as to the workability of the mandate works its way back up—or does it?

Perhaps resistance to a new understanding of implementation is linked to the pervasive influence of the notion of control. Things are controlled or they are not. If something is not controlled, it is perceived to be out of control, and nothing productive is rendered. When implementers are delegated control over some or all of the implementation process, they have been allowed "discretion"—not given control.

Most of the theoretical literature on implementation identifies "control" as a crucial determinant of process and outcome. Although it is generally agreed that the type of control exercized should reflect the characteristics of the policy being implemented, the role of the implementer as purposive evaluator, i.e., as a learner, is not emphasized.[24]

Giandomenico Majone demonstrates that "the prevailing mode of control is closely related to the structure (as well as the task environment) of the organization," for each of three basic types of organization. "Output control" is favored in market transactions and for-profit firms; "input control" and "process/behavior control" is utilized in public bureaucracies and bureaucratic components of private and nonprofit organizations; and "collegial control" is useful in professional organizations.[25] Majone explains his "modes of control" in terms of "two basic conditions: the availability of suitable output measures, and the knowledge of the production function." By dichotomizing these variables, he delineates four modes of control.[26]

24. Ladislav Cerych suggests that "strong central control facilitates implementation of higher education reforms provided that other (crucial) conditions are met." "Implementation of Higher Education Reforms in Europe," chapter 8, in *The Policy Perspective*, Burton R. Clark, ed. (Berkeley and Los Angeles: University of California Press, forthcoming).

25. Giandomenico Majone, "Modes of Control and Institutional Learning," no. 17 in the series Guidance, Control and Performance Evaluation in the Public Sector (Laxenburg, Austria: Research Group, Center for Interdisciplinary Research, University of Bielefeld, 1981/82), p. 12.

26. Ibid., p. 8. Controlled implementation, as described by Thompson, "features precise statutory mandates and much oversight activity." This type of implementation depends on "a well understood technology that is not

Majone on Modes of Control:

KNOWLEDGE OF PRODUCTION FUNCTIONS

	Complete	Incomplete
Unambiguous	Output Control or Behavior Control	Output Control
Ambiguous	Behavior/ Process Control	Input Control Collegial Control

(OUTPUT MEASURE)

The category combining "incomplete knowledge" and "ambiguous output measure" is the most important in our discussion of control. For where output measures are ambiguous and, at the same time, knowledge of the production function is incomplete, the tendency is to favor process over outcome evaluation. Majone offers the example of physician care, in which output (the rate of cure or remedy) may say little about the quality of care received or the relationship between that quality and the outcome of an illness. Yet, if the variables active in the process are this difficult to pinpoint, control cannot be exercised by measuring that process. Instead, Majone suggests two forms of control suitable to programs in which knowledge is incomplete and outcomes are ambiguous. One is input control (i.e., budgetary and accounting controls over administrative discretion by limiting the ability of the "bureaucratic manager to substitute one input for another in order to take advantage of new opportunities and changing circumstances"); the other is collegial control (i.e., the promotion of "mutual adjustment," "learning and effective cooperation" via

---

bottom heavy," "environmental stability," and "the efficaciousness of overhead institutions" and is most desirable in "a debilitating socio-political milieu" and in the "absence of tempered commitment to the policy within the implementing agency." See Frank Thompson, "Policy Implementation and Overhead Control," University of Georgia, Athens, Georgia, typescript, April 1983.

peer review based on information that is "largely 'tacit' and cannot be articulated in explicit standards and rules of behavior").[27]

The problem of "control design," or of generating an effective "control mechanism," lurks in every policy formulator's conference room. Whether it is recognized at that early point in the policy process or only evolves to recognizable proportions once an implementation process is under way, the control design dilemma is one forever torn between locating the evaluative perspective and the power at the top, or distributing it throughout the implementing organization.

On further analysis, the very assignment of implementation responsibility will determine much of the character of the implementation process. To wit, Jan-Erik Lane's "typology of implementation conditions" dichotomizes circumstances in which the actors find themselves.[28]

	Status of Conditions	
	Controllable	Uncontrollable
The Formulator	I	II
The Implementer	III	IV

The fourth box in Lane's table—the category where formally designed, officially designated control is least pronounced—is of special interest here. As in Majone's fourth category of incomplete knowledge and ambiguous measures, weak control design may result in greater freedom for and innovation on the part of actors at the bottom or even outside of the implementation hierarchy. Indeed, at the bottom of the hierarchy, where implementation and environment merge, actors and outsiders may bear so much influence that they share the role of implementer. Of course, this is the territory where the risks are greatest. As Lane argues,

27. Majone, "Modes of Control . . . ," p. 10.
28. Jan-Erik Lane, "The Concept of Implementation," *Statsvetenskaplig Tidskri* 1 (1983):36.

This is the instability of the implementation phenomenon: the larger the set of conditions that the implementer controls the greater is the probability that the behavior of the implementer will affect the outcomes which may work both ways; more latitude in decision making on the part of the implementer may be conducive to either successful implementation or to implementation failure; it will present the implementer with the opportunity to move the policy closer to the environment, overcoming major faults or minor inadequacies in the original outline of the policy, but simultaneously such local discretion on the part of the implementer opens up the possibilities for reinterpreting of the policy.[29]

Lane calls this reinterpretation or reinvention "reimplementation" and suggests that this concept is important to an understanding of implementation failure. But reimplementation can also be the source of implementation success, defined as successful exploration. Failure as an outcome, in our view, should only mean failure to learn how to do better.

Despite the risks involved, the least controlled implementation offers the most opportunity for exploration. For this reason, both Majone's and Lane's fourth boxes (where both agreement and knowledge are in short supply) deserve a second interpretation.

ROOTING LEARNING IN ORGANIZATIONAL LIFE

Organizations may wish to learn, but what they attempt to learn may be different. We can think of Majone's and Lane's categories as types of organizations or, better still, as ways of life in which organizational members share values legitimating their preferred social practices.

Take, for example, three types of organizations. Market organizations, based on competitive bidding and bargaining, seek to maximize the total gain to the group, provided that members are allowed to receive unequal rewards according to their contribution. The sole purpose of authority is to maintain freedom of contract. Programs are judged by results, not by the processes involved in achieving them. The idea is to do as well as possible, given available resources, not to get there in any prescribed way. Hierarchical organizations, by contrast, are based on inculcating inequality (i.e., specialization and the division of labor) in order to achieve and maintain social

29. Ibid., pp. 36–37.

order. Every substantive goal (say, improvement in reading) is, therefore, subordinate to the hierarchy's procedural goals. How things are done and who has the right to do them is at least as important as what is done because the overriding purpose of the organization is to maintain official differences among members. The purpose of the collegium is to diminish differences among members. Because differences in ability or expertise suggest that some people have a right to make decisions for others, there is no authority other than what members voluntarily agree to on a case-by-case basis.

What do members who adhere to these distinctive principles of organization, we ask, want to learn about the implementation of public policy? Supporters of market principles wish to maximize results, no matter who receives them. Thus a market approach might lead to the overall maximization of the group's reading scores, even if most of the gain is concentrated in a few students. Members of hierarchies wish to inculcate proper procedures so as to keep their organization together. Organizational structure and the maintenance of it is always at the forefront of their consciousnesses. In order to support this way of life, reading scores should increase differently according to each individual's respective ability or some other fixed criterion of demarcation. To adherents of a collegium, which seeks to live by egalitarian norms, reducing the spread in the group's reading ability is more important than the extent to which any one member's reading is improved. It would be better to lower overall levels so long as the disparity among readers is also diminished. Among learning in market organizations (to maximize total scores), in collegiums (to minimize differences among scores), and in hierarchies (to improve individual scores by recognized criteria of merit), there are considerable differences.

The student of implementation may well favor learning over non-learning, but that preference has to be modified by the realization that there is more than one way to organize social life. One consequence of living by different values and practices is that even if different organizations learn about implementation, conflict over policy will by no means be at an end. The second consequence is that different types of organizations are disposed by their structure (their patterns of values and practices) to learn different things. Hierarchies want to learn about who is entitled to have what by reason of status, markets about how to maximize total results, collegiums about the equalization of outcomes. Insofar as evaluation is concerned, hierarchies evaluate to make certain proper procedures are followed; collegiums evaluate to get the work analyzed from the vantage point of the worst off; and market organizations evaluate to utilize the optimum mix of resources to achieve the greatest overall gain, regardless of disparate individual outcomes.

A third consequence of attending to the plurality of organizational structures is a reminder of a home truth: the difficulty of implementation depends on how hard the task is to accomplish. Let us categorize this dimension as the extent of change in personal behavior that is desired. The dimensions that interest Majone (knowledge of production function) and Lane (status of conditions) can be exemplified by the amount of search for new information that will be utilized in the process of making public policy.

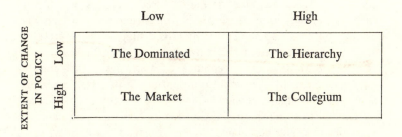

SEARCH FOR INFORMATION

		Low	High
EXTENT OF CHANGE IN POLICY	Low	The Dominated	The Hierarchy
	High	The Market	The Collegium

Hierarchies are concerned with maintaining the existing order. Where they used to rest their legitimacy on divine right, nowadays they rely on science and expertise: the right person in the right job most capable of making the right decision. So hierarchies search for new information to do a better job of holding together the existing social order. Hierarchies are by aspiration hypotheses-generating and knowledge-testing organizations, but they are slow to discard old truths, returning to the old until the new can be comfortably accommodated with the existing order. On the other end of the organization spectrum, collegiums are high both on search and on change. They search for new evidence of inequality and new knowledge of how to reduce it. They want to change not only disparities in resources but in human beings themselves so as to fit them for a life of power sharing. Their opposites, the people they want to change, may be called "the dominated." Being fatalistic, always awaiting orders, controlled by outsiders, the dominated search neither for information nor for change. The market organization is the home of Herbert Simon's "satisficing"; it inculcates change via a minimum of search, learning just enough to seek to satisfy the latest consumer needs—and never learning more. People who prefer market arrangements take individuals as they are (as economists say, preferences are "exogenously" determined). They search hard to satisfy existing preferences; new consumer goods, not new tastes, are the hallmarks of societies organized along market principles.

Organizations are more than instruments; they are themselves bundles of desires, for organizations encapsulate ways of life as well as modes of achievement. How, indeed, could people be persuaded to commit themselves to organizational life (omitting, of course, the dominated) unless the organizations themselves contain the ties that bind—their values legitimating their desired practices. For hierarchies, authority is in the organization, the structure specifying who has the right to act, to implement, and to evaluate. Collegiums reject authority as coercive (as in hierarchies) or inegalitarian (as in markets): only voluntary acceptance, each and every time, conveys that right to act. Markets want transient authority to act, to implement, and to evaluate, enough to defend the sanctity of contract but not enough to bring the permanent hierarchies policemen and the tax collectors. The dominated exemplify negative authority, so to speak, as others make the rules that run their lives.[30] They have no rights to act, to implement or to evaluate.

The different organizational life styles supply the missing link in

30. For development of these categories, see Aaron Wildavsky and Mary Douglas, *Risk and Culture* (Berkeley and Los Angeles: University of California Press, 1982); Mary Douglas, "Cultural Bias," in *In the Active Voice* (London and Boston: Routledge & Kegan Paul, 1982); and Aaron Wildavsky, "Models of Political Regimes; or Pluralism Means More Than One Political Culture in One Country at One Time," paper prepared for a conference on "The Meaning of American Pluralism," Center for the Study of Federalism, Temple University, May 16–19, 1982, and to be published in a volume edited by Ellis Katz and Daniel Elazar (Philadelphia: Institute for the Study of Human Issues Press, forthcoming).

the study of evaluation and implementation. The basic assumptions, so deep they are hardly ever challenged, are that all organizations are (a) basically the same, and (b) interested in evaluation and implementation, that is, error detection and error correction. And so they are, except that the objectives of these laudable endeavors are markedly different. Once that is understood—that evaluation and implementation may be desirable but are definitely different in various types of organizations—the exasperation surrounding the subject (why can't evaluators and implementers do the right thing or, sometimes, do anything at all?) should give way to sustained social analysis. For then, at long last, implementation and evaluation would become social studies, which means that we would seek to root explanations in social (or, as we say, organizational) life rather than, as is done now, leaving them suspended in mid-air, as if they were unconnected to human preferences. There is quite a difference between saying "evaluate!" "implement!" as if these were angelic activities, virtuous but disembodied, and deciding how much authority, competition, domination, or equality there ought to be in our public lives.

What organizational structure would we prefer and in what proportion if we wanted high degrees of search and change, that is, if we wanted to detect and correct mistakes, changing our preferences as well as the means of implementing them? Without strong market forces there could be no evaluative enterprise. Only members of markets believe in competition for its own sake and in evaluation for the sake of competition. Without evaluators that are multiple, external, and independent (as are bidders and bargainers in competitive markets), there can be no genuine evaluation. Toward what end, however, will this market-oriented evaluation and the implementation that follows from it be directed? A call for evaluation and implementation that represents a wider range of values would be unnecessary if those values held by all significant elements of the population were already represented in the market. Participation according to collegial principles is essential if those worst off in the possession of critical resources are to receive due consideration. But how do we know whether good intentions are likely to be realized? Without adherence to hierarchical principles, no one would be concerned with perfecting processes. Yet without strict causal knowledge linking resources to objectives, we often must rely on the next best harbinger of results, namely, processes. Evidently, then, some combination of different organizational structures—hierarchies, collegiums, and markets—facilitates evaluation and implementation.

Toward this end, a "multiorganizational analytic perspective," such as that suggested by Benny Hjern and David Porter, makes sense.[31] Hjern and Porter claim that an implementation structure is multiorganizational—"clusters" of public and private organizations carry out and influence all implementation, indirectly and directly.[32] In our understanding, this means that markets, hierarchies, and collegia cross paths during implementation processes. While these organizational components of the implementation process do not, by virtue of their differences, attain the ultimate in evaluation and implementation, their interactions should result in a reasonable level of multiorganizational learning. To say more than this would be to say more than we know—which combinations of organizational structures are optimal under what conditions for diverse purposes.

EXPLORATION

Policy implementation is hypothesis-testing: it is exploration. Any political body that argues otherwise mistakenly regards itself as omniscient and omnipotent. Its territory has been conquered and mapped: all unknowns have been banished from its kingdom. With the unquestioned assurance that the central plan is ethically, politically, and practically error-free, implementation can proceed without the expectation that learning will ensue.

Yet there is no amount of statutory specificity and top-down control that will prevent an implementation process from becoming a test of its own efficacy. Where coercion may subdue political obstructions to the implementation process, rarely can it compensate for a misshapen plan of action, for a misdiagnosis of the problem to be treated, or for a lack of foresight. Implementation failure, then, does not only affect democratically organized systems. It is common to all policy formulating and implementing processes.

31. Benny Hjern and David O. Porter, "Implementation Analysis: A New Unit of Administrative Analysis," *Organization Studies* 2/3 (1981):211–27.

32. Gordon Chase writes of the implementing agency head as "final arbiter of interagency struggles" between and among overhead and line agencies in "Implementing a Human Services Program," *Public Policy* 27 (Fall 1979): 431.

What an organization devoted to learning can do about implementation failure is to utilize it as a route to implementation success —successful exploration. Rather than seeking to make tractable eternally intractable social problems, or designing detailed problemsolving policies, a learning organization must avoid an unquestioning, uninquiring, myopic stance. It must analyze its policies for their informational yield. It should evaluate its implementation of these policies, not against prospectively stated objectives alone, but in light of discoveries made during implementation.

Evaluation that is insensitive to the problems of transforming policy makers' ideas into implementers' actions is obtuse; it leaves the best bits behind unexamined. Evaluators who hold implementers accountable for each increment of this transformation and nothing else are, in essence, only accountants.[33] Without denying the importance of accountability studies, there should also be an appreciation of evaluation as continuous learning. Locating all evaluation along a continuum, accountability will approach one extreme while learningoriented evaluation, searching for experience, falls toward the other.

ACCOUNTABILITY EVALUATION	LEARNING EVALUATION

←——————————————————————————————→

On this continuum, learning evaluation is the most abstract information-producing activity, because it does not merely compare outcomes against a single baseline of expectations. Instead, the evaluative criteria are fluid, dynamic, and open-ended. Baseline (preimplementation) and outcome (post-implementation) comparisons become differentials in a perpetual policy-analytic calculus. The rate at which baseline (original) objectives are redefined along the way represents the level of learning occurring during implementation.

Accountability seeks to preserve existing relationships by holding the actors at the bottom responsible to the expectations at the top. Learning evaluation strives to unearth faulty assumptions, reshape

33. "The bulk of evaluation presently being performed by most Federal agencies is not yet highly sophisticated but typically involves the simple counting of activities, transactions or services accomplished." Eleanor Chelimsky, *An Analysis of the Proceedings of a Symposium on the Use of Evaluation by Federal Agencies*, vol. 2, November 17–19, 1976 (MacLean, Va.: Metrek, 1977), p. 45.

misshapen policy designs, and continuously redefine goals in light of new information derived during implementation. That, the emphasis on learning, is why evaluation becomes more like policy analysis. That, also, is why analysis that hopes to facilitate learning should include the implementer among the crucial players and active agents in the policy process. Baseline objectives are often resculpted at the very scene of implementation (the site of service delivery, the locus of community interaction, or the interaction between layers of bureaucracy). The learning society views the implementer as a source of new information. On this basis, a case can be made for the reconceptualization of implementation as an exploratory rather than an unquestioning, instrumental, and even subservient type of behavior.

Appendix

EDA CHRONOLOGY

1965

August 26 Passage of the Public Works and Economic Development Act.

October Eugene Foley appointed assistant secretary of commerce in charge of the EDA.

December Short visit to Oakland by Foley and Amory Bradford; they meet with black community groups but do not see the mayor.

1966

January 28–29 Dunsmuir House conference between EDA officials and Oakland business and government leaders. Foley commits at least $15 million.

February Bradford conducts extensive interviews with business, labor, and political leaders to form an acceptable employment policy.

March Foley approves employment plan idea.

April 29 Announcement by Foley of $23 million in public works projects.

October 5 Foley resigns.

November 12 Employment Plan Review Board Committee approves World Airways plan; Bradford leaves.

1967

January Charles Patterson takes over as EDA Oakland representative.

January 27 Port of Oakland decides to move terminal project to new location, thus ending a controversy about filling material at the previous location.

May 6 Port signs agreement with Charles Luckman and Associates to design airline hangar.

1968

April 1 Navy complains about flight safety hazards at marine terminal.

April 2 Charles Luckman and Associates notify the port of a substantial cost overrun on the airline hangar; the port requests additional funding from the EDA.

April 7 Port submits to the EDA a plan for a revolving restaurant at the marine terminal.

June EDA agrees to fund the construction of the West Oakland Health Center.

June World Airways Compliance Report shows drop in total number of minority employed from 129 to 111.

August U.S. General Accounting Office is critical of the EDA's grant and loan arrangements with the Port of Oakland.

December 23 Charles Patterson is replaced as EDA Oakland representative by Hugh Taylor; Patterson becomes vice-president of World Airways.

1969

Early February Parties meet to sign a contract for construction of the West Oakland Health Center.

February 26 EDA head Ross Davis denies the request for additional funding for hangar project.

April 4 Robert A. Podesta replaces Davis as assistant secretary of commerce for EDA.

April 7 The navy and the port finally resolve their differences on construction of the terminal.

December Contracts are awarded for construction of the terminal.

December 11 EDA turns down the port's request for funds for the proposed revolving restaurant at the marine terminal.

1970

February 12 EDA notifies the port that final plans and specifications for a hangar costing *less* than $9.5 million will have to be submitted by December 31, 1970, and that employment guarantees will also have to be made.

April 8 The port hires a new architect for the hangar project.

May 15 World Airways submits an affirmative action plan, but it is criticized by federal employment offices.

June 30 EDA approves preliminary plans and specifications for the hangar which set the cost at $9.2 million.

1971

May Terminal completed.

June Contracts for constructing hangar are let.

Bibliography

BOOKS

Aaron, Henry J. *Politics and the Professors: The Great Society in Perspective.* Washington, D.C.: Brookings Institution, 1978.

Alkin, Marvin C., Richard Daillak, and Peter White. *Using Evaluations: Does Evaluation Make a Difference?* Beverly Hills, Calif.: Sage Publications, 1980.

Argyris, Chris, and Donald A. Schon. *Organizational Learning: A Theory of Action Perspective.* Menlo Park, Calif.: Addison-Wesley, 1978.

Bailey, Stephen K., and Edith K. Mosher. *ESEA: The Office of Education Administers a Law.* Syracuse, N.Y.: Syracuse University Press, 1968.

Barber, Theodore. *Pitfalls in Human Research: Ten Pivotal Points.* New York: Pergamon Press, 1976.

Bardach, Eugene. *The Implementation Game: What Happens After a Bill Becomes a Law.* Cambridge, Mass.: MIT Press, 1977.

Barrett, Susan, and Colin Fudge, eds. *Policy and Action: Essays on the Implementation of Public Policy.* London and New York: Methuen, 1981.

Barringer, H. R., G. I. Blanksten, and R. Mack, eds. *Social Change in Developing Areas.* Cambridge, Mass.: Scheukman, 1965.

Benson, Charles S., and Harold L. Hodgkinson. *Implementing the Learning Society: Strategies for Financing Social Objectives.* San Francisco: Jossey-Bass, 1974.

Berman, Paul, and Milbrey McLauglin. *An Exploratory Study of School District Adaptation.* Santa Monica, Calif.: Rand Corporation, 1979.

Bernstein, Ilene, and Howard E. Freeman. *Academic and Entrepreneurial Research: Consequences of Diversity in Federal Evaluation Studies.* New York: Russell Sage, 1975.

Beyer, Janice M., and Harrison M. Trice. *Implementing Change: Alcoholism Policies in Work Organizations*. New York: Free Press, 1978.

Bruess, Clint E., and John E. Gay. *Implementing Comprehensive School Health*. New York: Macmillan, 1978.

Caiden, Naomi, and Aaron Wildavsky. *Planning and Budgeting in Poor Countries*. New York: John Wiley & Sons, 1974.

Campbell, Donald T., and Julian C. Stanley. *Experimental and Quasi-Experimental Designs for Research*. Chicago: Rand McNally, 1963.

Comfort, Louise. *Education Policy and Evaluation: A Context for Change*. New York: Pergamon Press, 1982.

Cronbach, Lee J. *Toward Reform of Program Evaluation*. San Francisco: Jossey-Bass, 1980.

Derthick, Martha. *New Towns In-Town: Why a Federal Program Failed*. Washington, D.C.: Urban Institute, 1972.

Dunn, William N. *Public Policy Analysis: An Introduction*. Englewood Cliffs, N.J.: Prentice-Hall, 1981.

Dunsire, A. *Implementation in a Bureaucracy*. Oxford: Martin Robertson, 1978.

Edwards, George C., III. *Implementing Public Policy*. Washington, D.C.: Congressional Quarterly Press, 1980.

Etheredge, Lloyd. *Government Learning: An Overview*. Cambridge, Mass.: MIT Center for International Studies, 1976.

Gilbert, Neil, and Harry Specht. *Dimensions of Social Welfare Policy*. Englewood Cliffs, N.J.: Prentice-Hall, 1974.

Glaser, Daniel. *Routinizing Evaluation: Getting Feedback on the Effectiveness of Crime and Delinquency Programs*. Rockville, Md.: National Institute of Mental Health, U.S. Department of Health, Education and Welfare, 1973.

Gross, Neal, Joseph B. Giacquinta, and Marily Bernstein. *Implementing Organizational Innovations: A Sociological Analysis of Planned Change in Schools*. New York: Basic Books, 1971.

Hargrove, Erwin C. *The Missing Link: The Study of the Implementation of Social Policy*. Washington, D.C.: Urban Institute, 1975.

Hatry, Harry, Richard E. Winnie, and Donald M. Fisk. *Practical Program Evaluation for State and Local Governments*. Washington, D.C.: Urban Institute, 1981.

Hood, C. C. *The Limits of Administration*. London: John Wiley & Sons, 1976.

Huysmans, Jan H. B. M. *The Implementation of Operations Research*. New York: Wiley Interscience, 1970.

Ingram, Helen M., and Dean E. Mann, eds. *Why Policies Succeed or Fail*. Beverly Hills, Calif.: Sage Publications, 1980.

Johnson, R. M. *The Dynamics of Compliance*. Evanston, Ill.: Northwestern University Press, 1967.

Jones, Charles. *Clean Air*. Pittsburgh: University of Pittsburgh Press, 1975.

Judd, Charles M., and David A. Kenny. *Estimating the Effects of Social Interventions*. New York: Cambridge University Press, 1981.

Kaufman, Herbert. *Administration Feedback: Monitoring Subordinates' Behavior*. Washington, D.C.: Brookings Institution, 1973.

_____. *The Limits of Organizational Change*. University, Alabama: University of Alabama Press, 1971.

Lane, Jan-Erik. *Creating the University of Norrland: Goals, Structures and Outcomes.* USPA 7. Umea, Sweden: University of Umea, 1983.

Langbein, Laura Irwin. *Discovering Whether Programs Work.* Santa Monica, Calif.: Goodyear Publishing Co., 1980.

Levitan, Sar. *Federal Aid to Depressed Areas: An Evaluation of the Area Redevelopment Administration.* Baltimore, Md.: Johns Hopkins University Press, 1964.

Levy, Frank, Arnold Meltsner, and Aaron Wildavsky. *Urban Outcomes.* Berkeley and Los Angeles: University of California Press, 1973.

Lieber, Harvey. *Federalism and Clean Waters.* Lexington, Mass.: D. C. Heath, 1976.

Lowi, Theodore. *The End of Liberalism: The Second Republic of the United States.* New York: W. W. Norton, 1979.

Lucas, Henry C., Jr. *Implementing of Computer Based Models.* New York: National Association of Accountants, 1976.

Mazmanian, Daniel A., and Paul A. Sabatier. *Implementation and Public Policy.* Palo Alto, Calif.: Scott, Foresman, 1983.

Meltsner, Arnold J., and Christopher Bellavita. *The Policy Organization.* Beverly Hills, Calif.: Sage Publications, 1983.

Meyers, William R. *The Evaluation Enterprise.* San Francisco: Jossey-Bass, 1981.

Mumford, Enid, and Andrew Pettigrew. *Implementing Strategic Decisions: Business Strategy and Planning.* New York: Longman, 1975.

Nakamura, Robert T., and Frank Smallwood. *The Politics of Policy Implementation.* New York: St. Martin's Press, 1980.

O'Connor, James. *The Fiscal Crisis of the State.* New York: St. Martin's Press, 1975.

Orfield, Gary. *The Reconstruction of Southern Education: The Schools and the 1964 Civil Rights Act.* New York: Wiley Interscience, 1969.

Patton, Michael Quinn. *Utilization-Focused Evaluation.* Beverly Hills, Calif.: Sage Publications, 1978.

Radin, Beryl. *Implementation, Change, and the Federal Bureaucracy: School Desegregation Policy in HEW, 1964–1968.* New York: Teachers College Press, 1977.

Reichardt, Charles S., and Thomas D. Cook. *Qualitative and Quantitative Methods in Evaluation Research.* Beverly Hills, Calif.: Sage Publications, 1979.

Rein, Martin. *From Policy to Practice.* Armonk, N.Y.: M. E. Sharpe, Inc., 1983.

_____, and Francine Rabinovitz. *Implementation: A Theoretical Perspective.* Working Paper no. 43. Cambridge, Eng.: Joint Center for Urban Studies, 1977.

Rich, Robert F. *Translating Evaluation into Policy.* Beverly Hills, Calif.: Sage Publications, 1979.

Ripley, Randall B., and Associates. *The Implementation of CETA in Ohio.* Employment and Training Monograph no. 44. Washington, D.C.: U.S. Government Printing Office, 1977.

Ripley, Randall B., and Grace A. Franklin. *Bureaucracy and Policy Implementation.* Homewood, Ill.: Dorsey Press, 1982.

Rivlin, Alice. *Systematic Thinking for Social Action*. Washington, D.C.: Brookings Institution, 1971.

_____, and P. Michael Timpane. *Ethical and Legal Issues of Social Experimentation*. Washington, D.C.: Brookings Institution, 1975.

Rodgers, Harrell, and Charles Bullock. *Coercion to Compliance*. Lexington, Mass.: D. C. Heath, 1976.

Ryavec, Karl W. *Implementation of Soviet Economic Reforms: Political, Organizational and Social Progress*. New York: Praeger, 1975.

Sabatier, Paul, and Daniel Mazmanian. *Effective Policy Implementation*. Lexington, Mass.: D. C. Heath, 1981.

_____. *Toward a More Adequate Conceptualization of the Implementation Process—With Special Reference to Regulatory Policy*. Davis, Calif.: Institute of Governmental Affairs, 1979.

Sapolsky, Harvey. *The Polaris Missile System: Bureaucratic and Programmatic Success in Government*. Cambridge, Mass.: Harvard University Press, 1972.

Schachter, Esther. *Enforcing Air Pollution Controls*. New York: Praeger, 1974.

Schein, Jerome Daniel, et al. *Implementation of the Model State Plans for Vocational Rehabilitation of Deaf Clients*. Silver Spring, Md.: National Association of the Deaf, 1977.

Schultz, Randall L., and Dennis P. Slavin, eds. *Implementing Operations Research-Management Sciences*. New York: Elsevier, 1975.

Stake, Robert A. *Evaluating the Arts in Education: A Responsive Approach*. Columbus, Ohio: Charles E. Merrill, 1975.

Stephens, Thomas. *Implementing Behavioral Approaches in Elementary and Secondary Schools*. Columbus, Ohio: Charles E. Merrill, 1975.

Suchman, Edward. *Evaluative Research: Principles and Practice in Public Service and Social Action Programs*. New York: Russell Sage, 1967.

Ungson, G., and D. Braunstein, eds. *Decision Making: An Interdisciplinary Inquiry*. Boston: Kent Publishing Co., 1982.

Van Horn, Carl E. *Implementation in the Federal System: National Goals and Local Implementers*. Lexington, Mass.: Lexington Books, 1979.

Washington, R. O. *Program Evaluation in the Human Services*. Milwaukee: University of Wisconsin, n.d.

Weed, L. L., et al., eds. *Implementing the Problem-Oriented Medical Record*. Vol. 2. Seattle: Medical Communications, 1976.

Weick, Karl. *The Social Psychology of Organizing*. Menlo Park, Calif.: Addison-Wesley, 1979.

Weigand, James E., ed. *Implementing Teacher Competencies: Positive Approaches to Personalizing Education*. Englewood Cliffs, N.J.: Prentice-Hall, 1977.

Weiss, Carol H. *Evaluating Action Programs*. Boston: Allyn and Bacon, 1972.

_____. *Evaluation Research*. Englewood Cliffs, N.J.: Prentice-Hall, 1972.

Wildavsky, Aaron. *Speaking Truth to Power: The Art and Craft of Policy Analysis*. Boston: Little, Brown, 1979.

Wilensky, Harold. *Organizational Intelligence*. New York: Basic Books, 1969.

Williams, Walter. *The Implementation Perspective*. Berkeley: University of California Press, 1980.

_____, ed. *Studying Implementation*. Chatham, N.J.: Chatham House, 1982.

_____, and Richard F. Elmore. *Social Program Implementation*. New York: Academic Press, 1976.

ARTICLES

Allison, Graham. "Implementation Analysis: A Teaching Exercise." In *Benefit Cost and Policy Analysis*, edited by Richard Zeckhauser, chap. 19. Chicago: Aldine, 1975.

Altenstetter, Christa, and James Bjorkman. "Implementation of a Federal-State Health Program: Political and Administrative Lessons from Connecticut and Vermont." Paper presented at 1977 Annual Meeting of the American Political Science Association, September 1–4, 1977, in Washington, D.C.

Armor, David J. "The Evidence on Busing." *The Public Interest* 28 (Summer 1972):90–126.

Armor, David J., Thomas F. Pettigrew, and James Q. Wilson. "On Busing: An Exchange." *The Public Interest* 30 (Winter 1973):88–134.

Ball, Howard, Dale Krane, and Thomas Lauth. "Shadows on the Southern Cave Wall: Compliance Theory and Reality with Respect to the Enforcement of the Voting Rights Act of 1965." Paper presented at 1978 Annual Meeting of the Midwest Political Science Association, April 20–22, 1978, in Chicago.

Bardach, Eugene. "Implementation Studies and the Study of Implements." Presented at the 1980 meetings of the American Political Science Association, University of California, Berkeley, 1980.

_____. "On Designing Implementable Programs." In *Pitfalls of Analysis and Analysis of Pitfalls*, edited by G. Majone and E. Quade. London and New York: John Wiley and Sons, 1979.

Barth, Thomas. "Perception and Acceptance of Supreme Court Decisions at the State and Local Level." *Journal of Public Law* 17 (1968):308–50.

Baum, Lawrence. "Implementation of Judicial Decisions: An Organizational Analysis." *American Politics Quarterly* 4 (January 1976):86–114.

_____. "Implementation of Legislative and Judicial Politics: A Comparative View." Paper presented at Workshop on Policy Implementation, November 1978, at Pomona College, Pomona, Calif.

Becker, Thomas E., et al. "Information Resources for Program Evaluators." *Evaluation and Program Planning* 3 (1980):25–33.

Begun, Audrey L. "Social Policy Evaluation: An Example from Drinking Age Legislation." *Evaluation and Program Planning* 3 (1980):165–70.

Behn, Robert D. "Closing a Government Facility." *Public Administration Review* 38 (July/August 1978):332–38.

_____. "Closing the Massachusetts Public Training Schools." *Policy Sciences* 7 (June 1976):151–71.

_____. "The False Dawn of the Sunset Laws." *The Public Interest* 49 (Fall 1977):103–18.

Berman, Paul. "The Study of Macro- and Micro-Implementation." *Public Policy* 26 (Spring 1978):172–74.

_____, and Milbrey McLaughlin. "Implementation of Educational Innovation." *The Educational Forum* 40 (March 1976):345–70.

Biller, Robert P. "On Tolerating Policy and Organization Termination: Some Design Considerations." *Policy Sciences* 7 (June 1976):133–49.

Bowen, Elinor R. "The Pressman-Wildavsky Paradox: Four Addenda or Why Models Based on Probability Theory Can Predict Implementation Success and Suggest Useful Tactical Advice for Implementers." *Journal of Public Policy* 2 (February 1982):1–21.

Brady, Gorden L., and Blair T. Bower. "Effectiveness of the U.S. Regulatory Approach to Air Quality Management: Stationary Sources." *Policy Studies Journal* 11 (September 1982):66–76.

Brandl, John E. "Evaluation and Politics." *Evaluation.* Special Issue (1978): 6–48.

Brewer, Garry D., with James L. Foster. "And the Clocks Were Striking Thirteen: The Termination of War." *Policy Sciences* 7 (June 1976):225–43.

Browning, Rufus, and Dale Rogers Marshall. "Implementation of Model Cities and Revenue Sharing in Ten Bay Area Cities." In *Public Policy Making in a Federal System,* edited by Charles D. Jones and Robert D. Thomas. Beverly Hills, Calif.: Sage Publications, 1976.

_____. "Implementation of Model and Political Change: Sources of Local Variations in Federal Social Programs." Paper presented at Workshop on Policy Implementation, November 1978, at Pomona College, Pomona, Calif.

_____, and David Tabb. "Implementation and Political Change: Sources of Local Variation in Federal Social Programs." In *Effective Policy Implementation,* edited by Daniel Mazmanian and Paul Sabatier. Lexington, Mass.: D. C. Heath, 1981.

Bunker, Douglas R. "Policy Sciences Perspectives on Implementation Processes." *Policy Sciences* 3 (March 1972):72.

Bush, Malcolm, Andrew C. Gordon, and Robert LeBailly. "Evaluating Child Welfare Services: A Contribution from the Client." *Social Service Review* (September 1977):491–501.

Canada. Office of Auditor General. "Audit Guide: Auditing of Proceedings for Effectiveness, Subject Matter Series." 1981.

Canada. Treasury Board. "Guide on the Program Evaluation Function." Comptroller General, Program Evaluation Branch, May 1981.

Canon, B. C., and K. Kolson. "Rural Compliance with Gault: Kentucky, A Case Study." *Journal of Family Law* 10 (1971):300–326.

Cerych, Ladislav. "Implementation of Higher Education Reforms in Europe." To be published as chapter 8 in *The Policy Perspective,* edited by Burton R. Clark. Berkeley: University of California Press, forthcoming.

Chandler, Daniel. "Evaluating California's Mental Health Programs." Prepared for Assembly Health Committee. State of California, Assembly Office of Research, Sacramento, February 1978.

Chelimsky, Eleanor. "The Nature, Definition, and Measurement of Quality in Program Evaluation." *GAO Review* 17 (Fall 1982):41–47.

Chen, Huey-Tsych, and Peter H. Rossi. "The Multi-Goal, Theory-Driven Approach to Evaluation: A Model Linking Basic and Applied Social Science." *Evaluation Studies Review Annual* 6 (1981):38–54.

Churchman, C. West. "Managerial Acceptance of Scientific Recommendations." *California Management Review* 7 (Fall 1964):31–38.

Connolly, Terry, and Alan L. Porter. "A User-Focused Model for the Utilization of Evaluation." *Evaluation and Program Planning* 3 (1980):131–40.

Constable, Robert, and Rita Beck Black. "Mandates for a Changing Practice: PSRO and P. L. 94–142." *Social Service Review* 54:273–82.

Cook, Thomas D., and Charles Gruder. "Metaevaluation Research." *Evaluation Studies Review Annual* 4 (1979):469–513.

Cronbach, Lee J., et al. "Our Ninety-Five Theses." *Evaluation Studies Review Annual* 6 (1981):27–37.

de Leon, Peter. "Policy Evaluation and Program Termination." Rand Paper Series, P-680F. Santa Monica, Calif.: Rand Corporation, 1982.

Dery, David. "Evaluation and Problem Redefinition." *Journal of Public Policy* 2 (February 1982):23–30.

Dexter, Lewis Anthony. "Undesigned Consequences of Purposive Legislative Action: Alternatives to Implementation." *Journal of Public Policy* 1 (October 1981):413–31.

Downing, Paul B., and James N. Kimball. "Enforcing Pollution Control Laws in the U.S." *Policy Studies Journal* 11 (September 1982):56–67.

Elmore, R. F. "Backward Mapping: Implementation Research and Policy Decisions." In *Studying Implementation*, edited by Walter Williams. Chatham, N.J.: Chatham House, 1982.

————. "Lessons from Follow Through." *Policy Analysis* 1 (Summer 1977):549–84.

————. "Organizational Models of Social Program Implementation." *Public Policy* 26 (Spring 1978):185–228.

Engleberg, Sydney. "Network Analysis in Evaluation: Some Words of Caution." *Evaluation and Program Planning* 3 (1980):15–23.

Freeman, Howard E. "Boundaries of the Evaluation Research Field." *Evaluation Studies Review Annual* 2 (1977):24–30.

————. "The Present Status of Evaluation Research." *Evaluation Studies Review* (1977):17–51.

————, and Marian A. Solomon. "Evaluation and the Uncertain '80s." *Evaluation Studies Review Annual* 6 (1981):1–23.

Freeman, John, and Michael T. Hannan. "Growth and Decline Processes in Organizations." *American Sociological Review* 40 (April 1975):215–28.

Garey, Robert B., and John F. Sacco. "Everyday Bureaucratic Realities and Program Evaluation." *GAO Review* 17 (Fall 1982):29–32.

General Accounting Office. Report to the Administrator, Agency for International Development, ID–82–36, June 15, 1982.

Georgopoulos, Basil S., and Arnold S. Tannenbaum. "Subjective and Objective Output Indicators." In *Policies, Decisions and Organizations*, edited by Fremont J. Lyden, et al. New York: Appleton-Century-Crofts, 1969.

Goodsell, Charles T. "Client Evaluation of Three Welfare Programs." *Administration and Society* 12 (August 1980):123–36.

Goodwin, Leonard, and Phyllis Moen. "On the Evolution and Implementation of Welfare Policy." Paper presented at Workshop on Policy Implementation, November 1978, at Pomona College, Pomona, Calif.

Gould, Stephen Jay. "Darwinism and the Expansion of Evolutionary Theory." *Science* 216 (April 1982):380–86.

Gross, B. "Activating National Plans." In *Operational Research and the Social Sciences.* London: Tavistock, 1966.

Grossman, J. "The Supreme Court and Social Change." *American Behavioral Scientist* 13 (March/April 1970):545–46.

Hays, Allen R. "Social Welfare Programs and Political Conflict in Local Communities: The Mediating Function of the Implementing Agency." *Policy Studies Journal* 11 (December 1982):234–44.

Heclo, Hugh. "Review Article: Policy Analysis." *British Journal of Political Science* 2 (January 1972):83–108.

Hedberg, Bo L. T., Paul C. Nystrom, and William H. Starbuck. "Camping on Seesaws: Prescriptions for a Self-Designing Organization." *Administrative Science Quarterly* 27 (March 1976):41–65.

Hjern, Benny, and Chris Hull. "Implementation Research as Empirical Constitutionalism." *European Journal of Political Research* 10 (1982):105–15.

––––––, and D. Porter. "Implementation Structures: A New Unit for Administrative Analysis." *Organization Studies* 2 (1981):211–27.

Holling, C. S. "Resilience and Stability of Ecological Systems." *Annual Review of Ecology and Systematics* 4 (1979):1–23.

Hudson, Barclay. "Domains of Evaluation." *Social Policy* 6 (September-October 1975):79–81.

Ingram, Helen. "Policy Implementation Through Bargaining: The Case of Federal Grants-in-Aid." *Public Policy* 2 (Fall 1977):499–526.

"Intelligence Failures, CIA Misdeeds Studied." *Foreign Policy/National Security*, September 20, 1975, 20–25.

Johnson, Robert, Seymore Schwartz, and Thomas Klinkner. "Successful Plan Implementation: The Growth Phasing Program of Sacramento County." *AIP Journal* (October 1978):412–23.

Jones, E. Terrance. "Block Grants and Urban Policies: Implementation and Impact." *Policy Studies Journal* 8 (Summer 1980):906–12.

Kagle, Jill Doner. "Evaluating Social Work Practice." *Social Work* 24 (July 1979):292–96.

Knott, Jack, and Aaron Wildavsky. "If Dissemination Is the Solution, What Is the Problem?" *Knowledge* 1 (June 1980):537–78.

Lane, Jan-Erik. "The Concept of Implementation." *Statsvetenskaplig Tidskrift* 1 (1983):17–40.

Lave, Judy R., and Lester B. Lave. "Measuring the Effectiveness of Prevention." In *Economics and Health Care*, edited by John B. McKinlay. Cambridge, Mass.: MIT Press, 1981.

Lazin, F. A. "The Failure of Federal Enforcement of Civil Rights Regulations in Public Housing, 1963–1971: The Co-optation of a Federal Agency by Its Local Constituency." *Policy Sciences* 4 (1973):263–73.

Levine, Charles H. "Organizational Decline and Cutback Management." *Public Administration Review* 38 (July/August 1978):316–24.

Lipsky, Michael. "Standing the Study of Public Policy Implementation on Its Head." In *American Politics and Public Policy*, edited by Walter Dean Burnham and Martha Wagner Weinberg. Cambridge, Mass.: MIT Press, 1978.

Luft, Harold. "Benefit Cost Analysis and Public Policy Implementation." *Public Policy* 24 (Fall 1976):437–62.

Majone, Giandomenico, and Aaron Wildavsky. "Implementation as Evolution." In *Policy Studies Review Annual* 2, edited by Howard E. Freeman. Beverly Hills, Calif.: Sage Publications, 1978.

Marmor, Theodore. "Can the U.S. Learn from Canada?" In *National Health Insurance: Can We Learn from Canada?*, edited by S. Andreopoulos. New York, 1975.

Marshall, Dale Rogers. "Implementation of Federal Poverty and Welfare Policy: A Review Essay." *Policy Studies Journal* 2 (Spring 1974):152–58.

Maynard-Moody, Steven, and Charles C. McClintock. "Square Pegs in Round Holes: Program Evaluation and Organizational Uncertainty." *Policy Studies Journal* 9 (Spring 1981):644–66.

Mayntz, Renate. "External Pressures and Conflicts in the Formation and Implementation of Environmental Policy." International Institute of Management, Berlin, June 1975.

Mechanic, David. "Sources of Power of Lower Participants in Complex Organizations." *Administrative Science Quarterly* 7 (December 1962): 349–64.

Milcarek, Barry I., and Bruce G. Link. "Handling Problems of Ecological Fallacy in Program Planning and Evaluation." *Evaluation and Program Planning* 4 (1981):23–28.

Murphy, Jerome T. "The Education Bureaucracies Implement Novel Policy: The Politics of Title I of ESEA, 1965–72." In *Policy and Politics in America*, edited by Allan P. Sindler, pp. 160–98. Boston: Little, Brown, 1973.

————. "Title I of ESEA: The Politics of Implementing Federal Education Reform." *Harvard Educational Review* 41 (1971):35–49.

Nance, Kathy Newton, and Jolie Bain Pillsbury. "An Evaluation System for Decision Making." *Public Welfare* 34 (Spring 1976):45–52.

Neiman, Max, and Catherine Lovell. "Mandating as a Policy Issue." *Policy Studies Review Annual* 9 (Spring 1981):667–71.

Olson, Richard Stuart, and Douglas C. Nilson. "Public Policy Analysis and Hazards Research: Natural Complements." *The Social Science Journal* 19 (January 1982):89–103.

Palumbo, Dennis J., and David Nachmias. "The Pre-Conditions for Successful Evaluation: Is There an Ideal-Type?" Paper prepared for presentation at the International Political Science Association Meetings, August 9–14, 1982, in Rio de Janeiro, Brazil.

Pillsbury, Jolie Bain, and Kathy Newton Nance. "An Evaluation Framework for Public Welfare Agencies." *Public Welfare* (Spring 1976):47–51.

"Proposed Master Plan for Children and Youth: Executive Summary." Public Hearing Draft. State of California, Office of Statewide Health Planning, Sacramento, November 1980.

Rein, Martin, and Francine F. Rabinovitz. "Implementation: A Theoretical Perspective." In *American Politics and Public Policy*, edited by Walter Dean Burnham and Martha Wagner Weinberg, pp. 307–35. Cambridge: MIT Press, 1978.

Rein, Martin, and Sheldon H. White. "Policy Research: Belief and Doubt."

Working Paper no. 46, Joint Center for Urban Studies of MIT and Harvard University, April 1977.

Roosevelt, Franklin D., Jr. "Appalachia: Case Study for Regional Development." In *The Manpower Revolution: Its Policy Consequences,* edited by Garth L. Mangum. Garden City, N.Y.: Doubleday, 1965.

Rosenbaum, Nelson. "Statutory Stringency and Policy Implementation: The Case of Wetlands Regulation." Paper presented at Workshop on Policy Implementation, November 1978, at Pomona College, Pomona, Calif.

Rossi, Peter H., and Richard A. Berk. "An Overview of Evaluation Strategies and Procedures." *Human Organizations* 40 (1981):287–99.

Sabatier, Paul, and Daniel Mazmanian. "The Conditions of Effective Implementation: A Guide to Accomplishing Policy Objectives." *Policy Analysis* 5.

_____. "Toward a More Adequate Conceptualization of the Implementation Process—With Special Reference to Regulatory Policy." Research paper sponsored by the National Science Foundation under grant ENV77–20077. University of California, Davis, and Pomona College, Pomona, July 1978.

Salasian, Susan. "Evaluation as a Tool for Restoring the Mental Health of Victims." *Evaluation and Change,* Special Issue (1980):25–30.

Sayer, S. T. "Macroeconomic Policy Rules Versus Discretion: Some Analytical Issues." *Journal of Public Policy* 1 (October 1981):465–79.

Scheft, T. J. "Control over Policy by Attendants in a Mental Hospital." *Journal of Health and Human Behavior* 2 (1961):93–105.

Schick, Allen. "A Death in the Bureaucracy: The Demise of Federal PPB." *Public Administration Review* (March, April 1973):146–56.

_____. "Beyond Analysis." *Public Administration Review* 37 (May-June 1977):258–63.

Scriven, Michael. "Pros and Cons About Goal-Free Evaluation." *Evaluation Comment: The Journal of Education Evaluation* (UCLA Center for the Study of Evaluation, Los Angeles) 3 (December 1972):1–7.

_____. "The Methodology of Evaluation." In *Perspectives on Curriculum Evaluation,* edited by R. W. Taylor, et al. Skokie, Ill.: Rand McNally, 1976.

Segal, Steven P. "Issues in the Utilization and Evaluation of Social Work Treatment." *International Social Work* 21 (1978):2–18.

Smith, Thomas. "Policy Roles: An Analysis of Policy Formulators and Policy Implementors." *Policy Sciences* 4 (1973):297–307.

Smith, T. B. "The Policy Implementation Process." *Policy Sciences* 4 (1973): 197–209.

Solomon, Marian A. "Evaluation in the U.S. Department of Health, Education and Welfare." *Evaluation and Program Planning* 3 (1980):53–55.

Stufflebeam, Daniel L., and William J. Webster. "An Analysis of Alternative Approaches to Evaluation." *Evaluation Studies Review Annual* 6 (1981): 70–85.

Thomas, Robert. "Intergovernmental Coordination in the Implementation of National Air and Water Pollution Policies." In *Public Policy-Making in the Federal System,* edited by Charles D. Jones and Robert T. Thomas, pp. 129–48. Beverly Hills, Calif.: Sage Publications, 1976.

Ukeles, Jacob B. "Policy Analysis." *Public Administration Review* 37 (May-June 1977):223–28.

Van Horn, Carl E., and Donald S. Van Meter. "The Implementation of Intergovernmental Policy." In *Public Policy Making in a Federal System*, Sage Yearbooks in Politics and Public Policy, edited by Charles O. Jones and Robert Thomas, vol. 3, pp. 39–62. Beverly Hills, Calif.: Sage Publications, 1976.

Van Meter, Donald S., and Carl E. Van Horn. "The Policy Implementation Process: A Conceptual Framework." *Administration and Society* 6 (February 1975):445–87.

Weatherly, Richard, and Michael Lipsky. "Street Level Bureaucrats and Institutional Innovation: Implementing Special Education Reform." *Harvard Educational Review* 47 (May 1977):171–97.

Weiler, Philip, et al. "The Implementation of Model Standards in Local Health Departments." *American Journal of Public Health* 72 (1982):1230–37.

Weiss, Carol H. "Alternative Models of Program Evaluation." *Social Work* (November 1974):675–81.

Wenner, Lettie. "Enforcement of Water Pollution Control Law." *Law and Society Review* (May 1972):481–507.

Wholey, J. S. "Evaluation to Improve Program Performance." *Evaluation Studies Review Annual* 6 (1981):55–69.

Wildavsky, Aaron. "Doing Better and Feeling Worse: The Political Pathology of Health Policy." *Daedalus* 106 (Winter 1976):105–23.

_____. "The Self-Evaluating Organization." *Public Administration Review* 32 (September/October 1972):509–20.

_____. "Trial Without Error: Anticipation Versus Resilience as Strategies for Reducing Risk." Paper presented at the 1983 Faculty Seminar on "Private Enterprise, Regulatory Reform and Risk Assessment: The Role of the University," sponsored by the Chair of Free Enterprise in the College of Engineering at the University of Texas at Austin, April 15–17, 1983, and to be published in the proceedings of the seminar.

Williams, Walter. "Implementation Analysis and Assessment." *Policy Analysis* 1 (Summer 1975):531–66.

Wolman, Harold. "The Determinants of Program Success and Failure." *Journal of Public Policy* 1 (October 1981):433–64.

Subject Index

Index of Authors Cited

279